# Pretrain Vision and Large Language Models in Python

End-to-end techniques for building and deploying foundation models on AWS

**Emily Webber**

BIRMINGHAM—MUMBAI

# Pretrain Vision and Large Language Models in Python

**Group Product Manager**: Ali Abidi
**Publishing Product Manager**: Dhruv Jagdish Kataria
**Content Development Editor**: Priyanka Soam
**Technical Editor**: Rahul Limbachiya
**Copy Editor**: Safis Editing
**Project Coordinator**: Farheen Fathima
**Proofreader**: Safis Editing
**Indexer**: Subalakshmi Govindhan
**Production Designer**: Ponraj Dhandapani
**Marketing Coordinator**: Shifa Ansari and Vinishka Kalra

First published: May 2023

Production reference: 1250523

Published by Packt Publishing Ltd.
Livery Place
35 Livery Street
Birmingham
B3 2PB, UK.

ISBN 978-1-80461-825-7

www.packtpub.com

*To the beginner's mind in us all. May we all have the humility and the courage to face the unknown with curious minds.*

*- Emily Webber*

# Foreword

Welcome to the remarkable world of Machine Learning and foundation models! It has been rare that a new technology has taken the world by storm like these models have. These extraordinary creations have revolutionized the way we interact with technology and have opened up unprecedented opportunities for innovation and discovery.

In this book, penned with clarity and a genuine passion for the subject, Emily invites you on a journey. Whether you are a first-time user or someone seeking a fresh perspective on these fascinating tools and practical applications, you will find this book a valuable companion.

The field of ML can be daunting - complex algorithms, intricate mathematical formulas, and technical jargon. Yet Emily skillfully navigates through this intricacy, distilling the fundamentals into an accessible and easy-to-understand language. Emily's writing style takes you not only through the "how" but also the "why" behind these advancements. The clear examples, and the grounding in the very practical platform offered by Amazon SageMaker, offer you the ability to follow along and learn-by-doing. The broad coverage of fields such as dataset preparation, pretraining, fine-tuning, deployment, bias detection and ML operations are covered in a rare soup-to-nuts, deep-yet-readable description.

Ultimately, this book is a testament to Emily's passion for sharing knowledge and empowering others. By the time you reach the final page, you will have gained a solid foundation in the world of large language models, armed with the confidence to embark on your own exciting experiments and projects.

So, without further ado, let us embark on this captivating journey through the world of large language models. Join Emily as she illuminates the way, inspiring you to embrace the power of these remarkable creations and harness their potential to reshape the future.

Thank you, my friend, for the time, effort and - ultimately - love you put into this.

*Andrea Olgiati*

*Chief Engineer, Amazon SageMaker*

*Santa Clara, May 2023*

# Contributors

## About the author

**Emily Webber** is a principal **machine learning** (**ML**) specialist solutions architect at **Amazon Web Services** (**AWS**). In her more than five years at AWS, she has assisted hundreds of customers on their journey to ML in the cloud, specializing in distributed training for large language and vision models. She mentors ML solution architects, authors countless feature designs for SageMaker and AWS, and guides the Amazon SageMaker product and engineering teams on best practices in regard to ML and customers. Emily is widely known in the AWS community for a 16-video YouTube series (`https://www.youtube.com/playlistlist=PLhr1KZpdzukcOr_6j_zmSrvYnLUtgqsZz`) featuring SageMaker with 211,000 views, and for giving a keynote speech at O'Reilly AI London 2019 on a novel reinforcement learning approach she developed for public policy.

# Acknowledgment

It seems almost impossible to thank all of the talented, passionate, hardworking, and kind people who have helped me in my journey to this very moment. And yet I would be remiss if I didn't try!

To the Packt team, including Dhruv Kataria, Priyanka Soam, Aparna Ravikumar Nair, and Hemangi Lotlikar, thank you so much for all of your enthusiasm, careful checks, and for believing in me from the start. Ten years ago I would have never thought I'd be writing a book on artificial intelligence, and it truly took the whole village of us to pull it off.

There are quite literally hundreds of Amazonians I would like to thank for supporting me and the content of this book. This is due to services they've scoped and developed, customers they've onboarded and businesses they've built, design patterns they've developed, techniques they've perfected, the content they've built, and so much more. In particular, I'd like to call out Nav Bhasin, Mani Khanuja, Mark Roy, Shelbee Eigenbrode, Dhawal Patel, Kanwaljit Khurmi, Farooq Sabir, Sean Morgan, and all of the rest of the wonderful ML SA's I love working with every day. There are so many other teams at Amazon whose passion has helped create this work: from engineering to product, business development to marketing, all of my friends in the field, documentation, start-ups, public sector, and across the world, what an honor it is to make this dream come true with you.

To my customers, you truly bring everything to life! Whether we shared an immersion day, a workshop, a call, a talk, a blog post, or a Slack channel, it is such an honor to serve as your technology partner in so many. We truly do walk up every day thinking about how to optimize for your outcomes!

I spent quite a few days working on this book during the Winter Applications of Computer Vision (WACV) Conference in Hawaii, in January 2023. This was during a workshop I'd hosted https://sites.google.com/view/wacv2023-workshop with Fouad Bousetouane, Corey Barrett, Mani Khanuja, Larry Davis, and more. To all of my friends at WACV, it was such a perfect place to hash out ideas and misconceptions with you, thanks for all of your support!

Finally, I'd love to thank my loving husband and the rest of my family for all of their support throughout the winding road that's been my life. Who would have guessed that some crazy girl from Pennsylvania would be writing books on AI from Amazon? Not me!

To my readers, you make this all possible. I hope you'll consider reaching out to me and connecting! I'm live on Twitch every Monday, so you can always hop on for a question or a chat. For the future, stay tuned. I have a lot more words in me yet to write.

# About the reviewer

**Falk Pollok** is a senior **software engineer** in IBM Research Europe and a senior RSE for the MIT-IBM Watson AI Lab, specializing in foundation models and multimodal question answering. Falk was a member of the MIT-Harvard-Stanford team on the **Defense Advanced Research Projects Agency (DARPA) Machine Common Sense (MCS)** project, contributed to IBM Watson Core, Orchestrate, and ML, was the lead developer for IBM Sapphire, and founded IBM's Engineering Excellence program. He holds a master's degree in **computer science** from RWTH Aachen, leadership certificates from Cornell, and IBM's highest developer profession rank. Moreover, he has published eight papers in top conferences such as NeurIPS, AAAI, and Middleware, has two patents, was named a Face of IBM Research, and received multiple awards, including IBM's OTA and InfoWorld's **Open Source Software Awards (BOSSIE)** award.

# Table of Contents

# Part 2: Configure Your Environment

# Part 3: Train Your Model

# 7

## Finding the Right Hyperparameters    95

# 8

## Large-Scale Training on SageMaker    107

# 11

## Detecting, Mitigating, and Monitoring Bias    149

# 12

## How to Deploy Your Model    163

# Part 5: Deploy Your Model

# 13

## Prompt Engineering    177

# 14

## MLOps for Vision and Language                                    193

# 15

## Future Trends in Pretraining Foundation Models                    207

# Preface

So, you want to work with foundation models? That is an excellent place to begin! Many of us in the machine learning community have followed these curious creatures for years, from their earliest onset in the first days of the Transformer models, to their expansion in computer vision, to the near ubiquitous presence of text generation and interactive dialogue we see in the world today.

But where do foundation models come from? How do they work? What makes them tick, and when should you pretrain and fine-tune them? How can you eke out performance gains on your datasets and applications? How many accelerators do you need? What does an end-to-end application look like, and how can you use foundation models to master this new surge of interest in generative AI?

These pages hope to provide answers to these very important questions. As you are no doubt aware, the pace of innovation in this space is truly breathtaking, with more foundation models coming online every day from both open-source and proprietary model vendors. To grapple with this reality, I've tried to focus on the most important conceptual fundamentals throughout the book. This means your careful study here should pay off for at least a few more years ahead.

In terms of practical applications and guidance, I've overwhelmingly focused on cloud computing options available through AWS and especially Amazon SageMaker. I've spent more than the last five years very happily at AWS and enjoy sharing all of my knowledge and experience with you! Please do note that all thoughts and opinions shared in this book are my own, and do not represent those of Amazon's.

The following chapters focus on concepts, not code. This is because software changes rapidly, while fundamentals change very slowly. You'll find in the repository with the book links to my go-to resources for all of the key topics mentioned throughout these fifteen chapters, which you can use right away to get hands-on with everything you're learning here. Starting July 1, 2023, you'll also find in the repository a set of new pretraining and fine-tuning examples from yours truly to complete all of the topics.

You might find this hard to believe, but in my early twenties I wasn't actually coding: I was exploring the life of a Buddhist monastic. I spent five years living at a meditation retreat center in Arizona, the Garchen Institute. During this time, I learned how to meditate, focus my mind, watch my emotions and develop virtuous habits. After my master's degree at the University of Chicago years later, and now at Amazon, I can see that these traits are extremely useful in today's world as well!

I mention this so that you can take heart. Machine learning, artificial intelligence, cloud computing, economics, application development, none of these topics are straightforward. But if you apply yourself, if you really stretch your mind to consider the core foundations of the topics at hand, if you keep yourself coming back to the challenge again and again, there's truly nothing you can't do. That is the beauty of humanity! And if a meditating yogi straight from the deep silence of a retreat hut can eventually learn what it takes to pretrain and fine-tune foundation models, then so can you!

With that in mind, let's learn more about the book itself!

> **Note**
>
> Most of the concepts mentioned here will be accompanied by scripting examples in the repository starting July 1, 2023. However, to get you started even earlier, you can find a list of resources in the repository today with links to useful hands-on examples elsewhere for demonstration.

## Who is this book for?

If you're a machine learning researcher or enthusiast who wants to start a foundation modelling project, this book is for you. Applied scientists, data scientists, machine learning engineers, solution architects, product managers, and students will all benefit from this book. Intermediate Python is a must, along with introductory concepts of cloud computing. A strong understanding of deep learning fundamentals is needed, while advanced topics will be explained. The content covers advanced machine learning and cloud techniques, explaining them in an actionable, easy-to-understand way.

## What this book covers

*Chapter 1, An Introduction to Pretraining Foundation Models* In this chapter you'll be introduced to foundation models, the backbone of many artificial intelligence and machine learning systems today. We will dive into their creation process, also called pretraining, and understand where it's competitive to improve the accuracy of your models. We will discuss the core transformer architecture underpinning state of the art models like Stable Diffusion, BERT, Vision Transformers, CLIP, Flan-T5 and more. You will learn about the encoder and decoder frameworks that work to solve a variety of use cases.

*Chapter 2, Dataset Preparation: Part One* In this chapter, we begin to discuss what you'll need in your dataset to start a meaningful pretraining project. This is the first of two parts on dataset preparation. It opens with some business guidance on finding a good use case for foundation modeling, where the data become instrumental. Then, focusing on the content of your dataset, we use qualitative and quantitative measures to compare it with datasets used in pretraining other top models. You'll learn how to use the scaling laws to determine if your datasets are "large enough" and "good enough" to boost accuracy while pretraining. We discuss bias identification and mitigation, along with multilingual and multimodal solutions.

*Chapter 3, Model Preparation* In this chapter you'll learn how to pick which model will be most useful to serve as a basis for your pretraining regime. You'll learn how to think about the size of the model in parameters, along with the key loss functions and how they determine performance in production. You'll combine the scaling laws with your expected dataset size to select ceiling and basement model sizes, which you'll use to guide your experiments.

*Chapter 4, Containers and Accelerators on the Cloud* In this chapter, you'll learn how to containerize your scripts and optimize them for accelerators on the cloud. We'll learn about a range of accelerators for foundation models, including tradeoffs around cost and performance across the entire machine learning lifecycle. You'll learn key aspects of Amazon SageMaker and AWS to train models on accelerators, optimize performance, and troubleshoot common issues. If you're already familiar with using accelerators on AWS, feel free to skip this chapter.

*Chapter 5, Distribution Fundamentals* In this chapter, you'll learn conceptual fundamentals for the distribution techniques you need to employ for large scale pretraining and fine-tuning. First, you'll master top distribution concepts for machine learning, notably model and data parallel. Then, you'll learn how Amazon SageMaker integrates with distribution software to run your job on as many GPUs as you need. You'll learn how to optimize model and data parallel for large-scale training especially with techniques like sharded data parallelism. Then, you'll learn how to reduce your memory consumption with advanced techniques like optimizer state sharding, activation checkpointing, compilation, and more. Lastly, we'll look at a few examples across language, vision, and more to bring all of these concepts together.

*Chapter 6, Dataset Preparation: Part Two, the Data Loader* In this chapter, you'll learn how to prepare your dataset to immediately use with your chosen models. You'll master the concept of a data loader, knowing why it's a common source of error in training large models. You'll learn about creating embeddings, using tokenizers and other methods to featurize your raw data for your preferred neural network. Following these steps, you'll be able to prepare your entire dataset, using methods for both vision and language. Finally, you'll learn about data optimizations on AWS and Amazon SageMaker to efficiently send datasets large and small to your training cluster. Throughout this chapter we'll work backwards from the training loop; giving you incrementally all the steps you need to have functional deep neural networks training at scale. You'll also follow a case study from how I trained on 10TB for Stable Diffusion on SageMaker!

*Chapter 7, Finding the Right Hyperparameters* In this chapter, you'll dive into the key hyperparameters that govern performance for top vision and language models, such as batch size, learning rate, and more. First, we'll start with a quick overview of hyperparameter tuning for those who are new or new a light refresh, including key examples in vision and language. Then we'll explore hyperparameter tuning in foundation models, both what is possible today and where trends might emerge. Finally, we'll learn how to do this on Amazon SageMaker, taking incremental steps in a cluster size and changing each hyperparameter as we do.

*Chapter 8, Large-Scale Training on SageMaker* In this chapter, we cover key features and functionality available with Amazon SageMaker for running highly optimized distributed training. You'll learn how to optimize your script for SageMaker training, along with key usability features. You'll also learn about backend optimizations for distributed training with SageMaker, like GPU health checks, resilient training, checkpointing, script mode, and more.

*Chapter 9, Advanced Training Concepts* In this chapter, we will cover advanced training concepts at scale, like evaluating throughput, calculating model TFLOPS per device, compilation, and using the scaling laws to determine the right length of training time. In the last chapter you learned about how to do large-scale training on SageMaker generally speaking. In this chapter you'll learn about particularly complex and sophisticated techniques you can use to drive down the overall cost of your job. This lower cost directly translates to higher model performance, because it means you can train for longer on the same budget.

*Chapter 10, Fine-Tuning and Evaluating* In this chapter, you'll learn how to fine-tune your model on use case-specific datasets, comparing its performance to that of off-the-shelf public models. You should be able to see quantitative and qualitative boost from your pretraining regime. You'll dive into some examples from language, text, and everything in-between. You'll also learn how to think about and design a human-in-the-loop evaluation system, including the same RLHF that makes ChatGPT tick! This chapter focuses on *updating the trainable weights of the model.* For techniques that mimic learning but don't update the weights, such as prompt tuning and standard retrieval augmented generation, see Chapter 13 on prompt engineering or Chapter 15 on future trends.

*Chapter 11, Detecting, Mitigating, and Monitoring Bias* In this chapter, we'll analyze leading bias identification and mitigation strategies for large vision, language, and multimodal models. You'll learn about the concept of bias, both in a statistical sense and how it impacts human beings in critical ways. You'll understand key ways to quantify and remedy this in vision and language models, eventually landing on monitoring strategies that enable you to reduce any and all forms of harm when applying your foundation models.

*Chapter 12, How to Deploy Your Model* In this chapter, we'll introduce you to a variety of techniques for deploying your model, including real-time endpoints, serverless, batch options and more. These concepts apply to many compute environments, but we'll focus on capabilities available on AWS within Amazon SageMaker. We'll talk about why you should try to shrink the size of your model before deploying, along with techniques for this across vision and language. We'll also cover distributed hosting techniques, for scenarios when you can't or don't need to shrink your model. Lastly, we'll explore model serving techniques and concepts that can help you optimize the end-to-end performance of your model.

*Chapter 13, Prompt Engineering* In this chapter, we'll dive into a special set of techniques called prompt engineering. You'll learn about this technique at a high level, including how it is similar to and different from other learning-based topics throughout this book. We'll explore examples across vision and language, and dive into key terms and success metrics. In particular this chapter covers all of the tips and tricks for improving performance without updating the model weights. This means we'll be mimicking the learning process, without necessarily changing any of the model parameters. This includes some advanced techniques like prompt and prefix tuning.

*Chapter 14, MLOps for Vision and Language* In this chapter, we'll introduce core concepts of operations and orchestration for machine learning, also known as MLOps. This includes building pipelines, continuous integration and deployment, promotion through environments, and more. We'll explore options for monitoring and human-in-the-loop auditing of model predictions. We'll also identify unique ways to support large vision and language models in your MLOps pipelines.

*Chapter 15, Future Trends in Pretraining Foundation Models* In this chapter, we'll close out the book by pointing to where trends are headed for all relevant topics presented in this book. We'll explore trends in foundation model application development, like using LangChain to build interactive dialogue applications, along with techniques like retrieval augmented generation to reduce LLM hallucination. We'll explore ways to use generative models to solve classification tasks, human-centered design, and other generative modalities like code, music, product documentation, PowerPoints, and more! We'll talk through AWS offerings like SageMaker JumpStart Foundation Models, Amazon Bedrock, Amazon Titan, and Amazon Code Whisperer, and top trends in the future of foundation models and pretraining itself.

# To get the most out of this book

As mentioned earlier, you want to be very happy in Python development to absolutely maximize your time in this book. The pages don't spend a lot of time focusing on the software, but again, everything in the GitHub repository is Python. If you're already using a few key AWS services, like Amazon SageMaker, S3 buckets, ECR images, and FSx for Lustre, that will speed you up tremendously in applying what you've learned here. If you're new to these, that's ok, we'll include introductions to each of these.

| AWS Service or Open-source software framework | What we're using it for |
|---|---|
| Amazon SageMaker | Studio, notebook instances, training jobs, endpoints, pipelines |
| S3 buckets | Storing objects and retrieving metadata |
| Elastic Container Registry | Storing Docker images |
| FSx for Lustre | Storing large-scale data for model training loops |
| Python | General scripting: including managing and interacting with services, importing other packages, cleaning your data, defining your model training and evaluation loops, etc |
| PyTorch and TensorFlow | Deep learning frameworks to define your neural networks |
| Hugging Face | Hub with more than 100,000 open-source pretrained models and countless extremely useful and reliable methods for NLP and increasingly CV |
| Pandas | Go-to library for data analysis |
| Docker | Open-source framework for building and managing containers |

If you are using the digital version of this book, we advise you to access the code from the book's GitHub repository (a link is available in the next section), step through the examples, and type the code yourself. Doing so will help you avoid any potential errors related to the copying and pasting of code.

# Download the example code files

You can download the example code files for this book from GitHub at `https://github.com/PacktPublishing/Pretrain-Vision-and-Large-Language-Models-in-Python`. If there's an update to the code, it will be updated in the GitHub repository.

We also have other code bundles from our rich catalog of books and videos available at `https://github.com/PacktPublishing/`. Check them out!

# Conventions used

There are a number of text conventions used throughout this book.

`Code in text`: Indicates code words in text, database table names, folder names, filenames, file extensions, pathnames, dummy URLs, user input, and Twitter handles. Here is an example: "Mount the downloaded `WebStorm-10*.dmg` disk image file as another disk in your system."

A block of code is set as follows:

```
html, body, #map {
 height: 100%;
 margin: 0;
 padding: 0
}
```

**Bold**: Indicates a new term, an important word, or words that you see onscreen. For instance, words in menus or dialog boxes appear in **bold**. Here is an example: "Select **System info** from the **Administration** panel."

> **Tips or important notes**
> Appear like this.

# Get in touch

Feedback from our readers is always welcome.

**General feedback**: If you have questions about any aspect of this book, email us at `customercare@packtpub.com` and mention the book title in the subject of your message.

**Errata**: Although we have taken every care to ensure the accuracy of our content, mistakes do happen. If you have found a mistake in this book, we would be grateful if you would report this to us. Please visit www.packtpub.com/support/errata and fill in the form.

**Piracy**: If you come across any illegal copies of our works in any form on the internet, we would be grateful if you would provide us with the location address or website name. Please contact us at copyright@packt.com with a link to the material.

**If you are interested in becoming an author**: If there is a topic that you have expertise in and you are interested in either writing or contributing to a book, please visit authors.packtpub.com.

## Share Your Thoughts

Once you've read *Pretrain Vision and Large Language Models in Python*, we'd love to hear your thoughts! Scan the QR code below to go straight to the Amazon review page for this book and share your feedback.

https://packt.link/r/1-804-61825-X

Your review is important to us and the tech community and will help us make sure we're delivering excellent quality content.

# Download a free PDF copy of this book

Thanks for purchasing this book!

Do you like to read on the go but are unable to carry your print books everywhere?

Is your eBook purchase not compatible with the device of your choice?

Don't worry, now with every Packt book you get a DRM-free PDF version of that book at no cost.

Read anywhere, any place, on any device. Search, copy, and paste code from your favorite technical books directly into your application.

The perks don't stop there, you can get exclusive access to discounts, newsletters, and great free content in your inbox daily

Follow these simple steps to get the benefits:

1.  Scan the QR code or visit the link below

https://packt.link/free-ebook/9781804618257

2.  Submit your proof of purchase
3.  That's it! We'll send your free PDF and other benefits to your email directly

# Part 1: Before Pretraining

In part 1, you'll learn how to get ready to pretrain a large vision and/or language model, including dataset and model preparation.

This section has the following chapters:

# 1

# An Introduction to Pretraining Foundation Models

*The biggest lesson that can be read from 70 years of AI research is that general methods that leverage computation are ultimately the most effective, and by a large margin … The only thing that matters in the long run is the leveraging of computation.*

*– Richard Sutton, "The Bitter Lesson," 2019 (1)*

In this chapter, you'll be introduced to foundation models, the backbone of many artificial intelligence and machine learning systems today. In particular, we will dive into their creation process, also called pretraining, and understand where it's competitive to improve the accuracy of your models. We will discuss the core transformer architecture underpinning state-of-the-art models such as Stable Diffusion, BERT, Vision Transformers, OpenChatKit, CLIP, Flan-T5, and more. You will learn about the encoder and decoder frameworks, which work to solve a variety of use cases.

In this chapter, we will cover the following topics:

- The art of pretraining and fine-tuning
- The Transformer model architecture
- State-of-the-art vision and language models
- Encoders and decoders

# The art of pretraining and fine-tuning

Humanity is one of Earth's most interesting creatures. We are capable of producing the greatest of beauty and asking the most profound questions, and yet fundamental aspects about us are, in many cases, largely unknown. What exactly is consciousness? What is the human mind, and where does it reside? What does it mean to be human, and how do humans learn?

While scientists, artists, and thinkers from countless disciplines grapple with these complex questions, the field of computation marches forward to replicate (and in some cases, surpass) human intelligence. Today, applications from self-driving cars to writing screenplays, search engines, and question-answering systems have one thing in common – they all use a model, and sometimes many different kinds of models. Where do these models come from, how do they acquire intelligence, and what steps can we take to apply them for maximum impact? Foundation models are essentially compact representations of massive sets of data. The representation comes about through applying a *pretraining objective* onto the dataset, from predicting masked tokens to completing sentences. Foundation models are useful because once they have been created, through the process called pretraining, they can either be deployed directly or fine-tuned for a downstream task. An example of a foundation model deployed directly is **Stable Diffusion**, which was pretrained on billions of image-text pairs and generates useful images from text immediately after pretraining. An example of a fine-tuned foundation model is **BERT**, which was pretrained on large language datasets, but is most useful when adapted for a downstream domain, such as classification.

When applied in natural language processing, these models can complete sentences, classify text into different categories, produce summarizations, answer questions, do basic math, and generate creative artifacts such as poems and titles. In computer vision, foundation models are useful everywhere from image classification to generation, pose estimation to object detection, pixel mapping, and more.

This comes about because of defining a **pretraining objective**, which we'll learn about in detail in this book. We'll also cover its peer method, **fine-tuning**, which helps the model learn more about a specific domain. This more generally falls under the category of **transfer learning**, the practice of taking a pretrained neural network and supplying it with a novel dataset with the hope of enhancing its knowledge in a certain dimension. In both vision and language, these terms have some overlap and some clear distinctions, but don't worry, we'll cover them more throughout the chapters. I'm using the term *fine-tuning* to include the whole set of techniques to adapt a model to another domain, outside of the one where it was trained, not in the narrow, classic sense of the term.

### Fundamentals – pretraining objectives

The heart of large-scale pretraining revolves around this core concept. A **pretraining objective** is a method that leverages information readily available in the dataset without requiring extensive human labeling. Some pretraining objectives involve masking, providing a unique [MASK] token in place of certain words, and training the model to fill in those words. Others take a different route, using the left-hand side of a given text string to attempt to generate the right-hand side.

The training process happens through a **forward pass**, sending your raw training data through the neural network to produce some output word. The loss function then computes the difference between this predicted word and the one found in the data. This difference between the predicted values and the actual values then serves as the basis for the **backward pass**. The backward pass itself usually leverages a type of stochastic gradient descent to update the parameters of the neural network with respect to that same loss function, ensuring that, next time around, it's more likely to get a lower loss function.

In the case of BERT*(2)*, the pretraining objective is called a **masked token loss**. For generative textual models of the GPT *(3)* variety, the pretraining objective is called **causal language loss**. Another way of thinking about this entire process is **self-supervised learning**, utilizing content already available in a dataset to serve as a signal to the model. In computer vision, you'll also see this referred to as a **pretext task**. More on state-of-the-art models in the sections ahead!

Personally, I think pretraining is one of the most exciting developments in machine learning research. Why? Because, as Richard Sutton suggests controversially at the start of the chapter, it's computationally efficient. Using pretraining, you can build a model from massive troves of information available on the internet, then combine all of this knowledge using your own proprietary data and apply it to as many applications as you can dream of. On top of that, pretraining opens the door for tremendous collaboration across company, country, language, and domain lines. The industry is truly just getting started in developing, perfecting, and exploiting the pretraining paradigm.

We know that pretraining is interesting and effective, but where is it competitive in its own right? Pretraining your own model is useful *when your own proprietary dataset is very large and different from common research datasets, and primarily unlabeled*. Most of the models we will learn about in this book are trained on similar corpora – Wikipedia, social media, books, and popular internet sites. Many of them focus on the English language, and few of them consciously use the rich interaction between visual and textual data. Throughout the book, we will learn about the nuances and different advantages of selecting and perfecting your pretraining strategies.

If your business or research hypothesis hinges on non-standard natural languages, such as financial or legal terminology, non-English languages, or rich knowledge from another domain, you may want to consider pretraining your own model from scratch. The core question you want to ask yourself is, *How valuable is an extra one percentage point of accuracy in my model?* If you do not know the answer to this question, then I strongly recommend spending some time getting yourself to an answer. We will spend time discussing how to do this in *Chapter 2*. Once you can confidently say an increase in the accuracy of my model is worth at least a few hundred thousand dollars, and even possibly a few million, then you are ready to begin pretraining your own model.

Now that we have learned about foundation models, how they come about through a process called pretraining, and how to adapt them to a specific domain through fine-tuning, let's learn more about the Transformer model architecture.

# The Transformer model architecture and self-attention

The Transformer model, presented in the now-famous 2017 paper *Attention is all you need*, marked a turning point for the machine learning industry. This is primarily because it used an existing mathematical technique, self-attention, to solve problems in NLP related to sequences. The Transformer certainly wasn't the first attempt at modeling sequences, previously, **recurrent neural networks** (**RNNs**) and even **convolutional neural networks** (**CNNs**) were popular in language.

However, the Transformer made headlines because its training cost was a small fraction of the existing techniques. This is because the Transformer is fundamentally easier to parallelize, due to its core self-attention process, than previous techniques. It also set new world records in machine translation. The original Transformer used both an encoder and decoder, techniques we will dive into later throughout this chapter. This joint encoder-decoder pattern was followed directly by other models focused on similar text-to-text tasks, such as T5.

In 2018, Alex Radford and his team presented **Generative Pretrained Transformers**, a method inspired by the 2017 Transformer, but using only the decoder. Called **GPT**, this model handled large-scale unsupervised pretraining well, and it was paired with supervised fine-tuning to perform well on downstream tasks. As we mentioned previously, this *causal language modeling* technique optimizes the log probability of tokens, giving us a left-to-right ability to find the most probable word in a sequence.

In 2019, Jacob Devlin and his team presented *BERT: Pretraining of Deep Bidirectional Transformers*. BERT also adopted the pretraining, fine-tuning paradigm, but implemented a masked language modeling loss function that helped the model learn the impact of tokens both before and after them. This proved useful in disambiguating the meaning of words in different contexts and has aided encoder-only tasks such as classification ever since.

Despite their names, neither GPT nor BERT uses the full encoder-decoder as presented in the original Transformer paper but instead leverages the **self-attention mechanism** as core steps throughout the learning process. Thus, it is in fact the self-attention process we should understand.

First, remember that each word, or token, is represented as an embedding. This embedding is created simply by using a **tokenizer**, a pretrained data object for each model that maps the word to its appropriate dense vector. Once we have the embedding per token, we use **learnable weights** to generate three new vectors: **key**, **query**, and **value**. We then use matrix multiplication and a few steps to interact with the key and the query, using the value at the very end to determine what was most informative in the sequence overall. Throughout the training loop, we update these weights to get better and better interactions, as determined by your pretraining objective.

Your pretraining objective serves as a directional guide for how to update the model parameters. Said another way, your pretraining objective provides the primary signal to your stochastic gradient descent updating procedure, changing the weights of your model based on how incorrect your model predictions are. When you train for long periods of time, the parameters should reflect a decrease in loss, giving you an overall increase in accuracy.

Interestingly, the type of transformer heads will change slightly based on the different types of pretraining objectives you're using. For example, a normal self-attention block uses information from both the left- and right-hand sides of a token to predict it. This is to provide the most informative contextual information for the prediction and is useful in masked language modeling. In practice, the self-attention heads are stacked to operate on full matrices of embeddings, giving us multi-head attention. Casual language modeling, however, uses a different type of attention head: masked self-attention. This limits the scope of predictive information to only the left-hand side of the matrix, forcing the model to learn a left-to-right procedure. This is in contrast to the more traditional self-attention, which has access to both the left and right sides of the sequence to make predictions.

Most of the time, in practice, and certainly throughout this book, you won't need to code any transformers or self-attention heads from scratch. Through this book, we will, however, be diving into many model architectures, so it's helpful to have this conceptual knowledge as a base.

From an intuitive perspective, what you'll need to understand about transformers and self-attention is fewfold:

- **The transformer itself is a model entirely built upon a self-attention function**: The self-attention function takes a set of inputs, such as embeddings, and performs mathematical operations to combine these. When combined with token (word or subword) masking, the model can effectively learn how significant certain parts of the embeddings, or the sequence, are to the other parts. This is the meaning of self-attention; the model is trying to understand which parts of the input dataset are most relevant to the other parts.

- **Transformers perform exceedingly well using sequences**: Most of the benchmarks they've blown past in recent years are from NLP, for a good reason. The pretraining objectives for these include token masking and sequence completion, both of which rely on not just individual data points but the stringing of them together, and their combination. This is good news for those of you who already work with sequential data and an interesting challenge for those who don't.

- **Transformers operate very well at large scales**: The underlying attention head is easily parallelizable, which gives it a strong leg-up in reference to other candidate sequence-based neural network architectures such as RNNs, including **Long Short-Term Memory (LSTM)** based networks. The self-attention head can be set to trainable in the case of pretraining, or untrainable in the case of fine-tuning. When attempting to actually train the self-attention heads, as we'll do throughout this book, the best performance you'll see is when the transformers are applied on large datasets. How large they need to be, and what trade-offs you can make when electing to fine-tune or pretrain, is the subject of future chapters.

Transformers are not the only means of pretraining. As we'll see throughout the next section, there are many different types of models, particularly in vision and multimodal cases, which can deliver state-of-the-art performance.

# State-of-the-art vision and language models

If you're new to machine learning, then there is a key concept you will eventually want to learn how to master, that is, **state of the art**. As you are aware, there are many different types of machine learning tasks, such as object detection, semantic segmentation, pose detection, text classification, and question answering. For each of these, there are many different research datasets. Each of these datasets provides labels, frequently for train, test, and validation splits. The datasets tend to be hosted by academic institutions, and each of these is purpose-built to train machine learning models that solve each of these types of problems.

When releasing a new dataset, researchers will frequently also release a new model that has been trained on the train set, tuned on the validation set, and separately evaluated on the test set. Their evaluation score on a new test set establishes a new state of the art for this specific type of modeling problem. When publishing certain types of papers, researchers will frequently try to improve performance in this area – for example, by trying to increase accuracy by a few percentage points on a handful of datasets.

The reason state-of-the-art performance matters for you is that it is a strong indication of how well your model is likely to perform in the best possible scenario. It isn't easy to replicate most research results, and frequently, labs will have developed special techniques to improve performance that may not be easily observed and replicated by others. This is especially true when datasets and code repositories aren't shared publicly, as is the case with GPT-3. This is acutely true when training methods aren't disclosed, as with GPT-4.

However, given sufficient resources, it is possible to achieve similar performance as reported in top papers. An excellent place to find state-of-the-art performance at any given point in time is an excellent website, *Papers With Code*, maintained by Meta and enhanced by the community. By using this free tool, you can easily find top papers, datasets, models, and GitHub sites with example code. Additionally, they have great historical views, so you can see how the top models in different datasets have evolved over time.

In later chapters on preparing datasets and picking models, we'll go into more detail on how to find the right examples for you, including how to determine how similar to and different from your own goals they are. Later in the book, we'll also help you determine the optimal models, and sizes for them. Right now, let's look at some models that, as of this writing, are currently sitting at the top of their respective leaderboards.

# Top vision models as of April 2023

First, let's take a quick look at the models performing the best today within image tasks such as classification and generation.

| Dataset | Best model | From Transformer | Performance |
|---|---|---|---|
| ImageNet | Basic-L (Lion fine-tuned) | Yes | 91.10% top 1% accuracy |
| CIFAR-10 | ViT-H/14 *(1)* | Yes | 99.5% correct |
| COCO | InternImage-H (M3I Pre-training: `https://paperswithcode.com/paper/internimage-exploring-large-scale-vision`) | No | 65.0 Box AP |
| STL-10 | Diffusion ProjectedGAN | No | 6.91 FID (generation) |
| ObjectNet | CoCa | Yes | 82.7% top 1% accuracy |
| MNIST | Heterogeneous ensemble with simple CNN *(1)* | No | 99.91% accuracy (0.09% error) |

Table 1.1 – Top image results

At first glance, these numbers may seem intimidating. After all, many of them are near or close to 99% accurate! Isn't that too high of a bar for beginning or intermediate machine learning practitioners?

Before we get too carried away with doubt and fear, it's helpful to understand that most of these accuracy scores came at least five years after the research dataset was published. If we analyze the historical graphs available on *Paper With Code*, it's easy to see that when the first researchers published their datasets, initial accuracy scores were closer to 60%. Then, it took many years of hard work, across diverse organizations and teams, to finally produce models capable of hitting the 90s. So, don't lose heart! If you put in the time, you too can train a model that establishes a new state-of-the-art performance in a given area. This part is science, not magic.

You'll notice that while some of these models do in fact adopt a Transformer-inspired backend, some do not. Upon closer inspection, you'll also see that some of these models rely on the pretrain and fine-tune paradigm we'll be learning about in this book, but not all of them. If you're new to machine learning, then this discrepancy is something to start getting comfortable with! Robust and diverse scientific debate, perspectives, insights, and observations are critical aspects of maintaining healthy communities and increasing the quality of outcomes across the field as a whole. This means that you can, and should, expect some divergence in methods you come across, and that's a good thing.

Now that you have a better understanding of top models in computer vision these days, let's explore one of the earliest methods combining techniques from large language models with vision: contrastive pretraining and natural language supervision.

## Contrastive pretraining and natural language supervision

What's interesting about both modern and classic image datasets, from Fei-Fei Li's 2006 ImageNet to the LAION-5B as used in 2022 Stable Diffusion, is that the labels themselves are composed of natural language. Said another way, because the scope of the images includes objects from the physical world, the labels necessarily are more nuanced than single digits. Broadly speaking, this type of problem framing is called **natural language supervision**.

Imagine having a large dataset of tens of millions of images, each provided with captions. Beyond simply naming the objects, a caption gives you more information about the content of the images. A caption can be anything from *Stella sits on a yellow couch* to *Pepper, the Australian pup*. In just a few words we immediately get more context than simply describing the objects. Now, imagine using a pretrained model, such as an encoder, to process the language into a dense vector representation. Then, combine this with another pretrained model, this time an image encoder, to process the image into another dense vector representation. Combine both of these in a learnable matrix, and you are on your way to contrastive pretraining! Also presented by Alex Radford and the team, just a few years after their work on GPT, this method gives us both a way to jointly learn about the relationship between both images and language and a model well suited to do so. The model is called **Contrastive Language-Image Pretraining (CLIP)**.

CLIP certainly isn't the only vision-language pretraining task that uses natural language supervision. One year earlier, in 2019, a research team from China proposed a **Visual-Linguistic BERT** model attempting a similar goal. Since then, the joint training of vision-and-language foundation models has become very popular, with Flamingo, Imagen, and Stable Diffusion all presenting interesting work.

Now that we've learned a little bit about joint vision-and-language contrastive pretraining, let's explore today's top models in language.

## Top language models as of April 2023

Now, let's evaluate some of today's best-in-class models for a task extremely pertinent to foundation models, and thus this book: language modeling. This table shows a set of language model benchmark results across a variety of scenarios.

| Dataset | Best model | From Transformer | Performance |
|---|---|---|---|
| WikiText-103 | Hybrid H3 (2.7B params) | No | 10.60 test perplexity |
| Penn Treebank (Word Level) | GPT-3 (Zero-Shot) *(1)* | Yes | 20.5 test perplexity |
| LAMBADA | PaLM-540B (Few-Shot) *(1)* | Yes | 89.7% accuracy |
| Penn Treebank (Character Level) | Mogrifer LSTM + dynamic eval *(1)* | No | 1.083 bit per character |
| C4 (Colossal Clean Crawled Corpus) | Primer | No | 12.35 perplexity |

Table 1.2 – Top language modeling results

First, let's try to answer a fundamental question. What is language modeling, and why does it matter? Language modeling as known today appears to have been formalized in two cornerstone papers: BERT *(9)* and GPT *(10)*. The core concept that inspired both papers is deceptively simple: how do we better use unsupervised natural language?

As is no doubt unsurprising to you, the vast majority of natural language in our world has no direct digital label. Some natural language lends itself well to concrete labels, such as cases where objectivity is beyond doubt. This can include accuracy in answering questions, summarization, high-level sentiment analysis, document retrieval, and more.

But the process of finding these labels and producing the datasets necessary for them can be prohibitive, as it is entirely manual. At the same time, many unsupervised datasets get larger by the minute. Now that much of the global dialog is online, datasets rich in variety are easy to access. So, how can ML researchers position themselves to benefit from these large, unsupervised datasets?

This is exactly the problem that language modeling seeks to solve. Language modeling is a process to apply mathematical techniques on large corpora of unlabelled text, relying on a variety of pretraining objectives to enable the model to *teach itself* about the text. Also called **self-supervision**, the precise method of learning varies based on the model at hand. BERT applies a mask randomly throughout the dataset and learns to predict the word hidden by the mask, using an encoder. GPT uses a decoder to predict left-to-right, starting at the beginning of a sentence, for example, and learning how to predict the end of the sentence. Models in the T5 family use both encoders and decoders to learn text-to-text tasks, such as translation and search. As proposed in ELECTRA *(11)*, another alternative is a **token replacement** objective, which opts to inject new tokens into the original text, rather than masking them.

**Fundamentals – fine-tuning**

Foundational language models are only useful in applications when paired with their peer method, fine-tuning. The intuition behind fine-tuning is very understandable; we want to take a foundational model pretrained elsewhere and apply a much smaller set of data to make it more focused and useful for our specific task. We can also call this **domain adaptation** – adapting a pretrained model to an entirely different domain that was not included in its pretraining task.

Fine-tuning tasks are everywhere! You can take a base language model, such as BERT, and fine-tune it for text classification. Or question answering. Or named entity recognition. Or you could take a different model, GPT-2 for example, and fine-tune it for summarization. Or you could take something like T5 and fine-tune it for translation. The basic idea is that you are leveraging the intelligence of the foundation model. You're leveraging the compute, the dataset, the large neural network, and ultimately, the distribution method the researchers leveraged simply by inheriting their pretrained artifact. Then, you can optionally add extra layers to the network yourself, or more likely, use a software framework such as Hugging Face to simplify the process. Hugging Face has done an amazing job building an extremely popular open source framework with tens of thousands of pretrained models, and we'll see in future chapters how to best utilize their examples to build our own models in both vision and language. There are many different types of fine-tuning, from parameter-efficient fine-tuning to instruction-fine-tuning, chain of thought, and even methods that don't strictly update the core model parameters such as retrieval augmented generation. We'll discuss these later in the book.

As we will discover in future chapters, foundational language and vision models are not without their negative aspects. For starters, their extremely large compute requirements place significant energy demands on service providers. Ensuring that energy is met through sustainable means and that the modeling process is as efficient as possible are top goals for the models of the future. These large compute requirements are also obviously quite expensive, posing inherent challenges for those without sufficient resources. I would argue, however, that the core techniques you'll learn throughout this book are relevant across a wide spectrum of computational needs and resourcing. Once you've demonstrated success at a smaller scale of pretraining, it's usually much easier to justify the additional ask.

Additionally, as we will see in future chapters, large models are infamous for their ability to inherit social biases present in their training data. From associating certain employment aspects with gender to classifying criminal likelihood based on race, researchers have identified hundreds (9) of ways bias can creep into NLP systems. As with all technology, designers and developers must be aware of these risks and take steps to mitigate them. In later chapters, I'll identify a variety of steps you can take today to reduce these risks.

Next, let's learn about a core technique used in defining appropriate experiments for language models: the scaling laws!

# Language technique spotlight – causal modeling and the scaling laws

You've no doubt heard of the now-infamous model **ChatGPT**. For a few years, a San Francisco-based AI firm, OpenAI, developed research with a mission to improve humanity's outcomes around artificial intelligence. Toward that end, they made bold leaps in scaling language models, deriving formulas as one might in physics to explain the performance of LLMs at scale. They originally positioned themselves as a non-profit, releasing their core insights and the code to reproduce them. Four years after its founding, however, they pivoted to cutting exclusive billion-dollar deals with Microsoft. Now, their 600-strong R&D teams focus on developing proprietary models and techniques, and many open source projects attempt to replicate and improve on their offerings. Despite this controversial pivot, the team at OpenAI gave the industry a few extremely useful insights. The first is GPT, and the second is the scaling laws.

As mentioned previously, GPT-based models use **causal language modeling** to learn how best to complete text. This means using a left-to-right completion learning criteria, which updates the model's learnable parameters until the text is completely accurate. While the first GPT model of 2018 was itself useful, the real excitement came years later in two phases. First, Jared Kaplan lead a team at OpenAI to suggest a novel concept: using formulas inspired by his work in physics to estimate the impact the size of the model, dataset, and overall compute environment will have on the loss of the model. These *Scaling Laws for Neural Language Models (9)* suggested that the optimal model size for a given compute environment was massive.

The original GPT model of 2018 was only 117 million parameters, and its second version, aptly named GPT-2, increased the model size by up to 10x. This increase in parameter size more than doubled the overall accuracy of the model. Encouraged by these results, and fuelled by Kaplan's theoretical and empirical findings, OpenAI boldly increased the model parameter size by another 10x, giving us GPT-3.

As the model increased in size, from 1.3 billion parameters to 13 billion, ultimately hitting 175 billion parameters, accuracy also took a huge leap! This result catalyzed the field of NLP, unleashing new use cases and a flurry of new work exploring and extending these impacts. Since then, new work has explored both larger (PaLM *(9)*) and smaller (Chinchilla *(10)*) models, with Chinchilla presenting an update to the scaling laws entirely. Yann LeCunn's team at Meta has also presented smaller models that outperform the larger ones in specific areas, such as question-answering (Atlas *(9)*). Amazon has also presented two models that outperform GPT-3: the AlexaTM and MM-COT. Numerous teams have also undertaken efforts to produce open source versions of GPT-3, such as Hugging Face's BLOOM, EleutherAI'S GPT-J, and Meta's OPT.

The rest of this book is dedicated to discussing these models – where they come from, what they are good for, and especially how to train your own! While much excellent work has covered using these pretrained models in production through fine-tuning, such as Hugging Face's own *Natural Language Processing with Transformers* (Tunstall et al., 2022), I continue to believe that pretraining your own foundation model is probably the most interesting computational intellectual exercise you can embark on today. I also believe it's one of the most profitable. But more on that ahead!

Next, let's learn about two key model components you'll need to understand in detail: encoders and decoders.

## Encoders and decoders

Now, I'd like to briefly introduce you to two key topics that you'll see in the discussion of transformer-based models: encoders and decoders. Let's establish some basic intuition to help you understand what they are all about. An encoder is simply a computational graph (or neural network, function, or object depending on your background), which takes an input with a larger feature space and returns an object with a smaller feature space. We hope (and demonstrate computationally) that the encoder is able to learn what is most essential about the provided input data.

Typically, in large language and vision models, the encoder itself is composed of a number of multi-head self-attention objects. This means that in transformer-based models, an encoder is usually a number of self-attention steps, learning what is most essential about the provided input data and passing this onto the downstream model. Let's look at a quick visual:

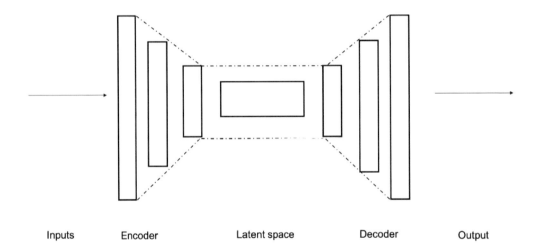

Inputs          Encoder                    Latent space              Decoder            Output

Figure 1.1 – Encoders and decoders

Intuitively, as you can see in the preceding figure, the encoder starts with a larger input space and iteratively compresses this to a smaller latent space. In the case of classification, this is just a classification head with output allotted for each class. In the case of masked language modeling, encoders are stacked on top of each other to better predict tokens to replace the masks. This means the encoders output an embedding, or a numerical representation of that token, and after prediction, the tokenizer is reused to translate that embedding back into natural language.

One of the earliest large language models, BERT, is an encoder-only model. Most other BERT-based models, such as DeBERTa, DistiliBERT, RoBERTa, DeBERTa, and others in this family use encoder-only model architectures. Decoders operate exactly in reverse, starting with a compressed representation and iteratively recomposing that back into a larger feature space. Both encoders and decoders can be combined, as in the original Transformer, to solve text-to-text problems.

To make it easier, here's a short table quickly summarizing the three types of self-attention blocks we've looked at, encoders, decoders, and their combination.

| Size of inputs and outputs | Type of self-attention blocks | Machine learning tasks | Example models |
|---|---|---|---|
| Long to short | Encoder | Classification, any dense representation | BERT, DeBERTa, DistiliBERT, RoBERTa, XLM, AlBERT, CLIP, VL-BERT, Vision Transformer |
| Short to long | Decoder | Generation, summarization, question-answering, any sparse representation | GPT, GPT-2, GPT-Neo, GPT-J, ChatGPT, GPT-4, BLOOM, OPT |
| Equal | Encoder-decoder | Machine translation, style translation | T5, BART, BigBird, FLAN-T5, Stable Diffusion |

Table 1.3 – Encoders, decoders, and their combination

Now that you have a better understanding of encoders, decoders, and the models they create, let's close out the chapter with a quick recap of all the concepts you just learned about.

## Summary

We've covered a lot in just this first chapter! Let's quickly recap some of the top themes before moving on. First, we looked at the art of pretraining and fine-tuning, including a few key pretraining objects such as masked language and causal language modeling. We learned about the Transformer model architecture, including the core self-attention mechanism with its variant. We looked at state-of-the-art vision and language models, including spotlights on contrastive pretraining from natural language supervision, and scaling laws for neural language models. We learned about encoders, decoders, and their combination, which are useful throughout the vision and language domains today.

Now that you have a great conceptual and applied basis to understand pretraining foundation models, let's look at preparing your dataset: part one.

# References

Please go through the following content for more information on a few topics covered in the chapter:

1.  *The Bitter Lesson*, Rich Sutton, March 13, 2019: `http://www.incompleteideas.net/IncIdeas/BitterLesson.html`

2.  Jacob Devlin, Ming-Wei Chang, Kenton Lee, and Kristina Toutanova. 2019. *BERT: Pre-training of Deep Bidirectional Transformers for Language Understanding*: `https://aclanthology.org/N19-1423/`. In *Proceedings of the 2019 Conference of the North American Chapter of the Association for Computational Linguistics: Human Language Technologies, Volume 1 (Long and Short Papers)*, pages 4171–4186, Minneapolis, Minnesota. Association for Computational Linguistics.

3.  Brown, Tom and Mann, Benjamin and Ryder, Nick and Subbiah, Melanie and Kaplan, Jared D and Dhariwal, Prafulla and Neelakantan, Arvind and Shyam, Pranav and Sastry, Girish and Askell, Amanda and Agarwal, Sandhini and Herbert-Voss, Ariel and Krueger, Gretchen and Henighan, Tom and Child, Rewon and Ramesh, Aditya and Ziegler, Daniel and Wu, Jeffrey and Winter, Clemens and Hesse, Chris and Chen, Mark and Sigler, Eric and Litwin, Mateusz and Gray, Scott and Chess, Benjamin and Clark, Jack and Berner, Christopher and McCandlish, Sam and Radford, Alec and Sutskever, Ilya and Amodei, Dario. 2020. *Language Models are Few-Shot Learners*. In *Advances in Neural Information Processing Systems, Volume 33*. Pages 1877-1901. Curran Associates, Inc.

4.  *AN IMAGE IS WORTH 16X16 WORDS: TRANSFORMERS FOR IMAGE RECOGNITION AT SCALE*: `https://arxiv.org/pdf/2010.11929v2.pdf`

5.  *AN ENSEMBLE OF SIMPLE CONVOLUTIONAL NEURAL NETWORK MODELS FOR MNIST DIGIT RECOGNITION*: `https://arxiv.org/pdf/2008.10400v2.pdf`

6.  *Language Models are Few-Shot Learners*: `https://arxiv.org/pdf/2005.14165v4.pdf`

7.  *PaLM: Scaling Language Modeling with Pathways*: `https://arxiv.org/pdf/2204.02311v3.pdf`

8.  *MOGRIFIER LSTM*: `https://arxiv.org/pdf/1909.01792v2.pdf`

9.  *BERT: Pre-training of Deep Bidirectional Transformers for Language Understanding*: `https://arxiv.org/pdf/1810.04805.pdf`

10. *Improving Language Understanding by Generative Pre-Training*: `https://s3-us-west-2.amazonaws.com/openai-assets/research-covers/language-unsupervised/language_understanding_paper.pdf`

11. *ELECTRA: PRE-TRAINING TEXT ENCODERS AS DISCRIMINATORS RATHER THAN GENERATORS*: `https://arxiv.org/pdf/2003.10555.pdf`

12. *Language (Technology) is Power: A Critical Survey of "Bias" in NLP*: `https://arxiv.org/pdf/2005.14050.pdf`

13. *Scaling Laws for Neural Language Models*: `https://arxiv.org/pdf/2001.08361.pdf`

14. *PaLM: Scaling Language Modeling with Pathways*: `https://arxiv.org/pdf/2204.02311.pdf`

15. *Training Compute-Optimal Large Language Models*: `https://arxiv.org/pdf/2203.15556.pdf`

16. *Atlas: Few-shot Learning with Retrieval Augmented Language Models*: `https://arxiv.org/pdf/2208.03299.pdf`

# 2

# Dataset Preparation: Part One

In this chapter, we will begin to discuss what you'll need in your dataset to start a meaningful pretraining project. This is the first of two parts on dataset preparation. It opens with some business guidance on finding a good use case for foundation modeling, where the data becomes instrumental. Then, focusing on the content of your dataset, we use qualitative and quantitative measures to compare it with datasets used to pretrain other top models. You'll learn how to determine whether your datasets are "large enough" and "good enough" to boost accuracy while pretraining. We discuss bias identification and mitigation, along with multilingual and multimodal solutions.

In this chapter, we will cover the following topics:

- A business-level discussion on finding datasets and use cases for foundation modeling

- Evaluating your dataset by comparing it to ones available in the open source research community

- Using scaling laws to size your dataset appropriately

- Bias detection and mitigation

- Dataset enhancements – multilingual and augmentation

## Finding a dataset and use case for foundation modeling

Datasets – we love them, we struggle with them, we rely on them, and we ignore them, oftentimes all at once. Every transaction, every digital moment, every archive, and every snapshot is a candidate for inclusion in a dataset. If your organization has already gone through a digital transformation, or if you're digitally native, odds are you are already heavily invested in some data storage solution. Whether it's on-premises or in the cloud, every organization needs a secure, reliable, operational, and robust solution to store countless types of data. The major question for you right now is, how can I monetize that? How can I lean into what is most unique about my organization's history and strengths, and capitalize on it to develop net-new capabilities that further my own competitive advantage?

For companies that already have machine learning models deployed into production applications, an easy way to find a candidate dataset for a foundation modeling project is to ask yourself, what is the single common denominator in all of my models? What domains, what modalities, and what signals do those models rely on, and what resources can I draw on to increase the overall intelligence of these models?

One common mental exercise is to consider the interactions that are core to your business. From search to customer support, supply chain, product development and maintenance, marketing, and so on, each of your lines of business involve decision making on a regular basis. Now, ask yourself the following:

- What if I could improve the accuracy of this decision making by 1%?

- What if I could increase my marketing lead conversion by 1%?

- What if I could recommend better content to customers by 1%?

- What if I could increase my operational efficiency by 1%?

- What if I could answer questions more accurately by 1%?

- What if I could deliver my products faster by 1%?

Once you've found a certain aspect of your business that's most interesting to you or where you think the impact of your investment could be the highest, try to quantify this number. Will an increase in accuracy by 1% give you $50,000? What about $500,000? Maybe even $1,000,000? Many multiples of that? I'm stating the obvious here, but all things being equal, higher is clearly better. You want to pick an area you think will have the absolute maximum return on your investment.

Now, once you have that area of your organization identified, take 10% of the total estimated earnings, or some other low percentage you feel more comfortable with. That is your maximum compute budget. Now, don't worry – we're not going to blow through that all at once. You may not even need to spend it all. As we step through this book, I'll help you figure out how to get early signals that your project is going to be successful, such as training on 1% of your data to ensure the performance is better than open source models. You want to hit key milestones throughout your pretraining project, and as you hit those milestones, you will get closer to achieving your end goal. That overall goal is also the same number you'll use to figure out how much time it's worth for you to spend on this project, how many people you'll want to pull in, how many sprints to use, and so on.

Once you have this target application in mind, along with both the estimated return and costs, you are ready to start bringing it to life! Start listing any datasets your organization already stores that are related to the application you want to build. Do you have relational databases with transactions relevant to this? Customer history? Click-stream data? Search results? What about images? Do you have any videos? Any audio files? Any experimental results? Push yourself to be creative in listing as many candidate datasets as you have. Consider taking a solid hour just to look around and see what your organization already has stored around this candidate application area. If it's already mission-critical, then most likely you have quite a bit stored already.

If you don't already have at least a few GB of data or, even better, a few 10s of GB, then you might want to consider gathering a new dataset from open source solutions. These might include any combination of over 6,000 datasets available through the *Papers With Code* site *(1)*. You can also look at the 8,000 datasets available from the *Hugging Face Hub (2)*. Remember, these datasets are available at no cost! Open source datasets are an excellent way to start proving the concept of your idea. Common datasets for language pretraining are *The Pile, Common Crawl, Wikipedia, CodeParrot*, and so on *(3)*. You can also look at the OSCAR corpus for multimodal pretraining. The **Vision Transformer** (**ViT**) *(4)* model was trained from scratch on ImageNet. You have plenty of options! You can also use all of these open source datasets to enhance your original dataset, using the best of both open source and proprietary options.

Something else to remember is that *pretraining explicitly benefits from unlabeled data.* The best pretraining projects happen when they leverage large volumes of unlabeled data and smaller volumes of labeled data. This is largely why pretraining foundation models is popular – most data in the world isn't labeled. However, when we use a pretraining objective, as we learned about in the first chapter, we can easily train models to learn about this. Then, we fine-tune them using supervised data, which is usually smaller in quantity.

So, if you find yourself in a scenario with multiple hundreds of GBs of data, such as images, files, records, transactions, metadata, and time-series data, you may want to consider that as a top candidate for custom pretraining.

## Top pretraining use cases by industry

Now, let's highlight a few top use cases to pretrain custom foundational models by industry. These are areas in our world where pretraining and finetuning are already having an impact today:

- **Software and internet**:

  - Search and discovery

  - Generating documentation and code

  - Questioning/answering

- **Hospitality and travel**:

  - Customer support and service

  - Booking recommendations

- **Consumer electronics**:

  - Design automation

  - Fashion design automation

- **Financial services**:

  - Document summarization and generation

  - Multimodal forecasts

- **Media and entertainment**:

  - Creativity enhancement

  - Speeding up the generation of creatives (new images, new movies, better artifacts, and so on)

  - Identifying the best creative to move to finals (best shot, best sequence, best melody, and so on)

- **Health care and life sciences**:

  - Protein modeling, drug discovery, and experimental prioritization

  - Notes synthesis and diagnosis confirmation

  - Visual results confirmation and experiment result prioritization

  - Scientific literature synthesis and experimental design suggestion

- **Manufacturing and agriculture**:

  - Part defects and building error detection

  - Overall design automation of parts and products

  - Autonomous product design

- **Public sector governance**:

  - Policy impact analysis automation

  - Policy suggestion automation

  - Political and philosophical difference reconciliation

  - Budget impact assessment and analysis automation

Let's now move on to see how different your dataset is.

# Delta – how different is your dataset?

Now that you have some idea of what use case you are most interested in, and what datasets will give your organization the most value, it's time to understand how unique your dataset is. This analysis matters because it will answer two questions:

1.  First, which models are already on the table for you to use, due to having been trained on similar data?

2.  Second, how well have those models performed?

This insight will start to give you a clue toward what performance you can hope to achieve on your datasets as a best-case scenario. Then, we'll plug that expected performance number back into our total project value and make sure we're still on track. The next chapter is completely dedicated to answering those questions. Here, we'll learn how to pick apart your dataset. This is a good section for those who are new to data analysis.

First, it's always a good idea to spend time really analyzing any dataset you're touching. Whether you are starting from something custom in your own database, or working with an open source option, anticipate spending at least a few hours getting to know it in little detail. Probably the best phrase I've heard to inspire this process is, *a good data science team asks more questions than they answer.* This is because *the act of analyzing a dataset is a living process, not a finite state.* Getting to know a dataset is a little bit like getting to know a person; it's just that the way you ask questions and make observations is totally different.

Start by verbally describing the contours of your dataset. How many rows does it have? How many columns? How large are the images? How many tokens does it have? What features does it have? Are they numeric or categorical? Is it based on time? What metadata does it have? Make sure you have a good picture in your mind of what this dataset looks like. Talk with other people on your team about it until you feel confident and can answer questions quickly about the basics of your dataset composition. Use common data analysis techniques, such as Jupyter notebooks, to produce summary statistics and charts, and perform exploratory data analysis.

Critically, ask yourself, what real-world process was this dataset drawn from? How was this dataset acquired? We call this a sampling mechanism. If you are new to data analysis, and especially new to data analysis in applied settings outside of theoretical research, the first thing you'll need to understand is that "not all sampling mechanisms are perfect." To put it another way, you should get into the practice of assuming that there may be something wrong with your dataset. You need to critically evaluate the way your dataset was developed. Was it randomly collected? Or does all of the data have some underlying similarities? Any errors? The most important part of your data analysis process is to disabuse yourself of any underlying errors, inconsistencies, oddities, and faults in the raw data itself. You need to gain certainty that the data itself is indeed valid and reliable. Why? Because this certainty serves as a fundamental guarantee for everything you produce from this dataset. If the data isn't reliable, your work can never be reliable.

When you have an idea about your dataset, before that idea is proven true by the results you empirically observe, it's called a **hypothesis**. A hypothesis is a concept you believe may be true about your dataset, or about any real-world process. However, because you currently lack empirical evidence validating the certainty of this hypothesis, you can't state at the current time that it is objectively true. That's why we call it a hypothesis!

A core part of the scientific process, and as a corollary, your own development in machine learning is learning how to state this hypothesis clearly. You can phrase it as a simple question, something as basic as "which model solves this problem the best?", "what does it mean to solve this type of problem optimally?", or even, "how can we improve upon the state of the art in this area?"

Once you have a hypothesis, also called a **research objective**, clearly stated, you then want to learn "how to design experiments that answer this question." Experimental design is a surprisingly challenging skill! This includes the work of evaluating current research in certain areas, considering open questions and results others have demonstrated, and attempting to build upon them empirically. At the end of your project, you want to have clear empirical results you can point to that validate your work. We'll discuss this more in the following chapters on model evaluation, but it's a critical topic to keep in mind.

Next, let's learn about sizing our datasets.

## Use the scaling laws to size your datasets

At this point, you should have identified your datasets, have a basic understanding of them, and be able to describe how they are similar to and different from previous datasets and research work in your chosen domain. It's helpful to have at least a handful of papers to refer to so that you can do so when you're stuck.

In this section, we'll explore how large your dataset should be in order to produce the expected results on a pretraining or fine-tuning project, which clearly validates the time and compute expenses you'll be racking up. We'll also discuss certain characteristics you'll want this dataset to have, such as sufficient variety, quality, and lack of duplicates. The entirety of the next chapter is dedicated to picking the right model, including the size and scope, but for now, we'll focus on the dataset.

First, it's helpful to know that there is a very large gray area between so-called large and small models and the corresponding size in datasets that they tend to run on. Under no circumstances should you think that you only need multiple terabytes and/or petabytes to think about pretraining, or even models that don't fit on a single GPU. You can produce meaningful results with unsupervised data simply by continuing to pretrain your model, rather than necessarily starting pretraining from scratch, and still hit your business and intellectual goals. Depending on your project, and how niche and interesting it may be, you can easily showcase some useful work on just under 1 GB of data. So, don't hesitate just because you aren't sitting on the Fort Knox of all web data; just start from where you are!

Next, you'll need to understand something called the scaling laws *(6)*. These are a set of theories and formulas about how large models behave at different scales, notably as power laws. These formulas themselves are derived from empirical behavior at varying scales. You can use them to determine what model and dataset sizes are optimal for a given compute budget, and vice versa. To some degree, these laws, and their updated versions as presented in *Chinchilla*, are independent of the model architecture itself. This implies that the biggest way to improve model accuracy is scaling up the size, rather than alterations in the model architecture itself. Kaplan originally presented scaling laws explicitly within the context of language models leveraging the transformer model architecture. However, given the 10x increase in accuracy that this validated hypothesis gave rise to in the GPT-3 paper, I and many others *(7)* believe there is a reason to explore this basic relationship outside of **large language models** (**LLMs**), including vision and multimodal especially.

You might be thinking, so what? Why is this such a big deal? Obviously, there's some balance you'd want to achieve across your dataset, compute size, and model, so what gives? The reason Kaplan's work was such a breakthrough is that *having a valid formula to quantify the optimal compute, data, and model values lets you estimate what range of loss your model might achieve*. To put it another way, now that we have scaling laws, we can figure out mathematically what loss we should expect at the end of our model training run, within a given range. And for training runs that can send compute costs into the hundreds of thousands of dollars, if not millions, this knowledge is incredibly valuable. OpenAI has validated this in its GPT-4 technical report, claiming to be able to accurately forecast its model's loss given changes in scale.

This opens a new area of questions. What other aspects of machine learning have empirically observable laws? In what other ways can we be inspired by physics to discover formulaic patterns that rely on mathematical relationships, beyond the inner workings of the model itself? This matters because, today, the vast majority of machine learning is trial and error. We hope something works, we try it out, learn from our experiment, and then take another step. However, I believe scaling laws point to a future where machine learning is increasingly enhanced with simple, efficient, and fast checks, rather than long-running computational experiments. What if we've simply been thinking about this in the wrong way for decades?

## Fundamentals – scaling laws of neural language models

If you take a look at the original paper: *Scaling Laws of Neural Language Laws*, you'll find out that one core concept is central to their analysis – proportionality. Kaplan et al here argue that changes in your dataset size or model size should be accompanied by proportional changes in the companion quantity. To put it another way, if you use a bigger dataset, you should use a bigger model, and vice versa. Now, exactly how strong this relationship is, what describes it, what constants are involved, and precisely how much scaling should be undertaken up or down is entirely at the heart of their paper.

While it is helpful to know that a relationship is proportional, it is insufficient. Kaplan et al suggest and find empirically that the optimal scaling of neural language models follows a power law. Power laws are actually quite simple; they're just about exponents at the end of the day. If two quantities follow a power law, you can assume that one side of the equation follows exponential change:

$$L(N, D) = \left[ \left( \frac{N_C}{N} \right)^{\frac{\alpha_N}{\alpha_D}} + \frac{D_C}{D} \right]^{\alpha_D}$$

To estimate the early-stopped test loss of a transformer-based training regime, given the size of both a dataset and a model, Kaplan et al suggest the following.

Let's try to unpack this in very simple terms – first, the left-hand side:

- **L** = the final loss of your model, stopped early, on your test set

- **N** = the number of trainable parameters in your model

- **D** = the size of your dataset in tokens (for language)

Now, you understand that the entire equation is about computing the potential loss of your model, which would be great to know ahead of time! The rest of the terms on the right-hand side are about how to get there. All four of $N_C$, $D_C$, $\alpha_N$, and $\alpha_D$ describe constants that must be discovered from the dataset and training regime. Think of these as hyperparameters; we want to find some constant terms that describe our specific dataset and model. In many cases, however, we can simply use the constants as presented in their work.

Kaplan et al found constant values for each of these in their training runs by fitting the loss curves with their scaling law functions. Using mathematical extensions of their core equations, they were able to accurately fit their learning curves. Making that fit helped them discover constants that proved useful throughout the rest of their studies.

In the real world, once you've performed some preliminary data analysis and have a good idea of what characteristics you'll need to train an adequate model, most data science teams will immediately move on to training your first model. This is because the machine learning process is generally iterative; you'll test a variety of methods, see which ones are the most promising at a given point in time, scale and evaluate, and then try again. For the purposes of a larger book on the topic, I'll go into more detail on two key topics that can help you improve your dataset. These are steps you probably wouldn't implement right at the beginning of your data science journey but that you should come back to over time to increase the overall quality of your work. The first is bias detection and mitigation, and the second is dataset enhancements.

# Bias detection and mitigation

The trajectory of the word "bias" is interesting in that, in the last 15 years, it's come full circle. Originally, *bias* was arguably a statistical term. Formally, it implied that a sample size was improperly constructed, giving excessive weight to certain variables. Statisticians developed numerous methods to identify and reduce bias to evaluate studies properly, such as those used in randomized control trials in public health or policy evaluations in econometrics. Basic tactics include making sure that the treatment and control groups are roughly the same size and have roughly the same characteristics. Without a guarantee of that basic mathematical equivalence, or more realistically as close to it as the research team can get, it's difficult to trust that the results of a study are truly valid. The results themselves are subject to bias, simply indicating the presence or absence of basic characteristics, rather than implying anything meaningful about the treatment itself.

In the last 5 years, however, numerous studies have demonstrated the inability of machine learning models to perform adequately for certain groups of people under certain scenarios. The most egregious examples include facial recognition, image detection, employment, judicial decision-making, and countless others. Large technology companies have been the first to come under fire here, with financial institutions and even public policy organizations also coming in tow. These accusations are valid. While bias in datasets has always been a big problem in machine learning, the impact on human lives across the world is now so obvious that it deserves significant dialogue, discussion, solutioning, and monitoring. If bias is present in any dataset, it is almost certain to creep into the model itself. Models certainly are not objective; they are effectively children of the datasets they were trained on. Bias has now come full circle, starting in statistics, resonating with human rights, and now driving machine learning research.

*The word bias has now come full circle; starting in statistics, resonating with human rights, and now driving machine learning research.*

For the purposes of developing and attempting to deploy a machine learning model, and especially a large one with its own pretraining regime, you need to know a few things. First, the most reliable way to mitigate bias is by increasing and decreasing the different aspects of your datasets. This is especially obvious in computer vision. If you add more images of certain groups – for example, African Americans – your model will be able to recognize them. If you don't have those images in sufficient numbers, your model won't be able to recognize them in applications.

For natural language, this question ends up being even more challenging. This is because most of the data in language isn't already tabulated into different social categories, such as gender, race, religion, and sexuality. For all of those types that we care about and know we want to protect, we need to introduce our own methods to identify, compare, and synthesize them across our datasets. Just doing this alone is tough, as you can imagine.

Identifying bias is the first critical step in your journey toward responsible ML. Right at the beginning, you need to be able to answer two critical questions about your dataset:

- First, what types of bias are present in my dataset currently?

- Second, how much risk does this bias expose to my organization?

Think about risk in terms of impact on your customers, particularly the predictions from a biased ML model. If your model has the potential to cause harm to your customers, such as denying a loan, downgrading an employment submission, recommending harmful content, or even denying bail or other legal sentencing, then by all means make bias detection and mitigation your highest priority!

While there are a variety of frameworks concerning responsible AI, I like to boil these down to four key actions to take. In terms of bias in ML models trained on biased datasets, your four key steps are **expect**, **identify**, **mitigate**, and **monitor**:

1.  **Expect**: When picking ML projects and datasets, expect that every dataset will have some type of bias at the root. Ask yourself, what problem is my ML model trying to solve, and what issues will I run into if I don't have enough of certain types of data?

2.  **Identify**: Then, use a variety of techniques to identify the bias present in your dataset. Make sure you know right at the outset how many attributes within certain groups you do or do not have. Keep working on this until you can quantify at least a handful of different types of bias metrics. See the following note box for some suggestions on how to identify bias.

3.  **Mitigate**: Once you've identified the bias in your dataset numerically, take steps to mitigate the bias. Increase or decrease certain aspects of your dataset. Use augmentation, up- or down-sampling, and data transformations to drive down your bias metrics until they hit a less dangerous threshold.

4.  **Monitor**: Once you've deployed your ML model, the adventure continues. You can use the same bias detection methods you leveraged in *step 2* to monitor the model deployed in your application. Ensure that your application and overall system design include statistical monitoring and set thresholds for acceptable statistical levels. When the model starts to meet or exceed your thresholds, start manually reviewing the model predictions and initiate your training pipeline. Keeping humans in the loop, particularly those who are both knowledgeable and caring, is the best way to reduce the risk of biased predictions.

### How to do bias detection and monitoring

Now that we know bias is important, how do we find it mathematically? And once we've done that, how do we mitigate and monitor? There are many ways of doing this, and we can categorize these in their respective domains:

**Tabular**: Detecting bias in tabular data amounts to computing some statistics. First, you'll need to have some ground truth label in your dataset, indicating the status inside or outside of a certain group. Notably, for many teams, this alone presents a sizeable problem. However, the logical counter to this is simple. Expect your data to be biased, regardless of whether or not you have a column labeling it as members of certain groups. Introducing this label *is the only way to identify bias intrinsic to your dataset and, ultimately, remove it*. Otherwise, try to use a proxy, although these are known to be faulty.

Assuming you have a label, such as gender or race, then you have two types of metrics – pretraining and post-training metrics. One simple pretraining statistic is **class imbalance**. Class imbalance is simply the number of observations from your advantaged group, minus the number in the disadvantaged group, divided by your overall dataset size. If your class imbalance is too high, your dataset and subsequent model are certain to be biased.

One common post-training metric is disparate impact, which is defined simply as the number of positive predicted labels in your disadvantaged group, divided by the same in your advantaged group. Intuitively, this measures your model's likelihood of predicting positive for different groups, which as you can imagine is critical in certain domains such as employment or law. There is some legal precedent for using 4/5, or 80%, as the lower threshold here.

**Vision and language**: Lastly, both vision and language have different approaches. In language, it's common to evaluate a language model's learned preference to suggest a given category under certain conditions, such as placing "he" or "her" under some employment criteria.

With vision, you might use a pretrained text classifier to ensure that datasets are balanced before training. Also, you can clearly indicate a model's poor behavior in detecting certain classes – for example, certain groups in image recognition.

# Enhancing your dataset – multilingual, multimodal, and augmentations

Finally, now that you've learned how to pick a dataset, compare it with research datasets, determine the right approximate size, and evaluate bias, let's dive into enhancing the dataset. In particular, we'll look at a few dimensions – **multilingual**, **multimodal**, and **augmentations**. All three of these typically come a bit later in your ML projects, especially after the first few versions of your models have been trained and you're looking for the next idea to give you a boost.

Personally, I think there are few applications in the world where multilingually *isn't* a strong added value. *Multilingual* just means multiple languages. While many of the state-of-the-art language models were originally trained on English-only text, researchers in the last few years have made strong efforts to increase the lingual diversity of these corpora. That means they're adding support for a lot of languages. In 2022, Hugging Face led a massive worldwide effort to democratize the creation of large language models, calling their program *Big Science (8)*. This led to the creation of a novel model they named the **BigScience Open-Science Open-Access Multilingual Language Model (BLOOM)**. Hugging Face hopes to improve upon the state of the art in multilingual use cases especially, such as zero-shot language translation. However, the model was shown to perform worse than GPT-3 in many cases, leading us to believe that the best models may be single-language only.

Frankly, being multilingual is just good business. For any product you develop, any program you run, and any service you offer, you are limited in interacting with your potential consumer through language at the end of the day. Think of a language as a market. While you're developing your product, you want to bring it to as many markets as you can. Ultimately, that means as many languages as you can. For this reason, I'm optimistic that the industry will find a better way to incorporate multiple languages in possibly the same model without worsening results. Perhaps this is as simple as formatting a dataset appropriately, as in the case of chain-of-thought or instruction tuning.

Briefly, let's explore adding additional modalities. Simply put, this means different types of datasets, such as adding vision to text, or vice versa. I introduced this concept in more detail at the close of *Chapter 1*. Here, I'd like to simply point out that *if you have text with images, or images with your text, try to use it*. Once you're invested in a project, with many hours spent on analyzing the data, training, evaluating models, deploying these, and so on, why would you not go the extra mile to explore adding other modalities? Particularly when it has the potential of raising accuracy, which it does. From the perspective of a model, another modality is just another type of embedding. You'll most likely want to use some model pretrained elsewhere to convert a raw image into embeddings – that is, before adding them as another input to your model.

There are trade-offs here; increasing the size of your model will increase its runtime. Increasing your dataset also increases your data transformation costs. Adding another step in the data transformation makes hosting more complex, meaning you may need to revisit the system design to deploy your model. All of these trade-offs are worthy of discussion, and ultimately, you'll need to prioritize the projects that add the most value for your teams and your customers, which could very well include language-only models.

The other reason I'm optimistic about multimodal projects generally, as opposed to language-only projects, is that the visual domain carries so much information to humans. Humans learn to see before they learn to speak, and so many of our experiences and knowledge are gathered visually. For this reason, I believe foundation models will continue to converge around joint vision and language tasks.

Finally, data augmentation is a simple and easy step to improve the accuracy of your models without adding a ton of extra work to get it. The core idea is that you're adding some degree of variety in your dataset and slight changes in the provided samples, which will help your model learn the difference between signal and noise. Both text and vision have well-tested methods for augmentation. With vision, this is frequently as simple as pixel manipulations, light color manipulations, or image rotations.

With text, this can be substituting synonyms, sentence-level reconstruction, or lightweight punctuation modifications. The trick is that you don't want to change the basic mechanism you are trying to learn. If you're training an image detection model, don't modify any of the images so that you can't detect the images. If you're training a text classifier, don't alter the text so much that it moves into a different class.

Augmentation is usually less of an issue in large-scale pretraining, where most datasets are so large, as they already include more than enough noise and variation. It does, however, seem like a promising avenue for bias reduction especially. Another key technique for pretraining is reducing duplicate text. This is especially key in web data, where memes, comments, and threads can easily render the same text many hundreds of times across platforms and users.

Now that you've learned all about the early stages of preparing your data, let's do a quick recap of what you just learned before we move on to preparing your model!

## Summary

In this chapter, we introduced a wide variety of use cases for foundation modeling, encompassing scenarios where you can fine-tune an existing foundation model and where pretraining itself is competitive. We provided a simple economics framework to help you make the case for your pretraining project, notably by tying it to how much you expect your business to increase based on a more accurate model. After that, we talked about evaluating your dataset, comparing it to research datasets, and learning how to think critically about its sampling mechanism. We set up some basic ideas to use this critical thinking for framing experiments, which we'll continue in the next chapter. We learned about the scaling laws and presented an open source notebook you can use to find which dataset size will help you hit performance levels, given fixed model and compute budgets. We talked about detecting and mitigating bias in your datasets, along with enhancing these with augmentation, modalities, and languages.

Next up is model preparation!

## References

Please go through the following content for more information on a few of the topics covered in this chapter:

1. *Papers With Code*: `https://paperswithcode.com/datasets`.

2. *Hugging Face Hub*: `https://huggingface.co/datasets`

3. *Hugging Face*: `https://huggingface.co/datasets?task_ids=task_ids:language-modeling&sort=downloads`

4. *AN IMAGE IS WORTH 16X16 WORDS: TRANSFORMERS FOR IMAGE RECOGNITION AT SCALE*: `https://arxiv.org/pdf/2010.11929.pdf`

5.  Scaling Laws for Neural Language Models: `https://arxiv.org/pdf/2001.08361.pdf`

6.  Training Compute-Optimal Large Language Models: `https://arxiv.org/pdf/2203.15556.pdf`

7.  *BigScience Episode #5 – Challenges & Perspectives in Creating Large Language Models*: `https://bigscience.huggingface.co/acl-2022`

# 3
# Model Preparation

In this chapter, you'll learn how to decide which model will be most useful to serve as a basis for your pretraining regime. You'll learn how to think about the size of the model in parameters, along with the key loss functions and how they determine performance in production. Finally, you'll combine the scaling laws with the expected size of your dataset to select ceiling and floor model sizes that you'll use to guide your experiments.

In this chapter, we will cover the following topics:

- Finding your best base model

- Finding your pretraining loss function

- Solving for your model size

- Planning future experiments

## Finding your best base model

At this point in the book, you should have learned how to pick your use case, how to find a dataset, and how to compare that with research datasets. You should have particularly learned how to compare that dataset with those available in the open source community. Now comes the fun part: picking your model!

Most likely, you already have a few candidates in mind. If you're working with natural language, you're probably thinking about something in the family of **Generative Pretrained Transformers** (**GPT**) for a generative use case, BERT for classification, or T5 for something akin to translation. For vision, you may be looking at CoCa *(1)*, CLIP *(2)*, or a jointly masked vision and language model *(3)*. For multimodal datasets, you might pick one straight from the vision examples or something much more unique based on your specific use case.

In *Chapter 1, An Introduction to Pretraining Foundation Models*, we briefly introduced some of these state-of-the-art models and dove into the core transformer-based neural network architecture that makes them tick. Let's briefly recap each of these models and reinforce why they matter:

- **Encoders**. Broadly speaking, an encoder architecture takes a lengthy input, such as a long sentence or a long embedding, and compresses it into something denser. An encoder might take an input of length 500 and, through a series of neural networks, compress this into an output of length 50. Encoder-only models were popularized by the BERT model and all of its subsequent relatives, including DeBERTa, RoBERTa, XLM, AlBERT, and so on. If you're curious, DeBERTa is included here because, despite its updated attention mechanism, which uses a disentangling objective function with a novel enhanced mask decoder, it is still generally appropriate for classification tasks.

> **Important note**
>
> Pick an encoder-only model architecture if you want to keep your model smaller and you're confident you won't need any generative abilities. This means you should plan on not using this model for text generation, zero-shot performance, summarization, and the final step in question answering.

- **Decoders**: A decoder model architecture does exactly the reverse of an encoder. It takes dense input, say, of length 50, and uses learnable feedforward networks to recompose that back into a larger space, for example, of length 250. We'll dive into the mechanics of how that happens later in this chapter (hint: it's all about the *pretraining loss function*). Decoder-only models came to the global stage with the GPT-4 model *(4)*, and open source options such as OPT and BLOOM are now available.

  Pick a decoder-only model (i.e., diffusion) if you want to focus on your model's generative ability. If you need strong summarization, generation, or the ability to generate quality images, decoder-only models are the way to go.

- **Diffusion models**: If you want to pretrain an image generation model, such as DALL-E 2 *(5)*, Imagen *(6)*, Flamingo *(7)*, and Stable Diffusion, then you're looking at using a diffusion model. Diffusion models, which we'll explore later in the book, are really interesting training systems that use multiple pretrained models to embed joint vision and language pairs. This ultimately joins them through a U-Net, which progressively adds, then removes, noise during the training process. The models learn to generate images by comparing the generated image from the provided caption and updating the model weights based on how far the image is from the caption provided.

- **Combination encoder-decoder models**: The most common use case for a mixture of encoders and decoders in the same neural network today is overwhelmingly translation. Models in this category came to fame with T5 *(8)*, which was known to be able to take strings in one language paired with their translations in another at very large scales. T5 has since evolved into BART, FLAN-T5, M2M, MBart, BigBird, and others.

Pick a combination encoder-decoder model when you are certain that translation is core to your use case. This might be the case for writing code from prompts, summarizing documents, or transferring styles.

Now, think to yourself, which of these do I need? Hopefully, at this point, you can settle on one of these major categories.

## Starting with the smallest base model you can

Throughout this chapter, we'll learn how to solve for the size of our model using scaling laws. However, at this point, it's helpful to introduce the concept of a **base model**. A base model is usually the absolute smallest version of a model available. You can find this on the Hugging Face Hub, for example, or on the GitHub site associated with the paper. Base models are usually in the order of a few hundred million parameters in size, so they tend to fit on a single GPU. They don't take up a lot of GPU memory, and they fit nicely when stored on disk in most environments. Base models are fast in production because the literal size of the neural network is smaller, computations can happen faster, and the data has fewer layers to pass through until the final output. All these benefits mean that putting a base model into production and working with it across your entire pipeline is going to be a lot easier than working with something larger. For this reason, when working with customers, I strongly recommend beginning experiments with the smallest model you can and increasing in size only when that stops giving you the mileage you need.

Later in this chapter, we'll talk about when, where, and how to design experiments that incorporate a larger model. In *Chapter 14*, we'll learn how to operationalize these with MLOps pipelines!

## Trade-off – simplicity versus complexity

One aspect that is helpful to consider when applying machine learning is this simple dimension: simplicity versus complexity. A simple model may be smaller. It might have fewer novel operations. Its writeup on the Hugging Face Hub may literally be shorter. It may have fewer GitHub issues but more associated papers. Starting with a simple artifact is a good way to give your teams a healthy beginning. You want to start projects with early success rather than failing to get off the ground. A simple project with a simple model may be fine-tuning BERT on just a few GB of data. After you've tested this on a real use case, and when you have more unsupervised data, you may simply try continuing to pretrain on this unsupervised set.

> **Important note**
> Starting with a simple artifact is a good way to give your teams a healthy beginning. You want to start projects with early success rather than failing to get off the ground.

On the other hand, complexity may be able to boost your model performance beyond what is possible with simpler models. This includes scaling the models, datasets, and computation sizes, in addition to incorporating multiple models throughout your preprocessing, training, and deployment pipelines.

As we've seen throughout the book, scale alone is a promising tactic for many use cases. In the chapter on fine-tuning, however, we'll explore how techniques such as instruction fine-tuning, chain-of-thought tuning, and reinforcement learning with human feedback can all boost model performance without necessarily scaling parameter size. These are promising trends!

### Trade-off – applying to many use cases versus being narrow to only one

Another key aspect to consider in the design of your overall solution, or product, is your ability to extend to as many use cases as possible. This follows the basic economics of maximizing a return on your investment. In this project, you will have two big investments:

- Your time
- Your compute costs, which we'll dive into in the upcoming chapter on GPUs

Both of these are allocations from your organization in order to produce some output, or, in this case, a model. Every use case this model is able to solve *is a potential path to value for your project*. Every time you fine-tune this model, deploy it into production for an application, use it for downstream analysis, or integrate it into a demonstration or report, you create a way for your organization to get value from its investment in your project. You set yourself up for success when your project is positioned to be able to solve as many use cases as you can.

In the case of pretraining and fine-tuning, this is an easy problem to solve. First, look at how many models are already deployed in your organization. If these are transformer-based models, then odds are they are fine-tuned artifacts from some set of open source models. Look at those open source models as your target range. Do your teams use BERT? RoBERTa? GPT-2? Pick the model that covers as many downstream tasks as you can.

Alternatively, you may consider solving a much smaller number of use cases if these are extremely high value. Search is a great example of this. From e-commerce to hospitality, customer service to product delivery, when a search engine gets a lot of traffic, it is probably a high-value business. Search is a top application for large, pretrained models, especially for new projects looking to leverage cutting-edge technologies for the highest impact.

### Tactical approaches to finding your best base model

Practically speaking, here's how I think about finding your best base model. First, as you did in *Chapter 2*, list out the key use cases you want your model to address. Look at model leader boards, such as those we discussed in *Chapter 1*, to see which ones seem to consistently hit the top. Consider the base architecture of this model and compare it to your top use cases. If you find a recent one with open source code samples and model weights, and it seems to map reasonably well to the use cases you're exploring, then I'd use that to start with.

If you want to push yourself, try to reimagine lower-level aspects of that model as areas for improvement. This might be updates to the neural networks, combinations of these, or even custom operators that might improve your overall goal. Remember that you want to keep both accuracy and efficiency as key indicators!

Once you've settled on your best base model or set of top models you want to consider, it's time to dig into a key element of this model that determines its ability to learn: the pretraining loss function.

# Finding your pretraining loss function

We introduced this topic in *Chapter 1* as a *pretraining objective*, or in vision as a *pretext task*. Remember that these are essentially different words for the same thing: the mathematical quantity your model will optimize for while performing **self-supervised learning**. This is valuable because it opens you up to a plethora of unsupervised data, which is, on average, more available than supervised data. Usually, this pretraining function injects some type of noise and then tries to learn what the real data patterns look like from the false ones (**causal language modeling as with GPT**). Some functions inject masks and learn how to predict which words have been masked (**masked language modeling as with BERT**). Others substitute some words with reasonable alternatives that reduce the overall size of the needed dataset (**token detection as with DeBERTa**).

> **Important note**
> When we pretrain our models, we use a pretraining loss function to create the ability for the model to recognize aspects of the dataset, which eventually predicts truth from falsehoods.

But what gives? Why do we care about pretraining objectives so much? How will it impact your project? The reason you should care about a pretraining loss function is that it is the primary factor in determining where your model can be used and how well it will perform. In the previous section, we mapped certain types of model architectures (encoders, decoders, and mixtures) to different machine learning use cases (classification, generation, and translation). The real reason why this mapping exists is because of the pretraining loss function!

Consider decoder-only models, notably GPT-3 and similar candidates. The pretraining function here is called *causal* because it works from left to right. The pretraining function picks up some base text string, say, half a sentence, and then uses the decoder to try to generate the rest of the sentence. Commonly, you'll pair this with an objective metric, such as perplexity, to consider how close to the root text your generated strings were. As the training run continues, the neural network optimizes this perplexity metric to change the weights such that the overall loss decreases, pushing up the performance of your model step by step.

Interestingly, given the recent performance of GPT-based models, we're starting to see these being applied across a variety of use cases with zero-shot performance. This means that once you train your GPT-based model at scale, you can then use it for prompting scenarios without providing previous examples, offering classification, entity extraction, sentiment analysis, question answering, and more. While you're still performing text generation, strictly speaking, the way this is used can solve more than just open-ended content generation.

Next, let's examine the pretraining loss functions across different models in vision, language, and multimodal scenarios.

## Pretraining loss functions in vision – ViT and CoCa

We've learned a lot about the core transformer model architecture, and now you should feel somewhat comfortable about how this works in natural language processing. But what about computer vision? The Vision Transformer *(9)* took a step in this direction, bridging the gap from advancements in NLP and making these available to the vision community. Notably, the **Vision Transformer, or ViT,** showed that convolution could be removed entirely from the model. A pretrained ViT reduced the overall amount of computational resources necessary to train downstream models that achieved results comparable with top convolution-based approaches of its time.

To be sure, CNNs are absolutely still in use today, and there are many cases where they clearly outperform ViTs. At its core, a CNN maintains the visual structure of an image well. The core process of convolution is a left-to-right, top-to-bottom rendering of all the pixels of the image into dense representations. One benefit of this approach is **inductive bias**, a learned preference the model develops for pixels in relation to each other while training. This is a core part of why CNNs learn vision well. ViTs lack this ability, instead working with the pixels as tokens. ViTs offer some benefits of scaling, due to their core self-attention operations, but CNNs may be more common in smaller datasets and models. Recent work *(5)* has begun bridging this gap for ViTs, bringing inductive bias to them.

But how does it work? Through an encoder! The solution starts with a basic data processing technique that flattens the input. A 2D image is taken and simply reshaped into a sequence of *flattened 2D patches*. Then, the encoder applies a *linear projection* process to merge all of the parts of the image into a single row, including positional terms, so the location of the content is still known to the model. This single row is fed into the transformer encoder, which itself uses the self-attention process. The encoder reduces the size of the rows until it hits the final row, the labels. The model then selects one of the available classes. Finally, the loss function, in connection with the ground truth, provides a learnable signal for the model to update its weights and improve accuracy on the next epoch. Let's take a look at this process.

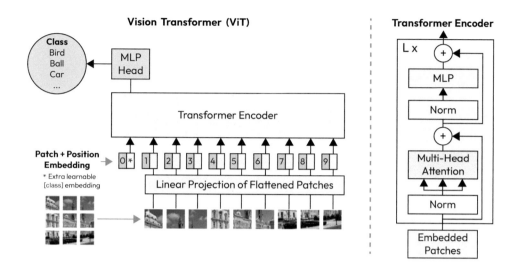

Figure 3.1 – The ViT

Notably, the ViT *is still effectively a supervised learning process*. Clearly, the learning method here relies on labels known ahead of time. This is a big difference from the pretraining regimes in language where the labels are unknown. But this base vision transfer still serves as an accuracy boost to enhance downstream models, so it's worth evaluating. While there are some projects *(10)* that attempt truly unsupervised approaches in vision, personally, I haven't yet seen a case in vision where this strictly outperforms a supervised approach. Perhaps this is a core difference between the two domains. Perhaps I'll be proved wrong next month.

Another pretraining loss function that is key to the vision domain is contrastive. We introduced this in the first chapter, but now I'd like to take you deeper. We'll spotlight one model using this: **CoCA**. Interestingly, the authors attempt to unify all three model architectures we've mentioned so far: encoder-only, decoder-only, and mixed encoder-decoder. Their trained model is able to solve use cases such as visual recognition, vision-language alignment, image captioning, end-to-end fine-tuning, frozen feature evaluation, and multimodal understanding with zero-shot transfer (more on zero-shot later in the book). In fact, CoCa uses two pretraining objectives: one to handle the images and the other to handle the text. Let's break it down!

The image part of the workflow looks similar to ViT; it takes an image, applies a flattening process, and feeds this into an encoder. In fact, the base implementation of CoCa uses ViT by default! However, instead of directly producing classification at the end of the encoder, these dense arrays are used in two ways:

- First, as an input to the final decoder
- Second, as an input to an *intermediary loss function*

This is called **contrastive loss** because it effectively contrasts the visual content with the textual. The final output then applies a **captioning loss**, increasing the accuracy of the text produced at the final stage of the model to label, or caption, the provided image. This is why the model is named CoCa: Contrastive Captioners.

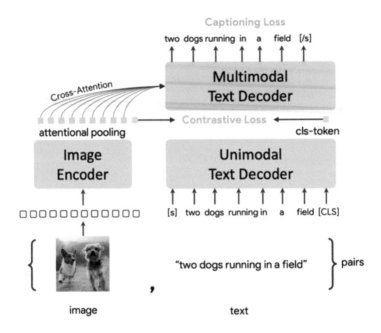

Figure 3.2 – Contrastive and captioning loss

On the language side of the workflow, we see a decoder. The decoder takes a provided textual input, such as the original caption of the image. Then, it applies another flattening process to tokenize and embed the words, preparing them for the decoder. The decoder then reduces the dimensionality of the words, outputting a denser representation of the caption. This is then provided as an input to the contrastive loss function, better enabling the joint comparison between image and text.

$$L_{(CoCa)} = \lambda_{Con} \cdot L_{Con} + \lambda_{Cap} + L_{Cap}$$

This is the weighted loss function for CoCa:

- $\mathcal{L}_{CoCa}$ = Overall loss for CoCa
- $\mathcal{L}_{Con}$ = Contrastive loss
- $\mathcal{L}_{Cap}$ = Captioning loss
- $\lambda_{Con}$ = Hyperparameter to weight the contrastive loss
- $\lambda_{Cap}$ = Hyperparameter to weight the captioning loss

Finally, the entire model uses a weighted combination of both loss functions to serve as the global loss function. How do they determine the weights, you ask? Through experimentation! This experimentation is almost certainly dependent on the dataset and task at hand. If you were using CoCa to solve a use case with extremely rich visual data but very weak language data, you might consider starting with a higher weight on contrastive loss. However, if your language data was excellent from the start and your visual data was only mildly informative, you might start with a higher weight on captioning.

In this way, you can start to understand how we pick hyperparameters for our models. This is the subject of a different chapter later on, so for now, I want you to develop the intuition that *the precise implementation of each of these models can be highly personalized to your datasets and use cases*. Reading these papers and learning about how these state-of-the-art models work is a helpful step to provide more depth to your own analysis and understanding. You can and should apply this knowledge for gain back at work!

## Pretraining loss functions in language – Alexa Teacher Model

At this point, you should feel pretty comfortable with the **masked language modeling** we discussed, especially how it makes encoder-only models happen in language, such as BERT. You should also know about **causal language modeling**, which enables decoder-only models such as GPT. Now let's find out what happens when we mix the two!

The Alexa Teacher Model (11) came out just a few weeks ago as of writing this, and as an Amazonian, I can tell you it feels great to see a large language model come out of your own organization! But that's not the only reason I'm mentioning it here. There are two reasons I think you should know about the **Alexa Teacher Model (AlexaTM)**:

- First, it uses a concept called *few-shot learning* to easily transfer its knowledge about human verbal communication from one language to another. As we'll learn in *Chapter 13* on prompt engineering, few-shot learning means you pass a few examples to the model on *inference*. These few examples work wonders in prompting the model to respond more accurately. This is especially useful for language, because it allows language researchers to develop solutions for *low-resource languages*, enabling some digital technology in relevant communities.

- Second, using this few-shot learning approach, a 20-billion parameter version of AlexaTM was able to outperform a model 27 times its size, PaLM, at 540B on the same problem *(12)*. This is a critical juncture to internalize and a trend that I hope we'll continue to see more of over the years. While bigger can sometimes be better in machine learning models, it isn't always, and sometimes it's worse. Remember, smaller models are faster to train, easier to work with, and faster for inference, so if the accuracy is the same or better, always move to a small model.

Now, how does it work? Similar to the CoCa example, there are now two loss functions we're tracking. The first you're already familiar with: **causal language modeling**, or **CLM** for short. Here, the CLM process tries to predict the end of a sentence. Now, AlexaTM 20B combines that with a **denoising loss function**. The denoising process was introduced in BART *(13)* as a way to jointly learn on the combination of encoders and decoders, notably *through introducing noise*. A given document is intentionally corrupted by introducing masks via the encoder. The decoder is then asked to predict the likelihood of the document being original. Actually, the process of adding noise and then trying to discriminate noise from truth is a bit similar to adversarial learning in general.

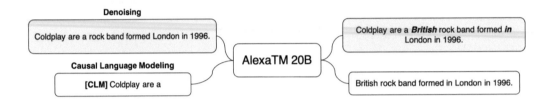

Figure 3.3 – Alexa Teacher Model

Interestingly, the AlexaTM 20B uses the CLM pretraining objective *only 20% of the time*. This is to introduce the ability of the model to work well in few-shot cases. During this time, the model does not produce noise at all; it simply tries to complete sentences. This is denoted via a signal provided to the beginning of 20% of the sentences [CLM]. The authors also randomly fed the model 20% and 80% of the document to ensure it performs well in both short and long cases. To start the training quickly, they also began with a 10B pretrained encoder, which they unfroze after hitting 100,000 steps. This overall process took 120 days on 128 A100 GPUs (NVIDIA hardware), which translates to only 16 `ml.p4d.24xlarge` on Amazon SageMaker distributed training. More on SageMaker training to come!

For your reference, the "Teacher" in AlexaTM refers to a process called **distillation**. **Distillation** is another way to transfer knowledge, comparable to fine-tuning. In fine-tuning, we attach extra layers to a larger base model, then we usually run it on a smaller set of supervised data. In distillation, we pair one larger "teacher" model with a much smaller "student" model. The student model is then trained to generate the same probability distribution as the teacher model but at a much smaller computational cost. All of *Chapter 10* is dedicated to methods for fine-tuning your model and comes with coding examples.

## Changing your pretraining loss function

Now that we've surveyed some of the top pretraining loss functions across vision, language, and multimodal scenarios, you might be wondering: is that it? What do I do with this information?

The answer to this question largely depends on your years of experience in machine learning. If you are just getting started, then you certainly don't need to be overly fixated on this aspect of your project. Simply pick your top model, understand how it learns, and get on with your project. However, as your level of experience increases, you may start to want to experiment with the pretraining loss regime itself, which is excellent! As you grow in machine learning, particularly as a developer or a scientist, it becomes extremely valuable to contribute your own novel ideas back to the community. Inventing new pretraining loss functions or, for that matter, any new optimization you come across in the entire modeling journey, is both incredibly valuable and deeply fulfilling. This is where you can truly establish a new state of the art in a given domain, possibly even a new domain that you yourself invent!

## Solving for your model size

Now that you've picked your best base model(s), you understand its pretraining regime, and you identified your dataset and its overall size in the last chapter, let's start to understand the sizes of models you can target!

You may remember that in *Chapter 1*, we introduced a core concept called *the scaling laws*. Introduced by Kaplan et al. in 2020, this bold idea suggests a formal relationship between the overall sizes of your compute training cluster, your dataset, and your model. Prior to Kaplan, most machine learning practitioners had understood there to be a general relationship between these three, but his team took the bold task of proving this empirically via power laws.

The basic thing you need to understand can be demonstrated with a simple graphic. To train your model well, both in terms of producing the highest accuracy you can and in getting the most value out of your overall compute budget, it's helpful to think about the following key items as a fundamental relationship.

Personally, I find it helpful to consider this visually. The fundamental way your model is going to learn anything about the real world is through the dataset itself. Naturally, you can see that as the size of the model increases, you'll want the dataset to also increase in some capacity. As the dataset increases, the model should also increase to some degree.

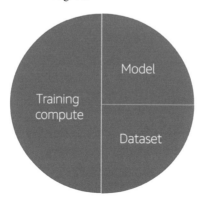

Figure 3.4 – The inter-relationship of machine learning

You can even think about it in terms of human learning. As we gain more experience, more knowledge, and more understanding, our brain literally builds new pathways to interpret, store, and learn from these experiences. The more new experiences you have and the more problems you solve, the more your brain evolves to store the necessary information. On the flip side, as our experiences and new challenges decrease, our brain loses some of its elasticity to respond in kind. This is an example of biological optimization at work!

To complete the analogy, our lived human experiences are like a dataset. Every new challenge, new relationship, new experience, and new problem is like adding extra records and aspects to the dataset. Similarly, our brains are like a model. Organically, our bodies handle building and releasing pathways in the brain dynamically with our most recent experiences. What we are trying to do as computer scientists is replicate this process with code through a process called *training*.

In terms of pretraining across vision, language, and multimodal scenarios, know that this relationship still applies. If you pair a large, complex model with a small dataset, it's likely that *your model will overfit*. Overfitting means you may get an extremely high level of accuracy on your training sets but completely fail to generalize well and provide meaningful results outside of the training procedure. On the other hand, if you pair a tiny model with an extremely large dataset, *you may well be underfitting*. This means you may not even perform well on the training set, let alone elsewhere.

Pairing the compute with the model and dataset sizes is all about cost optimization. There are inherent trade-offs in *scaling horizontally*, which means adding more compute to your cluster. This is different from *scaling vertically*, which means upgrading your instances to larger and more recent versions. Most teams find a natural balance between throwing as many machines as they can at a model to get the runtime low versus using as few machines as possible but taking many days, weeks, or even months to complete the training run. You want to find a natural middle ground between these two. We'll dive into these topics, including core distribution methods such as model and data parallelism, in *Chapter 5, Distribution Fundamentals*.

> **Case study – Amazon Search speeds up runtime seven-fold with distributed training**
>
> One great example of finding the natural balance between speed and per-hour cost is *Amazon Search*! Search is, as you might expect, the team responsible for helping you find the products you are most interested in on amazon.com. Every time you try to find something on Amazon, the query runs through our search engine to find exactly what you're looking for.
>
> Scientists and developers value the ability to iterate quickly. They love testing out ideas as fast as possible, getting feedback on them, and quickly jumping into the next version. This allows them to *optimize*, or simply improve their ideas rapidly. Staying agile on experimentation helps you keep the overall cost of research and development down, because it reduces the time it takes to move from initial product ideation to full release.
>
> At Amazon, SageMaker partnered with Search to release native support for PyTorch Lightning with an optimized inter-node communication project, Distributed Data Parallel. As a result, Search was able to move from training on 1 node up to 8 nodes, reducing the overall time to train from 99 minutes down to 13.5!

They didn't change the model size or dataset. They kept both constant and simply added a data parallel strategy to make copies of the model and shared the data out to all accelerators (GPUs). This allowed them to scale horizontally, adding extra nodes to their cluster and reducing the overall job time.

We'll dive into these distributed concepts in later chapters, but for now, simply know that *you can decrease the amount of time it takes to train your model when you use a distribution strategy with extra nodes in your cluster.*

## Practical approaches to solving for your model size

Now that you have a good understanding of the relationship between data, model, and compute sizes, let's get down to the nuts and bolts of figuring out which ones are right for you!

Most teams will consider the compute budget as fixed. Think of this number as what you should plan on asking your senior leadership to approve for your project. As we learned in *Chapter 2*, you should think of this number as some fraction of the overall value that increased accuracy will have on your business.

The second true bottleneck is your dataset size. Figure out how large your candidate dataset is. In vision, you might be counting images. In language, you might count tokens. I still like to baseline at GB, because this is easily understood and translatable across domains. Generally speaking, a good way to get started is just to find the models and ppaers you are inspired by, dive into them, understand how large their datasets were, and use that as your baseline. This will range from 10's of GB's to a few PB. For those of you who are new to machine learning, that's a great place to start. Following the standard paths of proven expertise is a great way to get yourself started toward successful projects. However, for those of you who aren't new to machine learning, let's take a quick look at using the scaling laws to solve for your optimal model size.

## Not all scaling laws are created equal

First, it's helpful to know that while the general relationship between your model, data, and compute size is intuitively understandable, the precise mathematical formulas actually can vary quite a bit. As we learned in *Chapter 2*, Kaplan used the mathematical term, $\propto$ which indicates that two quantities are "proportional" to each other. In other words, when two terms are equated by the proportional sign, we know that the two quantities are certainly linked, but we don't know precisely which constant terms govern that relationship.

This is the case in large deep learning models. Different papers and research terms have preferences for certain aspects of this, such as Kaplan preferring to keep model sizes large but datasets somewhat smaller and Hoffman suggesting to increase both equally. Kaplan originally presented autoregressive models, or decoder-based models, as the most *sample efficient*. However, the AlexaTM project indicated that joint encoders and decoders could actually be *more* efficient. All this is to say that while the scaling laws can suggest optimal model settings, results will vary.

Next, let's try to define the lower and upper model sizes you want to build up toward in your experiments.

# Planning future experiments

Now that you have an idea of what model size you'd like to target given your compute budget and data constraints, let's learn how to think about each run of your job *as an experiment*. Fundamentally, each stage in the machine learning process is ultimately a unique experiment. Some of your inputs to each stage in the project stay the same; you could call these your **dependent variables**. Some of your inputs to the project change; these are your *independent variables*. it takes time to build up skills on your project Simply put, change something and see what happens. Just make sure you're only changing one thing, so it's empirically clear what the result is!

It's critical to understand that the whole scope of your project is *not* going to happen all at once. A lot of this is because it takes time to build up skills on your time. Even if you are starting with a completely experienced team, which frankly happens very rarely, the ecosystem of machine learning itself changes so rapidly that every few months, you'll be learning about something new. So, plan on adding extra time to learn about all the newest releases.

At the beginning, start with the smallest possible experiment you can. Get the smallest version of your model up and running on your local IDE. Depending on the size of the model and the corresponding hardware you'll need, you can do this on a variety of compute options, from Jupyter notebooks and more robust options to your laptop, free compute experimental environments, and more. On AWS, we provide a wide variety of these options through our fully managed machine learning service, Amazon SageMaker.

After demonstrating interesting results on a tiny fraction of the dataset, I like to move directly into a remote SageMaker training job. You'll learn more about training on SageMaker in the next chapter, but for now, I'd simply like you to know that *you can easily and seamlessly scale up and down your training needs on Amazon SageMaker*. All of the practical guidance in this book will focus on how to do this efficiently. In terms of your project, you might consider working on the SageMaker Training API until you have a successful job run. I'd keep at this until you are running on a single instance with multiple GPUs: my go-to is the g family with four GPUs. This can be either `ml.g4dn.12xlarge`, or `ml.g5.12xlarge`. More on what this means in the chapters to come! Using multiple GPUs *will require a data and/or model parallelization strategy*, which is the entire content of *Chapter 5*.

Once you are running successfully both on SageMaker remote training and across multiple GPUs, then it's time to increase everything. Bump up the size of your data. Remember that model, data, compute, and key hyperparameters such as learning rate and batch size, in addition to the model architecture itself, are all interrelated. Finding the right settings for this is the entire content of *Chapter 7*.

As soon as you start increasing, extra complications arise. You want to make sure your loss is decreasing sufficiently, but you also want to keep GPU utilization high. You want to debug and improve the operators and communications in your job, but you also want to evaluate training throughput. When your job breaks, which it will with almost perfect certainty, you want to get it back online as quickly as possible, but accurately as well.

Diving into these nuances, unpacking them, and helping you get your project back on track to avoid as many of the roadblocks and capitalize on as many known issues is the entire focus of *Part 3*.

In short, there are many different discrete phases of pretraining a large model. This entire book aims to help you navigate them safely. In the next chapter, we'll dive into the GPU itself and uncover how to best utilize these efficient processors, also known as **accelerators**.

## Summary

In this chapter, you learned how to find your best base model, including the basics of architecture and the most common use cases and modalities, and you were given general guidance to start with the smallest model you can. You learned about key trade-offs, such as simplicity versus complexity, and applying  many use cases versus applying only one. You received tactical guidance on how to find a base model with good support. You learned how to find your pretraining loss function, including masked language modeling, causal language modeling, and those common in vision models such as ViT and CoCa. We looked at the Alexa Teacher Model, and we learned how to use the scaling laws to solve for our model size, with help from a case study from Amazon Search.

Next up: working with accelerators!

## References

Please go through the following content for more information on a few topics covered in the chapter:

1. *CoCa: Contrastive Captioners are Image-Text Foundation Models:* `https://arxiv.org/abs/2205.01917`

2. *CLIP: Connecting text and images:* `https://openai.com/blog/clip/`

3. *MASKED VISION AND LANGUAGE MODELING FOR MULTI-MODAL REPRESENTATION LEARNING:* `https://arxiv.org/pdf/2208.02131.pdf`

4. *Language Models are Few-Shot Learners:* `https://arxiv.org/abs/2005.14165`

5. *Hierarchical Text-Conditional Image Generation with CLIP Latents:* `https://cdn.openai.com/papers/dall-e-2.pdf`

6. *Photorealistic Text-to-Image Diffusion Models with Deep Language Understanding:* `https://arxiv.org/abs/2205.11487`

7. *Flamingo: a Visual Language Model for Few-Shot Learning:* `https://arxiv.org/pdf/2204.14198.pdf`

8. *Exploring the Limits of Transfer Learning with a Unified Text-to-Text Transformer:* `https://arxiv.org/pdf/1910.10683.pdf`

9. *AN IMAGE IS WORTH 16X16 WORDS: TRANSFORMERS FOR IMAGE RECOGNITION AT SCALE:* `https://arxiv.org/pdf/2010.11929.pdf`

10. *Unsupervised Pre-Training of Image Features on Non-Curated Data:* `https://arxiv.org/pdf/1905.01278.pdf`

11. *Alexa Teacher Model: Pretraining and Distilling Multi-Billion-Parameter Encoders for Natural Language Understanding Systems:* `https://arxiv.org/pdf/2206.07808.pdf`

12. *Alexa Teacher Model: Pretraining and Distilling Multi-Billion-Parameter Encoders for Natural Language Understanding Systems:* `https://arxiv.org/pdf/2208.01448.pdf`

13. *BART: Denoising Sequence-to-Sequence Pre-training for Natural Language Generation, Translation, and Comprehension:* `https://arxiv.org/pdf/1910.13461.pdf`

# Part 2: Configure Your Environment

In part 2, you'll learn how to configure your environment for large-scale pretraining. We'll dive into **graphics processing units** (**GPUs**), parallelization basics, and the second part of dataset preparation.

This section has the following chapters:

- *Chapter 4, Containers and Accelerators on the Cloud*
- *Chapter 5, Distribution Fundamentals*
- *Chapter 6, Dataset Preparation: Part Two, the Data Loader*

# 4

# Containers and Accelerators on the Cloud

In this chapter, you'll learn how to containerize your scripts and optimize them for accelerators on the cloud. We'll learn about a range of accelerators for foundation models, including trade-offs around cost and performance across the entire machine learning lifecycle. You'll learn about key aspects of Amazon SageMaker and AWS to train models on accelerators, optimize performance, and troubleshoot common issues. if you're already familiar with containers and accelerators on AWS, feel free to skip this chapter.

In this chapter, we're going to cover the following main topics:

- What are accelerators and why do they matter for foundation models?

- Containerize your scripts for accelerators on AWS

- Using accelerators with Amazon SageMaker

- Infrastructure optimizations on AWS

- Troubleshooting accelerator performance

## What are accelerators and why do they matter?

There's something remarkable about human behavior. We care a lot about our own experiences. Many of the arts and sciences, particularly social science, specialize in quantifying, predicting, and understanding the implications and particularities of human behavior. One of the most obvious of these is human responses to technical performance. While this certainly varies among human groups, for the subset that chooses to spend a sizeable portion of their time interacting with technology, one theorem is self-evident. Faster and easier is always better.

Take video games, for example. While the 1940s and 50s saw some of the earliest video games, these didn't come to massive popularity until arcade games such as *Pong* emerged in the early 70s. Perhaps unsurprisingly, this was nearly exactly the same time as the introduction of the original **Graphics Processor Unit** (**GPU**), in 1973 *(1)*! 1994 gave us the *PlayStation1* with its Sony GPU. As a child, I spent many hours loving the graphics performance on my Nintendo 64, with games such as *Zelda*, *Super Smash Brothers*, *Mario Kart 64*, and more! These days you only need to look at games such as *Roblox*, *League of Legends*, and *Fortnite* to understand how crucial graphics performance is to the success of the gaming industry. For decades, gaming has served as one of the most important signals in the market for GPUs.

Until machine learning, that is. In *Chapter 1*, we learned about the ImageNet dataset and briefly introduced its 2012 champion, AlexNet. To efficiently train their model on the large ImageNet dataset, the authors used GPUs! At the time, the GPUs were quite small, only offering 3 GB of memory, so they needed to implement a *model parallel strategy*. This used two GPUs to hold the entire model in memory. These enhancements, in addition to other modifications such as using the ReLU activation function and overlapped pooling, led AlexNet to win the challenge by a landslide.

Since that achievement more than 10 years ago, most of the best machine learning models have used GPUs. From transformers to reinforcement learning, training to inference, and vision to language, the overwhelming majority of state-of-the-art machine learning models require GPUs to perform optimally. For the right type of processing, GPUs can be many orders of magnitude faster than CPUs. When training or hosting deep learning models, the simple choice of using GPUs or CPUs can frequently make a difference of hours to days in completing a task.

We know GPUs have a lot of promising benefits as compared to standard CPU processing, but how? What's so different about them at a fundamental level? The answer may surprise you: *distribution*! Let's take a look at this figure to understand the differences between CPUs and GPUs:

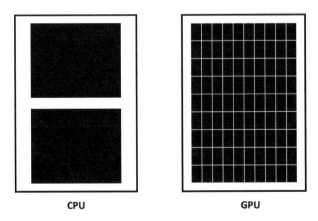

Figure 4.1 – Differences between CPU and GPU

CPUs have just a few cores but a lot of memory. This means they can do only a few operations at once, but they can execute these very quickly. Think of low latency. CPUs operate almost like a cache; they're great at handling lots of tasks that rely on interactivity.

On the other hand, GPUs have thousands of cores. NVIDIA's latest generation GH100 chips, for example, have 18,432 cores. This means they are excellent at processing many operations at once, such as matrix multiplication on the millions to billions of parameters in your neural networks. Think of high throughput.

Don't we care about both low latency and high throughput? Yes, absolutely! This is why the majority of compute you work with today, from your cell phone to your laptop, your notebook instance to the fleet of instances you need to train that state-of-the-art model, use both CPUs and GPUs. The question is, how?

As you might imagine, writing a software program to successfully run complex operations across tens of thousands of microprocessors isn't exactly the easiest thing in the world. This is why, in order to write code for a GPU, you need a specialized software framework purpose-built for hyper-distribution of operations. Enter **CUDA**, NVIDIA's **Compute Unified Device Architecture**. CUDA abstracts away the orchestration of those underlying distributed microprocessors from the consumer, allowing them to leverage the massive distribution without needing to be an expert in its specific architecture. CUDA comes in two parts: drivers that work directly with the hardware, and a toolkit that exposes this hardware to developers. Python can work directly with CUDA, for example. PyTorch and TensorFlow interact with CUDA as well.

NVIDIA certainly isn't the only vendor providing high-performance distributed microprocessors. Commonly called **accelerators**, GPU-like massively parallel processing units are available from Amazon (Inferentia and Trainium), Google (TPUs), Intel (Habna Gaudi), AMD (ROCm), and more. However, each of these requires specialized steps to utilize the underlying distributed hardware. While there are clear advantages when these apply to your use case, for the purposes of a beginner's book, we'll just stick with GPUs. We'll dive into using Amazon's accelerators, Trainium and Inferentia, in *Chapter 9, Advanced Training Concepts*.

Now you've been introduced to accelerators, let's figure out how to use them!

## Getting ready to use your accelerators

Let's start with learning how to use your accelerators:

1. *Step one: acquisition*. You definitely can't train a model on a GPU without first getting your hands on at least one of the GPUs. Fortunately, there are a few free options for you. One of my projects at Amazon was actually writing the original doc for this: SageMaker Studio Lab! Studio Lab is one way to run a free Jupyter Notebook server in the cloud. If you'd like to use a no-cost notebook environment on CPUs or GPUs, store your files, collaborate with others, and connect to AWS or any other service, Studio Lab is a great way to get started.

2. *Step two: containers.* Once you're in a Jupyter notebook and are trying to run some example code, you'll realize that everything hinges on installing the right packages. Even once you have the packages installed, connecting them to the GPU depends on the CUDA installation in your notebook. If the version of PyTorch or TensorFlow you're trying to use doesn't work nicely with that specific CUDA install, you're out of luck!

This is why using the right container as your base image is the perfect way to start developing, especially for deep learning on GPUs. AWS, NVIDIA, PyTorch, and TensorFlow all provide base images you can use to start working with deep learning frameworks. At AWS, we have 70+ containers across multiple frameworks and key versions of these *(2)*. We provide these containers across CPU, GPU, training, hosting, SageMaker, and our container services.

What's a container, you ask? Imagine writing a Python script with 5, 10, 15, or even more than 100 software packages. Installing all of those is really time-consuming and error-prone! Think how hard it is just to install one package successfully on your own; all of that complexity, time, and careful solution you found can literally be transferred anywhere you like. How? Through containers! Containers are a powerful tool. Learn how to make them your friend.

Now that you have some idea about working with containers, especially how they serve as the intermediary between your model and your GPUs, let's talk through the options for where to run your GPUs.

Here, I'd like to emphasize that obviously, I've spent many years working at AWS. I love it! It's been an amazing place for me to grow my skills, learn about the world, practice deep learning, serve customers, and collaborate with some amazing people. I've also spent many hours obsessing about the trade-offs in running compute on the cloud versus running compute on-premises. Actually, before working at AWS, I spent time at many different organizations: a few start-ups, a bank, a university, restaurants, policy organizations, and a non-profit. Each of these handled their compute slightly differently.

On the one hand, purchasing compute to store on-premises might seem like a safer bet upfront. Importantly, you're actually getting something physical for your dollars! You don't need to pay to use the machine, and it seems easier to secure. After all, you can just stash it under your desk. What gives?

There are five big problems with running compute on-premises:

- First is **logistics**. Say you actually do buy some local servers with GPUs. Where would you put them? How would you connect them to your laptop? How would you keep them cold? Power them sufficiently? What would you do if the power spontaneously shut down in that room in the middle of your experiment? You also need to wait for the GPUs to physically arrive in the mail. Then you need to "rack and stack" the boxes, putting them into your growing local data center. Soon enough, these auxiliary tasks can become your full-time job, and you'll need a team of people if you intend to run these for your whole organization.

- Second is **scale**. Say you only buy eight GPUs upfront. You can run a handful of experiments, executing them one at a time. But what if you have a great idea about a new project you'd like to test out? If you have only your eight GPUs, you are physically bound by them and unable to run extra experiments elsewhere. At this point, most people simply move to acquire more GPUs to run their extra experiments, which leads to the third problem.

- Third is **under-utilization**. When everyone goes home at night and isn't training any models, what's happening with those expensive GPUs? Probably nothing. They may be sitting totally unutilized. If you're running some experiments overnight, or for multiple days /weeks, you may see higher levels of GPU utilization. However, it's not at all uncommon for organizations to heavily invest in expensive GPU infrastructure only to see it actually go completely untouched by the very teams who requested it! Usually, you'll see a tiny number of power users, with a very long tail of lightly interested parties who may log in occasionally.

- Fourth is **currency**. Hardware updates, rapidly. Many companies are fully invested in releasing newer, faster, better versions of their hardware every year. Each year, you should expect to see a performance increase with the latest version. It's not a great feeling to have made a big investment in on-premises GPUs, only to see them deprecated in a matter of months. It also introduces a risk to your experiments; you may not be able to produce state-of-the-art results if you're not able to get the most performance out of your compute budget possible.

- Fifth is **carbon footprint**. How much do you know about the type of energy supplying your grid? Is it sustainable? How much extra energy will all of those GPUs add to the carbon footprint of your community, not to mention your bill? Amazon is actually the largest corporate purchaser of renewable energy in the world. We are incredibly careful about the grids supplying our regions and can demonstrate that moving to the AWS cloud can reduce the carbon footprint of the average data center by up to 80%, with a goal of up to 96% once we're powered with 100% renewable energy.

Another benefit of running your GPUs on Amazon SageMaker specifically is that *you are not paying for the instances if you're not running a job*. When using SageMaker to train your machine learning models, the GPUs come online *only when you are training the model itself*. This means your overall GPU utilization is significantly better by moving to SageMaker, simply because of the system architecture. Most data centers aren't built for the dynamism that deep learning training really requires, because when you aren't training a model, the nodes are still running! The same logic holds for Amazon EC2.

Finally, you'll need to make sure that your project actually uses the GPUs. This is much more complex than it sounds. First, the software framework itself needs to connect to the underlying CUDA kernels. Then, you'll want to use some tooling to ensure that you keep the GPU utilization as high as possible. There are a variety of techniques that you'll learn about later in the chapter to dive deeper into these topics.

Now that you've learned how to get ready to use your accelerators, let's learn how to use them on Amazon SageMaker!

# How to use accelerators on AWS – Amazon SageMaker

As you learned in the previous section, AWS is a great way to get your hands on GPUs without needing to provision, store, physically secure, and maintain GPUs. Now, we'll take a look at an easy, efficient, and high-performance way to leverage GPUs on AWS – Amazon SageMaker. Let me be clear, SageMaker certainly is not the only way to run GPUs or accelerators on AWS. However, it is my personal favorite, so we'll start there.

There are many books, blog posts, webinars, and re:Invent sessions dedicated to introducing and discussing SageMaker. I myself have a 16-video YouTube series you can use to learn more about it from me! However, for the purposes of this book, there are really three key pieces of SageMaker I want to you understand: **Studio**, **Training**, and **Hosting**. And each of these comes down to one single common denominator: **instances**.

*Instances* is the term we use to describe virtual machines at AWS. The service is called **Elastic Compute Cloud**, or **EC2**. Every time you turn on a virtual machine, we call it an **instance**. You may have worked with EC2 instances in the past, such as turning them on in the AWS console, SSHing into them, and trying to write some code. But didn't you find it a little frustrating when you needed to change the size? What about downloading the logs or the output? Sharing your notebook? Not to mention your surprise at the bill when you forgot to turn it off!

Now, what if I told you there was an easy way to run notebooks, train models, and build business applications around your own data science work products, without you needing to manage really anything about that underlying infrastructure? You'd probably be interested, right?

That's the core idea of SageMaker. We democratize machine learning by making it extremely easy for you to run your notebooks, models, jobs, pipelines, and processes from one single pane of glass. We also deliver extremely high performance at affordable prices. Let's take a closer look at some of the key pieces of SageMaker.

## *SageMaker Studio*

SageMaker Studio is our flagship development environment that is fully integrated with machine learning. What I love most about Studio is that *we decouple the compute backing your user interface from the compute running your notebook*. That means AWS is managing a Jupyter Server on your behalf, per user, to host your visual experience. This includes a huge volume of features purpose-built for machine learning, such as Feature Store, Pipelines, Data Wrangler, Clarify, Model Monitor, and more.

Then, every time you create a new Jupyter notebook, *we run this on dedicated instances*. These are called **Kernel Gateway Applications**, and they let you seamlessly run many different projects, with different package requirements and different datasets, without leaving your IDE. Even better, the notebooks in Studio are incredibly easy to upgrade, downgrade, and change kernels. That means you can switch from CPU to GPU, or back, without very much work interruption.

## SageMaker Training

Now you have some idea about how to run a notebook on SageMaker, but what about a large-scale job with distributed training?

For this topic, we'll need to introduce the second key pillar of SageMaker: **Training**. SageMaker Training lets you easily define job parameters, such as the instances you need, your scripts, package requirements, software versions, and more. Then, when you fit your model, we launch a cluster of remote instances on AWS to run your scripts. All of the metadata, package details, job output, hyperparameters, data input, and more are stored, searchable, and versioned by default. This lets you easily track your work, reproduce results, and find experiment details, even many months and years after your job has finished.

In addition, we've put a lot of muscle into updating our training backend platform to enable extreme-scale modeling. From data optimizations with FSx for Lustre to distributed libraries such as Model and Data Parallel, we're enabling the next generation of large models across vision and text to train seamlessly on AWS. The next chapter covers this in more detail. Most of the GPUs we'll analyze in this book come under SageMaker Training.

## SageMaker hosting

Lastly, you can also run GPUs on SageMaker hosting. This is valuable when you want to build a scalable REST API on top of your core model. You might use a SageMaker hosting endpoint to run a search experience, deliver questions and answers, classify content, recommend content, and so much more. SageMaker hosting supports GPUs! We'll dive into this in more detail in *Chapter 12, How to Deploy Your Model*.

Now that you understand some of the key pillars of SageMaker, let's break down this concept underlying all of them: instances.

## Instance breakdown for GPUs on SageMaker

As of November 2022, we support two primary instance families with GPUs on SageMaker, two custom accelerators, and Habana Gaudi accelerators. Here, I'll break down how to understand the naming convention for all our instances, in addition to describing what you might use each of these for.

The naming convention for all instances is really three parts: first, middle, and last. For example, `ml.g4dn.12xlarge`. The `ml` part indicates that it's actually a SageMaker instance, so you won't see it in the EC2 control plane. The `g` part tells you what series of compute the instance is part of, especially the type of compute itself. Here, `g` indicates it's a specific type of GPU accelerator: the `g4` instance has NVIDIA T4, and the `g5` has NVIDIA A10G. The number immediately after the letter is the version of this instance, with a higher number always being more recent. So, `g5` came out more recently than `g4`, and so on. The latest version of each instance will always give you better price performance.

Here, g4 indicates you are using NVIDIA T4 GPUs. The letters after the number tell you what else is available on that instance, in this case, d gives us **directly attached instance storage** through **Non-Volatile Memory Express (NVME)**. The letter n is for **networking optimized**. All of them together are called the **instance family**. Everything after the instance family is the size of this particular instance. You might use something quite small, such as ml.t3.medium to run your Jupyter notebook, but then upgrade to something large such as ml.g4dn.12xlarge for development, and ultimately, perhaps, ml.p4dn.24xlarge for extreme-scale training.

Generally speaking, the g instance is great for smaller models. This could include development and testing for you, such as running a complex notebook on this, using warm pools, or simply a multi-GPU model training with data-parallel. The g5 instance is especially competitive here.

However, if you want to train large language models, the p instance series is strongly recommended. This is because the GPUs are actually more performant, and also larger. They support larger models and larger batch sizes. ml.p4dn.24xlarge, with 8 NVIDIA A100s, has 40 GB of GPU memory per card. ml.g5.48xlarge, with 8 NVIDIA A10Gs, has only 24 GB of GPU memory per card.

As of this writing, Trainium has just become available! This is a custom accelerator developed by Amazon to deliver up to 50% better cost performance for customers.

Now that you've learned about how to use GPUs on AWS, especially on Amazon SageMaker, and which instances you want to stay on top of, let's unpack how to optimize GPU performance.

# Optimizing accelerator performance

There are two ways of approaching this, and both of them are important. The first is from a hyperparameter perspective. The second is from an infrastructure perspective. Let's break them down!

## Hyperparameters

All of *Chapter 7* is devoted to picking the right hyperparameters, and optimizing GPU performance is a large driver for that. Importantly, as the number of GPUs changes in your cluster, what we call your **world size**, you'll need to modify your hyperparameters to accommodate that change. Also, there's a core trade-off between increasing your overall job throughput, say by maxing out your batch size, and finding a smaller batch size, which ultimately will give you higher accuracy. Later in the book, you'll learn how to use hyperparameter tuning to bridge that gap.

## Infrastructure optimizations for accelerators on AWS

Here, you're going to learn about five key topics that can determine how well your scripts use the GPU infrastructure available on AWS. At this point in your journey, I am not expecting you to be an expert in any of these. I just want to you know that they exist and that you may need to update flags and configurations related to them later in your workflows:

- **EFA**: Amazon's **Elastic Fabric Adapter** is a custom networking solution on AWS that provides optimal scale for high-performance deep learning. Purpose-built for the Amazon EC2 network topology, it enables seamless networking scale from just a few to a few hundred to thousands of GPUs on AWS.

- **Nitro**: Amazon's custom purpose-built hypervisor system decouples physical hardware, CPU virtualization, storage, and networking that provides heightened security and faster innovation. You're using the Nitro system on SageMaker on many of the large GPU instances, such as `ml.p4d.24xlarge`, `ml.p3dn.24xlarge`, `ml.g4dn.12xlarge`, and more.

- **NCCL: NVIDIA Communication Collectives Library** is a tool you will want to gain some familiarity with when you're ready to actually improve your GPU performance. A common step is to ensure that you're using the latest version of NCCL. There are five key algorithms that NCCL provides: `AllReduce`, `Broadcast`, `Reduce`, `AllGather`, and `ReduceScatter`. Most distributed training software frameworks you will work with use a combination of these or custom implementations of these algorithms in a variety of ways. *Chapter 5* is devoted to exploring this in more detail. Another key NVIDIA library to know about is CUDA, as mentioned previously, which lets you run your deep learning framework software on the accelerators.

- **GPUDirectRDMA**: This is an NVIDIA tool that allows GPUs to communicate directly with each other on the same instance without needing to hop onto the CPU. This is also available on AWS with select instances.

- **Open MPI: Open Message Passing Interface** is an open source project that enables remote machines to easily communicate with each other. The vast majority of your distributed training workloads, especially those that run on SageMaker, will use MPI as a base communication layer for the various workers to stay in sync with each other.

If you're thinking, "*Now, how do I go use all of these things?*", the answer is usually pretty simple. It's three things, as follows:

1. First, ask yourself, *which base container am I using*? If you're using one of the AWS deep learning containers, then all of these capabilities will be provided to you after our extensive tests and checks.

2. Second, take a look at which instance you are using. As you learned previously, each instance type opens up your application to using, or not using, certain features on AWS. Try to make sure you're getting the best performance you can!

3. Third, look at ways to configure these in your job parameters. In SageMaker, we'll use hyperparameters and settings in your scripts to ensure you're maxing out performance.

Now that you've learned a bit about optimizing GPU performance, let's take a look at troubleshooting performance.

# Troubleshooting accelerator performance

Before we can analyze our GPU performance, we need to understand generally how to debug and analyze performance on our training platform. SageMaker has some really nice solutions for this. First, all of your logs are sent to **Amazon CloudWatch**, another AWS service that can help you monitor your job performance. Each node in your cluster will have a full dedicated log stream, and you can read that log stream to view your overall training environment, how SageMaker runs your job, what status your job is in, and all of the logs your script emits. Everything you write to standard out, or print statements, is automatically captured and stored in CloudWatch. The first step to debugging your code is to take a look at the logs and figure out what really went wrong.

Once you know what's wrong in your script, you'll probably want to quickly fix it and get it back online, right? That's why we introduced **managed warm pools** on SageMaker, a feature that keeps your training cluster online, even after a job has finished. With SageMaker warm pools, you can now run new jobs on SageMaker Training in just a few seconds!

With a script working, next, you'll need to analyze the overall performance of your job. This is where debugging tools come in really handy. SageMaker offers a debugger and profiler, both of which actually spin up remote instances while your job is running to apply rules and check on your tensors throughout the training process. The profiler is an especially nice tool to use; it automatically generates graphs and charts for you, which you can use to assess the overall performance of your job, including which GPUs are being utilized, and how much. NVIDIA also offers tooling for GPU debugging and profiling.

As we mentioned before, writing software to seamlessly orchestrate tens of thousands of GPU cores is no small task. And as a result, it's really common for GPUs to suddenly go bad. You might see NCCL errors, CUDA errors, or other seemingly unexplainable faults. For many of these, SageMaker actually runs GPU health checks ahead of time on your behalf! This is why the p4d instances take much longer to initialize than the smaller instances; we are analyzing the health of the GPUs prior to exposing them to you.

Outside of these known GPU-centric issues, you may see other faults such as your loss not decreasing or suddenly exploding, insufficient capacity, oddly low GPU throughput, or small changes in the node topology. For many of these, it's common to implement a **Lambda function** in your account to monitor your job. You can use this Lambda function to analyze your Cloudwatch logs, trigger alerts, restart a job, and more.

Just remember to *checkpoint your model at least every 2 to 3 hours*. We'll cover most of these best practices for training at scale on SageMaker in the coming chapters, but for now, simply know that you need to write a full copy of your most recently trained model with some regularity throughout the training loop.

Now that you've learned about some techniques for troubleshooting GPU performance, let's wrap up everything you've just learned in this chapter.

# Summary

In this chapter, we introduced accelerators for machine learning, including how they are different from standard CPU processing and why you need them for large-scale deep learning. We covered some techniques for acquiring accelerators and getting them ready for software development and model training. We covered key aspects of Amazon SageMaker, notably Studio, Training, and hosting. You should know that there are key software frameworks that let you run code on GPUs, such as NCCL, CUDA, and more. You should also know about the top features that AWS provides for high-performance GPU conception to train deep learning models, such as EFA, Nitro, and more. We covered finding and building containers with these packages preinstalled, to successfully run your scripts on them. We also covered debugging your code on SageMaker and troubleshooting GPU performance.

Now that we've learned about GPUs in some detail, in the next chapter, we'll explore the fundamentals of distributed training!

# References

Please go through the following content for more information on a few topics covered in the chapter:

1. A micro-controlled peripheral processor: `https://dl.acm.org/doi/10.1145/800203.806247`

2. *AWS, deep learning*: `https://github.com/aws/deep-learning-containers`

# 5

# Distribution Fundamentals

In this chapter, you'll learn conceptual fundamentals for the distribution techniques you need to employ for large-scale pretraining and fine-tuning. First, you'll master top distribution concepts for **machine learning** (**ML**), notably model and data parallel. Then, you'll learn how Amazon SageMaker integrates with distribution software to run your job on as many GPUs as you need. You'll learn how to optimize model and data parallel for large-scale training, especially with techniques such as sharded data parallelism. Then, you'll learn how to reduce your memory consumption with advanced techniques such as optimizer state sharding, activation checkpointing, compilation, and more. Lastly, we'll look at a few examples across language, vision, and more to bring all of these concepts together.

In this chapter, we're going to cover the following main topics:

- Understanding key concepts—data and model parallelism

- Combining model and data parallel

- Distributed training on Amazon SageMaker

- Advanced techniques to reduce GPU memory

- Bringing it all home with examples from models today

## Understanding key concepts – data and model parallelism

Some of my most extreme memories of working with ML infrastructure came from graduate school. I'll always remember the stress of a new homework assignment, usually some large dataset I needed to analyze. However, more often than not, the dataset wouldn't fit on my laptop! I'd have to clear out all of my previous assignments just to start the download. Then, the download would take a long time, and it was often interrupted by my spotty café network. Once I managed to download, I realized to my dismay that it was too large to fit into memory! On a good day, the Python library *pandas*, which you were introduced to in *Chapter 2*, had a function built to read that file type, which could limit the read to just a few objects. On a bad day, I needed to build a streaming reader myself. After I managed to run some analysis, I would pick a handful of models I thought would be relevant and well suited.

However, they seemed to take forever to train! I would sit in front of my laptop for hours, making sure the connection didn't fail and that my Jupyter kernel stayed alive, reading my debug statements, and hoping the loop would finish in time for my report due the following morning.

Fortunately for ML developers today, many of these issues have excellent solutions now—as we covered in the last chapter, Amazon SageMaker and the AWS cloud generally being one of them. Now, let's unpack one aspect of these in great detail: the *training runtime*. As it turns out, distribution is a concept you can master to train extremely large models and datasets. In this chapter, we'll explore two key concepts that, when used properly, will help you scale your training up to as large as your dreams. The two concepts are set out here:

- **Data parallelism**

- **Model parallelism**

Data parallelism *makes copies of your model per GPUs*, breaking up your dataset to help you train faster, and model parallelism *splits your model across GPUs*, helping you train even larger models. Put another way, data parallelism splits the data across accelerators in both single and multi-node settings. It applies different splits of the data to exactly the same model, copied N times. Model parallelism, on the other hand, splits this same model across multiple accelerators and nodes, using the same data for every model split.

## What data parallel is all about

Data parallel is useful when you are working with extremely large datasets. In the simplest case, you might have an instance with two GPUs. Assuming you're working with a model that is small enough to fit only a single GPU—say, something south of 1 billion parameters—your data parallel software framework might make two copies of your model, one per GPU. This same framework will also need a **distributed data loader**. This data loader will need to point to a single source—for example, your train and test files—but *split each batch by the number of model copies*. For example, if your global batch size were 32, your batch size per GPU would then become 16. Your data loader manages this for you, ensuring that each global batch is split and allocated correctly across your entire *world size*, or the total number of GPUs you are using to train across all machines.

How do you get one model—you ask—instead of two? By a simple average! The forward pass is simple to understand: each copy of the model executes a single forward pass through the network using the per-GPU batch. However, for the backward pass, the gradients *are averaged across all model copies*. After the forward pass, each model copy sends its output to the centralized control plane. This control plane computes a weighted average of the outputs of all the copies, compares this to the ground truth, and runs the gradient descent algorithm via the optimizer. The optimizer then sends new model weights out to each of the model copies. Each batch completion is called a **step**, and a full pass through your dataset is called an **epoch**.

This basic concept will scale as long as you keep adding GPUs. This means that good data parallel software, such as **SageMaker Distributed Data Parallel** (**SM DDP**), will help you run on multiple GPUs in both single- and multi-instance cases. We'll learn more about SageMaker-managed libraries for distributed training later in this chapter.

But first, now that you have a working understanding of data parallelism, let's unpack the second dimension of distribution: model parallel.

## What model parallel is all about

As we've come to find out, many of the state-of-the-art models in today's world are extremely large. Commonly, these range from anything as small as a few billion parameters to hundreds of billions of parameters, and occasionally trillions. Remember—**parameters** are the weights in your neural network. They are what is inside all of your layers. As data passes through your network, each step is a mathematical function that transforms the input data itself, using some formula defined by the type of layer, frequently applying some activation function, and sending the results into the next layer. Computationally, the layer is fundamentally a list. The list is composed of parameters! When set to **trainable**, these parameters will change during the stochastic gradient descent of the backward pass. When set to **not trainable**, these parameters will not change, allowing you to either deploy your model or fine-tune it with downstream layers.

But how do we deal with large models? Model parallelism is the answer!

Model parallelism encompasses a variety of methods that help you split your model across multiple GPUs. The simplest of these is called **pipeline parallel**. In pipeline parallel, your software framework will simply take layers of your neural network and place them on different GPUs. If your neural network had two extremely large layers, and you wanted to train this on an instance with two GPUs, you might place one layer on each GPU.

Similarly, with the preceding data parallel example, you'll still need a distributed data loader. This distributed data loader will still break up each global batch size into per-GPU **microbatches**. Each part of the model—in this case, each layer of the model—can then receive one microbatch at a time for the forward pass. The centralized control plane will then *execute each layer asynchronously*, passing the microbatches to relevant layers at the right points in time. Every layer will still see every item from the dataset, so mathematically it's the same as if all layers were packed into some massive single GPU. Thank you, commutative property!

You can see an illustration of the process in the following diagram:

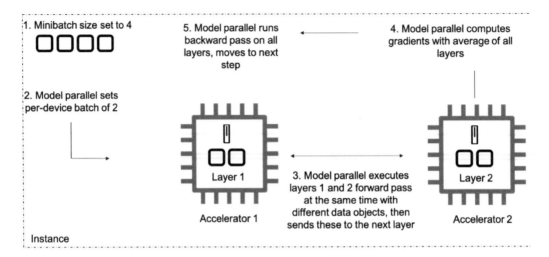

Figure 5.1 – Model parallelism

Another key aspect of model parallel is working with layers that are *too large to fit on a single GPU*. This is especially common in large language models, where the transformer attention head we learned about in the first chapter can easily surpass the memory limitations of modern GPUs. How do we do this? **Tensor parallelism**, which is the third dimension of distributed training. In a tensor parallel framework, you might have part of one tensor on one GPU, while the other part of that same tensor is placed onto a different GPU. The centralized distributed software still passes microbatches to them so that logically there is no difference in the operations. Tensor parallelism is strictly necessary for training the GPT-3-sized models of the world today, with 175 billion parameters and more.

To learn more about model parallelism, and especially the distributed library available through SageMaker model parallelism, take a look at our paper on the topic here (4). Now that you've learned about two foundational topics in distributed training, notably data and model parallelism, let's learn how to combine them!

## Combining model and data parallel

As you may have suspected previously, and as is empirically evidenced by scaling laws, large models *are only effective when combined with large datasets*. That is to say, if you use an extremely large model with a small or moderately sized dataset, you are extremely likely to overfit your model. This means it may eventually learn how to replicate the core examples you've provided, but it is very unlikely to handle new challenges well.

Surprisingly, the reverse is not necessarily true. As a general rule of thumb, it is helpful to increase the model size with the dataset size. However, in most computer vision cases, model sizes rarely surpass the memory sizes of single GPUs. I can say the majority of vision customers I work with, from autonomous vehicles to manufacturing, financial services to health care, tend to work with models that can fit quite nicely onto single GPUs. In these cases, data parallel alone is a strong candidate to improve the throughput of the training loop, because with every copy of the model on additional GPUs, your ability to train faster increases.

However, this is usually not the case in **natural language processing** (**NLP**), where the most performant models regularly require at least a few GPUs, and sometimes hundreds or even thousands. In these cases, *you can expect to use a combination of model and data parallelism*, as demonstrated by an early example from Alpa (5). Model parallel enables you to simply hold the model in active memory on GPUs, and data parallel improves your overall speed by copying your model and increasing the overall amount of data your model can process per step. When holding even one copy of the model requires multiple GPUs, it just means that each additional copy will require the same amount. So, if your model needs 4 GPUs, and based on your data size you used scaling laws to determine that your total compute budget includes 64 GPUs (8 instances with 8 GPUs each), then you'd have 16 copies of the model! This is because each 8-GPU instance could hold 2 copies of the model each. Let's break it down with a visual:

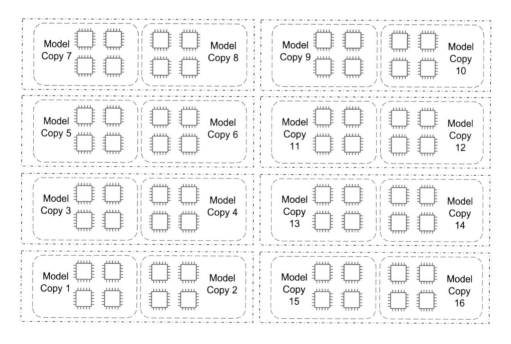

Figure 5.2 – Model and data parallelism

Remember—each copy of the model is handled through model parallelism. Then, merging all copies of the model is handled through data parallelism. Seems complex, right? But hopefully, these concepts are starting to sink in—once they do, suddenly all these terms and ideas will start making sense. Remember—you aren't alone in this journey. We have a fully managed service to help you train models at incredible scales! In the next section, I'd like to share with you some of what Amazon SageMaker automates, manages, and brings to the table to help you get to your science, faster.

## Distributed training on Amazon SageMaker

In the last chapter, we learned about SageMaker generally. Now, I'd like to dive into distributed training capabilities. We can break these up into four different categories: containers, orchestration, usability, and performance at scale.

As we learned in an earlier chapter, AWS offers **deep learning** (**DL**) containers that you can easily point to for your own scripts and code. These are strongly recommended as the first starting point for your project because all of the frameworks, versions, and libraries have been tested and integrated for you. This means that you can simply pick a container based on whichever DL framework you are using—for example, PyTorch or TensorFlow—*and this container has already been tested on AWS and SageMaker.* You can also select the GPU version of this container, and it will already have all of the NVIDIA libraries compiled and installed to run nicely on your GPUs. If you have your own container, however, you can simply push that to Amazon's **Elastic Container Registry** (**ECR**) and use it for training. You'll want to add the training toolkit to enable all of the training features for custom containers, such as the entrypoint script, log emissions, warm pools, and so on.

Once you have your image selected, you're ready to format your script! On SageMaker we use the **estimator** concept heavily. This is a Python wrapper around the API, `CreateTrainingJob`, and it's a concept you'll want to get very familiar with. The core idea is that you use your estimator to point to basic objects, such as your DL container, your scripts, and all of your job parameters. Then, you simply call `estimator.fit()`. This submits your call to the `CreateTrainingJob` API, which then executes the command to create the job!

Remember that SageMaker training *initializes remote instances for you during training.* This means that once you've executed `estimator.fit()`, then in the console under **Training Jobs**, you'll see new instances initialized. These are managed by the service. Once the instances are initialized, they'll copy your data onto them, download your image, and run your training script on your data. All the logs are sent to CloudWatch, and all the metadata for your job is maintained. This means your experiments are reproducible by default! Once your job is finished, the trained model artifact is sent to Amazon **Simple Storage Service** (**S3**) on your behalf.

Now, you must be thinking: This seems doable for a script that uses just one GPU. But how do I use multiple GPUs? The answer is easy: software!

## Distributed training software

The critical step in scaling your code from one to multiple GPUs is using the right software for this. And fortunately for you, there are many options available today. On SageMaker, you can use any open source software you want; it's easy to bring extra packages, scripts, and frameworks onto the `training` API. This means you can certainly implement any one of the top distributed training frameworks in our Training API. Some of these include DeepSpeed ZeRO-3D, Megatron-LM, PyTorch **DistributedDataParallel** (**DDP**), Horovod, and more. If you have code running in one of these frameworks already, your first step in scaling will likely be to just move this onto AWS and SageMaker especially. However, if you only use open source distributed frameworks, *you are leaving efficiency gains on the table*.

The reason for these efficiency gains comes fundamentally from a concept we use a lot at Amazon: *there's no compression algorithm for experience*. What this literally means is that Amazon constantly makes a lot of improvements in optimizing DL on the cloud, especially DL at scale. In particular, we have a software solution, SageMaker distributed training libraries, that helps you achieve state-of-the-art performance on AWS.

We'll dive more into the nuances of this different distributed training software, including key design decisions such as the difference between parameter servers and ring-based approaches, in *Chapter 8*. For now, let's explore the libraries available at a high level.

## SM DDP

Remember in *Chapter 4*, we learned about a concept called **communication collectives**. These are core algorithms designed to facilitate distributed gradient descent on multiple GPUs. However, the **NVIDIA Collective Communication Library** (**NCCL**) is actually designed with a target infrastructure in mind: InfiniBand. This is an extremely generous networking solution that enables more than 1 TB of communication transfer. Operationalizing this is quite expensive and requires a large upfront investment to acquire and utilize this on-premises.

At AWS, we design our own custom communication collectives that are purpose-built for the **Elastic Compute Cloud** (**EC2**) network topology. These enable the best performance on AWS, scaling to thousands of GPUs and beyond without the overhead requirement of massive networking. The primary way you can interact with these custom collectives is through SM DDP (*3*). SM DDP is a fully managed data parallel software that integrates with your training script via the backend. This means that you can bring your own data parallel neural network software—notably, PyTorch DDP, Hugging Face's Accelerate, or TensorFlow's Horovod—and simply set SM DDP as your backend.

The primary reason for setting SM DDP as your backend is to **increase scaling efficiency**. Without SM DDP, you are likely to use communication collective algorithms that aren't designed explicitly for the AWS EC2 instance topology. As a result, when you add more instances to your overall cluster size, you will experience *decreasing returns*. From a theoretical perspective, in a perfect world, you should be able to exactly halve your training time by moving from one to two nodes. Moving from one to three should cut down your train time by 3 times. Moving from one to four should cut down your train time by 4 times. This theoretical frontier is called **linear scaling efficiency**.

However, we don't live in a perfect world. Computationally, this linear scaling efficiency is effectively impossible to reach. What you will see are attempts at approaching better and better scaling efficiency, such as with better communication collective algorithms as provided by SM DDP. The gains from SM DDP are especially notable at larger scales. For example, if you compare an 8-node cluster using PyTorch DDP with the same one using SM DDP, the SM DDP job can be as much as 40% better. Those gains are on a massive scale. It means not only do your experiments come back faster, giving you more time to try new ideas and get your solution to market faster, but the actual compute cost of training is that much lower!

Now that we've learned about the SM DDP library, let's explore another option for clocking efficiency gains at scale on AWS: the **SageMaker Model Parallel** (**SMP**) library.

## SMP library

Remember that earlier in this chapter we introduced large-scale training on Amazon SageMaker. We also clarified that this enables you to run any open source library on as many GPUs as you like, without limitations around distribution software. In terms of model parallelism, this includes DeepSpeed, Megatron-LM, and others. However, to truly take advantage of all the performance enhancements SageMaker offers, I'd strongly recommend that you evaluate the SMP library. This is what we will use in detail throughout the book.

SMP is a Python SDK built and managed by AWS that helps you easily scale your neural network models across multiple GPUs. SMP integrates nicely with PyTorch and offers advanced features to help you scale models to anywhere from only a few to a few hundred or even thousands of GPUs. These include pipeline parallelism, tensor parallelism, optimizer state sharding, activation offloading and checkpointing, sharded data parallelism, and more. Later in this chapter, we'll explore the advanced features, but first, let's understand simply how to configure and use the library for basic model distribution.

Generally speaking, once you have a working PyTorch model that can train on a single GPU, it's time to evaluate scaling that up. First, ensure that the base container you are working with is compatible with SMP. If you are using an AWS-managed DL container with support for GPUs, SageMaker, and training, then you are ready to move to the next step. If not, follow the documented steps (*1*) to extend a prebuilt Docker container from any arbitrary base image.

Once you've ensured your container supports SMP, it's time to integrate the library into your training script. This centers on three key aspects, as follows:

1.  Import the library into your script. As of November 2022, this is as simple as executing the following command: `import smdistributed.modelparallel.torch as smp`.

2.  Wrap your model and optimizer with the relevant `smp` objects. This is actually pretty straightforward. After you've finished using PyTorch to define your neural network, or simply after you've loaded a PyTorch model from Hugging Face, simply pass it as an argument to the `smp.DistributedModel()` object. Then, continue passing your model throughout the rest of your script as you normally would. The optimizer follows a similar syntactic structure.

3.  Refactor your training loop to include two distinct functions, a **training step** and a **test step**. Both of these should take your model, optimizer, and other relevant parameters. The train step should pass your data forward through the network, compute the loss, propagate it backward through the network via the optimizer, and return the loss. The test step should simply compute the loss, also returning it.

For both the train and test step functions, you'll need to *add a Python decorator* declaring them as `@smp.step`. This decorator is critical because *everything included in this function will be sharded onto multiple GPUs*. The SMP library will explicitly evaluate the activity in these functions, notably your model and how data passes through it, to optimally place your model across multiple GPUs.

Once your script has these and a few other relevant changes, you'll need to make one last configuration. In your SageMaker training job estimator, add another parameter called `distribution`. As we'll see throughout the book, this parameter will allow us to configure many aspects of SageMaker training's backend, including both SMP and SM DDP. Pass a flag to enable SMP, along with any other relevant parameters. You'll also need to enable **Message Passing Interface** (**MPI**), which we learned about earlier in the book. MPI is an open source framework that enables your nodes to communicate with each other while training. SMP uses MPI to communicate across nodes.

Finally, test out your script! An easy way to test model parallelism within SageMaker Training is called **local mode**. Local mode is an extremely useful technique that lets you develop the SageMaker Training API, including containers, data pointers, scripts, and job parameters, without waiting for the overhead of your cluster to spin up. You can use SageMaker local mode from anywhere that runs Docker, such as a SageMaker notebook instance or even your local laptop. As of this writing, Studio does not support local mode. Local mode helps you take steps quickly and easily as you write your code, ensuring that everything is designed and working nicely.

Once you have increased the size of your model, either through importing a larger version from Hugging Face or through increasing the number of parameters manually in your PyTorch definition, and you have proof that this works nicely on at least two GPUs, it's time to explore advanced techniques in the SMP library to reduce your overall GPU memory footprint.

# Advanced techniques to reduce GPU memory

Now, let's imagine that you are pretty far into your project. You've already identified your dataset, your use case, and your base model. You've tested this at a small scale on SageMaker, such as by using 1% of your data on the smallest version of your model, and this seems to be working well. You've used scaling laws, or have simply seen through another example that a large model would help you increase your accuracy, and you're confident that you have enough data to justify that larger model. You've increased your model enough to run on at least two GPUs and have successfully tested this on AWS.

If you haven't hit all of those stages, then frankly I'd recommend you simply skip to the next section. Here, we're about to seriously dive into very complex, detailed, and niche topics in the cutting-edge space of model parallelism. If you aren't ready for them, such as through having hit all of the preceding stages in your project I just listed previously, then you'd be better off skipping this topic altogether for now. You can always come back and reference this material later on. Particularly if you are truly a beginner in this space, the topics we're about to discuss may overwhelm you, making it harder for you to continue in distributed training. You can still train state-of-the-art models, such as Stable Diffusion, without using extreme-scale model parallelism. However, for those of you who truly are ready to dive completely into the world of model parallelism, let's get started!

You may have noticed that splitting a model across multiple accelerators has the natural effect of *reducing the model's GPU memory footprint*. Put another way, when a model is too big to fit on a single GPU, it is bottlenecked by the available memory of that GPU, so we need a way to reduce its memory footprint. Splitting the model across GPUs is one way of doing this, but it isn't the only way. Let's introduce a few more.

Once you've integrated your training script with the SMP library, using the rest of the features is as simple as adding and removing hyperparameters. While coding for them is quite simple, understanding them and designing for them successfully is quite challenging. First off, let's recap the basics. The `pipeline_parallel_degree` parameter indicates how you'll be splitting your model across multiple GPUs. For example, if you have 8 GPUs on your box, and you set a `pipeline_parallel_degree` value of 2, then depending on how you allocate parameters in your model you will possibly have split your model in half. If each half of the model were using 4 GPUs, then the entire model could consume 8 GPUs, with each half consuming 4 GPUs. If you wanted to add a data parallel degree to this, you'd need another instance.

You'll also need to consider how large your batch size is per GPU. In the SMP library, we call this `microbatches`. All of *Chapter 7* is about finding the right hyperparameters, but here you need to understand that *increasing the batch size directly increases your GPU utilization*. The central goal in model parallelism is finding efficient ways to decrease the GPU memory footprint of your model, allowing you to increase batch size—and hence GPU utilization—which reduces the overall runtime of your job, and hence its price tag. However, as you'll learn in *Chapter 7*, accurate models generally need lower batch sizes. Yann LeCunn is famous for stating on Twitter that "*friends don't let friends use batch sizes over 32*".

Apart from pipeline parallelism and microbatches, a few other key terms to understand in model parallelism include tensor parallelism, optimizer state sharding, activation checkpointing, and sharded data parallelism.

## Tensor parallelism

While pipeline parallelism allowed us to place different layers in our neural network on different devices, in tensor parallelism we take this another step further to *break up the layers themselves*. Typically, this is common in cases of extreme model parallelism, such as with GPT-3-type models with more than 100 billion parameters. In SMP, you can enable this simply with `tensor_parallel_degree`. Try to make sure that you're keeping all aspects of a single layer within a single node, as this is critical in maximizing the bandwidth in your training cluster.

If you're especially curious, for scaling up to 1 trillion parameters another useful technique is a spare network. This was originally proposed in 2017 (6) as a **mixture-of-experts** (**MoE**) technique to activate only part of a neural network during training, enabling more efficient scaling to massive parameter sizes. A distributed training team out of Huawei proposed an update to this focused on transformers, implementing what they call **random routed experts**. Impressively, they claim this was trained on only 512 accelerators in over 100 days, improving the state of the art for Chinese NLP tasks (7). For the rest of this book, however, we will mostly focus on dense networks that are applicable for models up to a few hundred billion parameters.

## Optimizer state sharding

When the number of trainable weights, or parameters, in your neural network is large, you can expect the optimizer to be equally large. If you have multiple copies of your model in your training cluster, such as by using data parallelism in concert with model parallelism, then consider splitting the optimizer by setting `shard_optimizer_state : True`. Interestingly, this scopes the `DistributedOptimizer` object to only the parameters held in that data parallel rank. These are then called **virtual parameters**, and they share the underlying storage with the original parameters.

## Activation checkpointing

Activation checkpointing is actually a technique that *trades extra computation time for reduced memory overhead*. Put another way, when you have activation checkpointing enabled, you'll be able to load more objects into your cleared GPU memory, but at the price of each step taking a bit longer. This works through clearing activations of some layers and recomputing these while backpropagating the network.

## Sharded data parallelism

One of our teams at Amazon in 2022 developed a novel strategy to optimize for large-scale distributed training on AWS. In particular, they realized that *not all GPUs should be treated equally*. This is relevant when you are trying to optimize communication collectives *assuming some combination of model and data parallel*. They designed a hierarchical approach to **certificates of completion** (**CCLs**) for distributed training, one that looks first *within* a data parallel group (or shard, as it's called in the documentation), and then *across* data parallel groups. This minimizes the amount of overall communication required to synchronize the gradients during backpropagation and increases the overall speed of this job. Hence their name: **minimize communication scale**, or **MiCS** (*8*). This MiCS technique is available on SageMaker within the SMP library; it's known as **sharded data parallelism**.

Now that you've learned about some advanced ways to reduce your overall GPU consumption and speed up your job, let's explore examples from interesting models that will help you bring all of these concepts together.

# Bringing it all home with examples from models today

Remember we learned earlier in the book that *truly every state-of-the-art model requires some amount of distribution*. This is because good models come from good datasets, and good datasets are large. These take time to process, so you need to distribute your processes in order to complete them in a timely manner. Some of them have models that are too big to fit on a single GPU, so they'll require some amount of model parallelism. But others have models that are quite small, meaning they will only require data parallelism. Let's step through two examples from top models today: Stable Diffusion and GPT-2.

## Stable Diffusion – data parallelism at scale

Stable Diffusion is a fascinating model that enables you to *create images from text*. Once trained, you can simply provide textual input to Stable Diffusion, and it will generate a new picture for you! While researchers have been attempting this since at least 2017, Stable Diffusion achieves performance that begins to approach human-level creativity. Models with similar performance, but not shared publicly, include Imagen (*9*) and DALL-E (*10*). The quality of the images it generates is almost immediately usable. There are still certainly issues around bias, control of the images, resolution, and common-sense reasoning, but the jump up since the state-of-the-art performance in 2017 is truly exciting.

Fortunately for the average Python developer, Stable Diffusion is a small model! It can fit on a single GPU, by design, which means with just a tiny bit of scripting and a moderate GPU, you can easily stand up your own demo. The drivers behind Stable Diffusion's success are fewfold and are set out as follows:

1.  They use four models during training: a CLIP tokenizer, a CLIP text encoder, a **variational autoencoder** (**VAE**), and a 2D convolutional U-Net. The tokenizer and encoder use intelligent language models to process the textual data, while the VAE encodes the images and converts them to a smaller latent space.

2.  They add noise to those same latent images during the "diffusion", or learning process. Using the text encoded by a language model, they try to predict the noise residuals, computing the loss and propagating this back through the UNet.

3.  They use multiple billions of images! Their training data and code are both available publicly. Personally, I've written scripts to download 50 million images onto an optimized distributed filesystem on AWS, FSx for Lustre, and used almost 200 GPUs on Amazon SageMaker to take a few steps through this massive dataset. Their original dataset is **LAION-5B**, with the "**5B**" standing for 5 billion. These billions of images come straight from the internet, and the dataset includes textual captions for each image. Then, their model combines the images with the captions during training.

What this means is that having read this chapter, if you now have a solid understanding of data parallelism, you have everything you need to embark on training your own Stable Diffusion model! This will be the case both for pretraining and fine-tuning. In the next chapter, we'll dive into the data loader, and you'll learn how to prepare a new dataset for pretraining or fine-tuning at scale. But first, let's walk through a complex model parallel case study: GPT-3.

## GPT-3 – model and data parallelism at scale

As we learned in *Chapter 1*, GPT-3 is a really important model. When the team at OpenAI 10xed their model size and tripled their accuracy, moving from GPT-2 to GPT-3, they unleashed a worldwide movement that is now practically synonymous with **artificial intelligence** (**AI**). Core to this step in scaling, as we've learned throughout this chapter, is model parallelism. Let's unpack how this works for models with more than 100 billion parameters!

Let's start by estimating the memory size of the model itself. First, let's count this in parameters—say, 100 billion parameters. Then, for a job that uses FP16 data types and Adam optimizers, you can assume a single FP16 parameter takes about 2 bytes, and an FP16 gradient takes about the same. So, for a model with 10 billion parameters, you'll need at least 200 GB of GPU memory. A model with 100 billion would then need about 2 TB of GPU memory!

Assuming you have 40 GB of GPU memory available per device, as is the case for the p4d.24xlarge instances, that's 50 GPUs just to hold one full copy of the model in memory. Each p4d.24xlarge instance has 8 GPUs, so you're looking at just over 6 p4d instances per model copy. Assuming you both want an accurate model and not have to wait years for the job to finish training, you'll want many, many copies of this model. I've helped customers train on 128 p4d instances on SageMaker for large language models of this size, which in this calculation would give them about 20 copies of the model across all of those 1,024 GPUs.

For scripting examples to wrap your head around what this would look like in action, consider our notebooks at the *SageMaker Examples* repository on GitHub. You should find it if you search for GPT-2, or even model parallel in the repository. Currently, the link is here: (2).

If you inspect the notebook, you'll notice a few things:

- It offers different sizes for training the model, starting from the very smallest and going up to a few tens of billions of parameters
- Each of these different settings requires slightly different hyperparameters

All of *Chapter 7* is about selecting these. And now, you've just learned why this is so challenging and important! When you configure the job, you need to determine your distribution strategy, integrating the model and data parallel, your overall world size, any extra GPU memory reduction techniques, the model size and relevant parameters, and so much more.

But don't lose heart—we still have a lot to learn. For now, let's close out the chapter with a quick summary.

## Summary

In this chapter, you learned about the basics of distributed training. You learned about data parallelism and model parallelism as key concepts that will enable you to scale your training up to sizes that approach state of the art. You learned how to combine them, and especially how managed orchestration platforms such as Amazon SageMaker help you seamlessly work with hundreds to thousands of GPUs with optimized distributed training libraries. You then learned about advanced GPU memory reduction techniques and brought this to life with real-world examples such as Stable Diffusion and GPT-3.

In the next chapter, we'll dive into the engineering fundamentals and concepts you need to build your own data loader!

## References

Please go through the following content for more information on a few topics covered in the chapter:

1. *SMP library*: https://docs.aws.amazon.com/sagemaker/latest/dg/model-parallel-sm-sdk.html#model-parallel-customize-container

2. *Amazon SageMaker example*: https://github.com/aws/amazon-sagemaker-examples/blob/main/training/distributed_training/pytorch/model_parallel/gpt2/smp-train-gpt-simple.ipynb

3. *SM DDP library*: https://docs.aws.amazon.com/sagemaker/latest/dg/data-parallel.html

4. *Amazon SageMaker Model Parallism: A General and Flexible Framework for Large Model Training* https://arxiv.org/pdf/2111.05972.pdf

5. *Alpa: Automating Inter- and Intra-Operator Parallelism for Distributed Deep Learning*: https://www.usenix.org/conference/osdi22/presentation/zheng-lianmin

6. *Outrageously Large Neural Networks: The Sparsely-Gated Mixture-of-Experts Layer*: https://arxiv.org/pdf/1701.06538.pdf

7.  *Pangu-Σ: Towards Trillion Parameter Language Model With Sparse Heterogenous Computing*: `https://arxiv.org/pdf/2303.10845.pdf`

8.  *MiCS: Near-linear Scaling for Training Gigantic Model on Public Cloud*: `https://arxiv.org/pdf/2205.00119.pdf`

9.  *Photorealistic Text-to-Image Diffusion Models with Deep Language Understanding*: `https://arxiv.org/pdf/2205.11487.pdf`

10. *Zero-Shot Text-to-Image Generation*: `https://arxiv.org/pdf/2102.12092.pdf`

# Dataset Preparation: Part Two, the Data Loader

*Become one with the data. – Andrej Karpathy*

In this chapter, you'll learn how to prepare your dataset to immediately use it with your chosen models. You'll master the concept of a data loader, learning why it's a common source of errors in training large models. You'll learn about creating embeddings, using tokenizers, and other methods to featurize your raw data for your preferred neural network. Following these steps, you'll be able to prepare your entire dataset, using methods for both vision and language. Finally, you'll learn about data optimization on AWS and Amazon SageMaker to efficiently send datasets large and small to your training cluster. Throughout this chapter, we'll work backward through the training loop, incrementally giving you all the steps you need to have functional deep neural networks training at scale. You'll also follow a case study on how I trained on 10 TB for Stable Diffusion on SageMaker!

Never underestimate the power of data. Whether it's getting the highest quality samples and labels you can, failing to catch subtle corruptions, or optimizing your compute selections, data can truly make or break the success of your project. Many top deep learning models actually came about through the development of a novel dataset, from MNIST to AlexNet, and from GPT-3 to Stable Diffusion! When we think big in machine learning, frequently that means thinking big about your dataset.

You can't have a functional training loop without a functional data loader, so let's unpack it! In this chapter, we're going to cover the following main topics:

- Introducing the data loader through key concepts in Python
- Building and testing your own data loader: a case study from Stable Diffusion
- Embeddings and tokenizers
- Optimizing your data pipeline on AWS
- Transforming deep learning datasets at scale on AWS

# Introducing the data loader in Python

The data loader is a concept that is fairly unique to deep learning. In statistical machine learning, you still see many models using gradient updating, which requires mini-batches, but the *loading* aspect is more hidden – more integrated with the algorithm itself. PyTorch leaned into this concept from the early days, explicitly offering a data loader object and exposing the entire training loop to the developer. While somewhat more complex than early TensorFlow, this actually enabled developers to have a lot more flexibility and control over the training process, which helped them more easily develop custom solutions. This was a part of the reason more and more research projects eventually embraced PyTorch over TensorFlow as their deep learning framework of choice. Now, the majority of models I encounter are first implemented in PyTorch, and occasionally in TensorFlow.

What is a data loader? A data loader *hydrates your training loop with data.* Most PyTorch training loops are actually just nested loops. First, there's an outer loop through the number of epochs. Each epoch is a full pass through the dataset. This means – you guessed it – *the inner loop is just a pass through your data loader.* This means that your data loader needs to use, under the hood, a really useful object in Python known as an **iterator**.

First, let's take a quick look at objects in Python, and build up to the data loader.

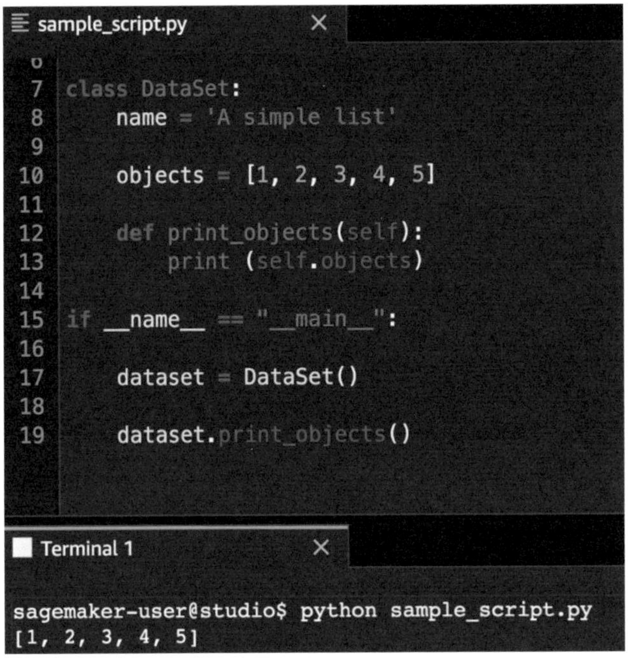

```
sample_script.py                    ×

 6
 7  class DataSet:
 8      name = 'A simple list'
 9
10      objects = [1, 2, 3, 4, 5]
11
12      def print_objects(self):
13          print (self.objects)
14
15  if __name__ == "__main__":
16
17      dataset = DataSet()
18
19      dataset.print_objects()


Terminal 1                          ×

sagemaker-user@studio$ python sample_script.py
[1, 2, 3, 4, 5]
```

Figure 6.1 – Classes in Python

Remember, Python is an **object-oriented** language. This means that, most of the time, when you're working in Python you're working with objects. A class is then just a convenient way of building, maintaining, and using objects.

Most of the time, in the real world, you won't be building objects, unless you're building a new software SDK. Usually, as a service consumer, you're just using an object someone else has built, and developing a script to integrate it into your tasks. This is also true in deep learning; most of our objects are already written in software packages such as PyTorch, pandas, sklearn, and so on.

Now, what if I wanted to point to a really large list all at once, but have it return only a predefined number of objects every time I call that function? Would I have to build this entire construct myself? Now that I'm not in grad school anymore, I can happily say no way! I'd just use an iterator, as shown in the following screenshot.

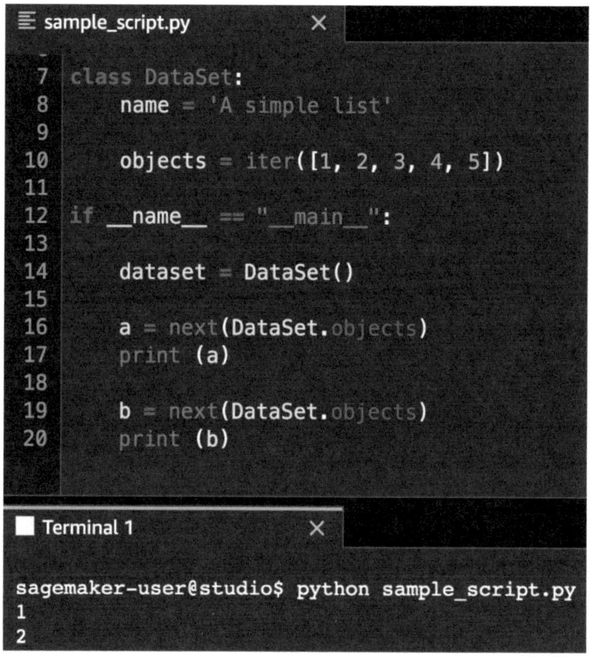

```
≣ sample_script.py            ×

 7  class DataSet:
 8      name = 'A simple list'
 9
10      objects = iter([1, 2, 3, 4, 5])
11
12  if __name__ == "__main__":
13
14      dataset = DataSet()
15
16      a = next(DataSet.objects)
17      print (a)
18
19      b = next(DataSet.objects)
20      print (b)
```

```
■ Terminal 1                  ×

sagemaker-user@studio$ python sample_script.py
1
2
```

Figure 6.2 – A simple iterator class in Python

Python iterators are purpose-built for scenarios like this, calling an object multiple times but retrieving a different item each time. Many objects in Python support iterators, such as lists and dictionaries. Turning one of them into an iterator is usually pretty simple. You'll do it in two steps, first when you define the core object as an iterator, here with the `iter()` syntax. Second, when you call the iterator to provide you with the next batch of items, here with `next()`. Expect the syntax to change, but most of the concepts to stay the same.

Your job in building a data loader is *not* to necessarily build a class from scratch. It's to use some software framework, such as NumPy, Hugging Face, PyTorch, or TensorFlow, to accept the data you want to work with. Then, you need to use that pre-built data loader to walk through your batches and populate your training loop with them.

Now that you know what a data loader is supposed to do, let's explore how to build your own data loader.

# Building and testing your own data loader – a case study from Stable Diffusion

The syntax for data loaders is guaranteed to change, so I don't want to rely on PyTorch's current implementation too heavily. However, let me provide you with one simple screenshot:

```
461    train_dataloader = torch.utils.data.DataLoader(
462        train_dataset, shuffle=True, collate_fn=collate_fn, batch_size=args.train_batch_size,
       num_workers=4
463    )
464    eval_dataloader = torch.utils.data.DataLoader(eval_dataset, collate_fn=collate_fn,
       batch_size=args.eval_batch_size, num_workers=4)
```

Figure 6.3 – Using data loaders in PyTorch

This is actually from my re:Invent demo on large-scale training in 2022, with Gal Oshri from SageMaker and Dan Padnos from AI21: https://medium.com/@emilywebber/how-i-trained-10tb-for-stable-diffusion-on-sagemaker-39dcea49ce32. Here, I'm training Stable Diffusion on 10 TB of data, using SageMaker and FSx for Lustre, which is a distributed file system built for high-performance computing. More on that and related optimizations later in the chapter!

As you can see, really the only hard part about this is building the input training dataset. Once you have a valid dataset object, getting a valid data loader is as simple as copying the latest syntax into your script and ensuring it's valid. So, you ask, how do we get our own training dataset? One word: dictionaries!

In my setup right now, I have a Jupyter notebook running on Studio. I upgrade and downgrade the instance running my kernel gateway application, or ephemeral notebook, continuously based on whether and when I need to do some large- or small-scale processing. In this notebook, I have developed scripts and functions that I'm sure will work, then I copied them into the main script that runs on my SageMaker training jobs. This is where I built out a custom data loading function.

Hugging Face provides a nice `load_dataset()` function from its dataset library, but after more than a few hours of searching and testing, I wasn't able to get this to work with my custom dataset. So, I ended up building my own data loader backend, which I then pointed to the `DatasetDict()` object. In my notebook, it looks like this:

```
from datasets import Dataset, DatasetDict

# should load the entire dataset into one massive DatasetDict object
def custom_load_dataset(args):

    part_list = glob.glob("{}/part-*".format(args['train_data_dir']))

    dataset_dicts = []

    for full_part_path in part_list[0:1]:

        # should continue adding to this dict through the loop iteration over images in 1 part
        dataset_dicts = add_part(dataset_dicts, full_part_path, unzip = False)

    dataset_list = Dataset.from_list(dataset_dicts, split='train')

    dataset_d = DatasetDict({'train': dataset_list})

    return dataset_d

dataset = custom_load_dataset(args)
• • •

dataset

DatasetDict({
    train: Dataset({
        features: ['image', 'caption'],
        num_rows: 1736
    })
})
```

Figure 6.4 – Create your own DatasetDict object in Hugging Face

Pretty simple, right? You can see I clearly have a training set, which itself is just the word `train` pointing to a Hugging Face `Dataset` object. You can also see that I only have 1,736 objects in this dataset, which is good, because I'm only using an `ml.t3.medium` instance to run my notebook, and it's tiny. When I need to point to and test a larger dataset, then in Studio, I upgrade my instance in a few clicks and suddenly I have hundreds of GB of instance memory with tens of CPU cores at my fingertips!

When it's simple, that is due to elegant design decisions. Your code should be like poetry: short, simple, effective, and evocative. Powerful. This goes all the way back to Shakespeare:

*Brevity is the soul of wit.*

For my Stable Diffusion dataset, I downloaded 50 million image and caption pairs. More on how I did that is presented later in the chapter!

After this, I realized that it would be extremely inefficient to waste expensive GPU time loading that entire dataset into memory. This is because my implementation, which no doubt could be improved, lazily lists all of the images, walks through them one by one, reads the caption, and stores it with the pointer.

Now, fortunately, I could at least use Python's multiprocessing package to list the images concurrently, one per CPU core, but for 50 million images that could easily take 24 hours to do. On top of that, I only needed one machine to execute this task. My training cluster has 24 `ml.p4d.24xlarge` machines, so I was not going to let all of those hosts sit idle while I listed the images and walked through them. So, I built an index!

Here, the index is simply a JSON Lines object. Let's inspect it!

```
!head -10 data_index.jsonl
{"image": "/opt/ml/input/data/training/laion-fsx/part-00018/07846037.jpg", "caption": "Join Ms. M
onica for Virtual Storytime each Tuesday and Thursday at 10:30 a.m."}
{"image": "/opt/ml/input/data/training/laion-fsx/part-00018/09755358.jpg", "caption": "Free Print
able Ace Hardware Coupons"}
{"image": "/opt/ml/input/data/training/laion-fsx/part-00018/03759897.jpg", "caption": "A physical
distancing sign is seen during a media tour of Hastings Elementary school in Vancouver on Septemb
```

Figure 6.5 – Inspect the data index

I spent a few days building this whole process end to end:

1. First, I tested my training script with some toy data on SageMaker to make sure it worked properly.

2. Then, I downloaded a new dataset using more than a few large CPU machines on SageMaker.

3. Next, I put the dataset onto FSx for Lustre. I tested this on SageMaker, pointing to the relevant **Virtual Private Cloud** (**VPC**) location.

4. Then I replicated a tiny version of this, with just a few objects, in Studio. I built some scripts to parse these objects, ensuring they scaled and were operational as I went. I moved those scripts onto my SageMaker training jobs and executed a run on a large-CPU machine overnight.

The next morning, I built and tested my index loader, moving it onto SageMaker training as it worked. Now I am running on 16 `ml.p4d.24xlarge` instances, or 128 A100 GPUs. Tomorrow, I'll do the full run for one full epoch with 50 million images on 24 `ml.p4d.24xlarge` instances, or 192 GPUs. If I could do this end to end, so can you!

Throughout this chapter, I'll share optimizations about that entire pipeline with you, but for now, let's unpack one key aspect of this training flow that is critical to preparing your data for your chosen model: tokenizers.

# Creating embeddings – tokenizers and other key steps for smart features

Now that you have your data loader tested, built, and possibly scaled, you're thinking to yourself, what do I do with all of these raw images and/or natural language strings? Do I throw them straight into my neural network? Actually, the last five years of learning representations have proven this definitively: no, you should not put raw images or text into your neural network right off the bat. You should convert your raw inputs to embeddings by using another model.

The intuition for this is simple: before you teach your model how to recognize relationships in your dataset, you first have to introduce it to the concept of a dataset. Creating embeddings is basically a way of doing this; you use a data structure that has been trained from another process to create vector representations of your data. That is to say, you provide your raw text and images as input, and you get high-dimensional vectors as output. Those vectors are produced through what you hope is a valid process that should catch nuanced details in their inter-relationship. Commonly in multimodal settings, such as with Stable Diffusion, you will actually use different processes for the vision and language embeddings, putting them into your model and integrating them through the learning loop distinctly.

Natural language tends to use a process called **tokenization**. Each model has a unique tokenizer that was trained on a specific vocabulary. If you want to pretrain or finetune a GPT-3 type model, you'll need to download the tokenizer that ships with the model and apply that tokenizer to your dataset. This will have a unique way of breaking down strings into words, subwords, or characters depending on the model. Eventually, each token is converted to a high-dimensional vector, or in more simple terms, a really long list of numbers. We call them **vector embeddings**. Many word embeddings also include **positional encoding**, a numerical way of representing to the neural network where that specific word, or token, sits in the sentence relative to other words. This positional encoding helps your transformer-based model pick up on the meaning of words in that specific dataset. If you are pretraining a net new model or dataset, you will likely end up needing to train your own tokenizer.

In computer vision, a common way of creating embeddings for images is *using a pretrained vision model to create features*. This means you can use a fully-trained computer vision model, such as **Contrastive Language-Image Pretraining** (**CLIP**), while setting the weights to inference only. This is the same as freezing the weights. That means as images pass through this network, the network creates a dense representation of the image, without actually formally producing a prediction. This dense representation then interacts with your trainable model, the one you actually are running gradient descent against.

Now, let's make these ideas more concrete through our example training Stable Diffusion on SageMaker.

```
25  from diffusers import AutoencoderKL, DDPMScheduler,
    PNDMScheduler, StableDiffusionPipeline,
    UNet2DConditionModel
26
27  from transformers import CLIPFeatureExtractor,
    CLIPTextModel, CLIPTokenizer
```

Figure 6.6 – Importing libraries

First, you'll see I'm pointing to two critical libraries: `diffusers` and `transformers`. Both of them are from our friends over at Hugging Face!

The `transformers` library provides a lot of helpful methods and techniques for working with natural language. The `diffusers` library does the same, just for models based on diffusion. Diffusion models tend to enable high-quality image generation, commonly by providing a prompt from natural language. This means you can provide a natural language prompt and have the model generate an image for you!

In the preceding code snippet, we're just pointing to the base models and tokenizers we'll use to featurize the image and text pairs we need to train a Stable Diffusion model. After that, we need to download them properly.

```
298  # Load models and create wrapper for stable diffusion
299  tokenizer = CLIPTokenizer.from_pretrained(
300      args.pretrained_model_name_or_path,
301      subfolder="tokenizer",
302      use_auth_token=args.use_auth_token,
303  )
304  text_encoder = CLIPTextModel.from_pretrained(
305      args.pretrained_model_name_or_path, subfolder="text_encoder", use_auth_token=args.use_auth_token
306  )
307  vae = AutoencoderKL.from_pretrained(
308      args.pretrained_model_name_or_path, subfolder="vae", use_auth_token=args.use_auth_token
309  )
310  unet = UNet2DConditionModel.from_pretrained(
311      args.pretrained_model_name_or_path, subfolder="unet", use_auth_token=args.use_auth_token
312  )
```

Figure 6.7 – Importing models to train Stable Diffusion

To save time on my massive GPU cluster, I downloaded each of these models ahead of time. I saved them in my S3 bucket, then created a *training channel* to point to that S3 path when I run my SageMaker training job. The script then reads them from the path on the training cluster where they've been downloaded at the start of the job.

A channel is just a pointer from your SageMaker training job to any supported data input. That can be an S3 path, an FSx for Lustre mount, or an EFS volume. Channels are handy ways to organize different inputs for your job. You can create them for pointing to different splits in your data, such as training and validation, base models, scripts, or anything else you want. These are tracked for you as job parameters, so you can see them stored with the rest of the job metadata. They're also searchable. SageMaker will copy, stream, or mount your channels after the instances start, so make sure you keep the copy time to a minimum, as this will reduce costs.

Next, we need to *freeze the weights*. This is the same as setting them to "untrainable," or "inference only." It means we only want the result of data passing through this model, not a prediction. Fortunately for us, the syntax for this is dead simple.

```
# Freeze vae and text_encoder
freeze_params(vae.parameters())
freeze_params(text_encoder.parameters())
```

Figure 6.8 – Freezing parameters for the non-trainable models

After this, we need to process our raw data to feed it into our neural network. This is where tokenization and featurization come into play.

```
377    # this function expects the image path
378    def preprocess_train(examples):
379        images = [Image.open(image).convert("RGB") for image in examples[image_column]]
380        examples["pixel_values"] = [train_transforms(image) for image in images]
381        examples["input_ids"] = tokenize_captions(examples)
382
383        return examples
```

Figure 6.9 – Preprocessing the images

This snippet should be fairly understandable. We pass in our training set. This function is explicitly expecting two columns, one with a path to images and one with captions. Then it uses a Python `Image` object to simply read all the images from disk and convert them into a machine-readable format. Typically this is three channels, one each for red, green, and blue. Each channel is a two-dimensional array or a simple list of lists of floating-point pixel values. After reading the images, the function next tokenizes the captions. This script uses `ClipTokenizer` to parse the provided natural text.

This function is then applied after we've created the `DataSetDict()` object, as in the notebook earlier in this chapter. We point to the training set, apply the transformation, and we are ready to finally pass this into our data loader!

```
451        # Set the training transforms
452        train_dataset = dataset["train"].with_transform(preprocess_train)
```

Figure 6.10 – Pointing to the training dataset

Now that we've learned how to build, test, and scale our data loader, let's learn about different optimizations for the entire data flow available on AWS.

# Optimizing your data pipeline on Amazon SageMaker

Remember that we've learned about ephemeral training on Amazon SageMaker, where you can seamlessly spin up anywhere from a few to hundreds, to thousands of GPUs on remote instances that are fully managed. Now, let's learn about different options to optimize sending data to your SageMaker Training instances.

If you've worked with SageMaker Training, you'll remember the different stages your job moves through: starting the instances, downloading your data, downloading your training image and invoking it, then uploading the finished model.

Here's a screenshot from my 2022 re:Invent demo, featuring Stable Diffusion. You might ask yourself, how is it that I'm downloading 50 million image/text pairs in only two minutes? The answer is an optimized data pipeline. In this case, I used FSx for Lustre.

**Status history**                                                                                      ✕

| Status | Start time | End time | Description |
|---|---|---|---|
| Starting | Nov 28, 2022 18:16 UTC | Nov 28, 2022 18:25 UTC | Preparing the instances for training |
| Downloading | Nov 28, 2022 18:25 UTC | Nov 28, 2022 18:27 UTC | Downloading input data |
| Training | Nov 28, 2022 18:27 UTC | Nov 28, 2022 18:44 UTC | Training image download completed. Training in progress. |
| Uploading | Nov 28, 2022 18:44 UTC | Nov 28, 2022 19:02 UTC | Uploading generated training model |

Figure 6.11 – Training job status

For much smaller datasets, such as those that are only a few tens of GB, it's fine to simply point to S3 as your input training channel. When you use S3 as your training input, SageMaker can either *copy* (File Mode) or *stream* (Pipe Mode or Fast File Mode) your files during training. Moving data around is generally a slow process, and here it's bottlenecked by the bandwidth of your lead training machine. Using File Mode with S3 as your input can easily add tens of minutes to your training time, and possibly hours or more as your dataset scales. When I train on 100 GB, for example, using S3 as my input data mode without streaming would add a solid 20 minutes to my training time. Sadly, I am paying for that wait time, because the instances have already initialized, so it's in my best interest to optimize my data pipeline.

In some cases, a simple and cost-effective alternative to the S3 copy option is **streaming**, using either Pipe Mode or Fast File Mode. Pipe Mode requires some scripting modifications on your end, but happily, Fast File Mode does not! However, Fast File Mode is known to have some scaling issues when you work with a larger number of files. To solve this issue, and to handle data loading at scale for hundreds to thousands of GPUs, we typically recommend FSx for Lustre.

FSx for Lustre is a distributed file system that easily connects to a data repository in S3, mounts to your SageMaker Training jobs, and executes a high throughput training loop on your behalf. This is because it reads the data from S3 once, then stores it in a cache and *scales reads horizontally with your mounts*. Said another way, once your data is loaded into Lustre, the training loop throughput reads and writes scale linearly as a function of your accelerators.

You'll need to create Lustre in a VPC, that is to say, in your virtual private cloud, on AWS. This is good news for those who work with personally identifiable information or in heavily regulated industries. Using VPCs, you can build and maintain a private network on the cloud, using security and networking controls to manage traffic and secure access to your highly restricted content.

Honestly, manage traffic and secure access from an S3 data repository is pretty straightforward. It usually takes me about twenty minutes, with a few of my own hiccups along the road, and that includes the volume creation time.

Here's how to establish the data repository when you are creating Lustre:

1. First, point to your S3 path with all of the data.

2. Second, determine what type of policies you'd like to set. An import policy will determine how Lustre automatically grabs data from S3, and an export policy determines how Lustre automatically pushes data to S3.

Lastly, here's a view of my volume after I loaded it with 9.5 TB of Stable Diffusion image/text pairs:

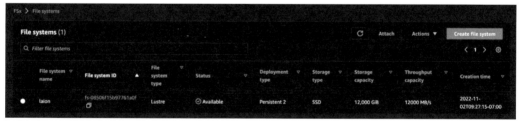

Once you have Lustre created, you'll need to spend another thirty minutes or so testing and perfecting the connection from SageMaker to Lustre. This entails configuring the VPC and its relevant subnet. Currently, these are the key steps:

1. Make sure you have an internet gateway in your target VPC.

2. Make sure the subnet where you created Lustre has a route to that gateway.

3. Ensure the security group for that subnet allows inbound and outbound traffic, defined in multiple ways.

4.  Establish an S3 VPC endpoint for your target buckets to allow SageMaker to upload the finished model artifacts to S3 on completion.

I've seen some configurations with two subnets, one to interact with the actual public internet to `pip install` new packages, and one to run the training jobs. Personally, I skipped over this by building a Docker container with all my packages, then loaded this to ECR, and pointed to it when starting my training job.

When you run your training jobs, if you want to point to a specific VPC, make sure you pass in the relevant credentials to the estimator. You'll also need to pass a few extra parameters to point to FSx for Lustre.

Lastly, you can also mount Lustre to your notebooks directly! In this setup, you'll need to *rebuild the notebook instance to connect to the same VPC credentials*. That actually isn't necessary to launch a job on Lustre, but it is required to mount the volume directly. Here's a nice script that helps you do this *(1)*. For an even more detailed consideration of the pros and cons of each of these options, see our blog post on the topic *(2)*.

Now that you have a better idea of how to optimize your data pipeline options to point to SageMaker for the training loop, let's take a step back and evaluate a few options for downloading and transforming datasets at scale on AWS!

# Transforming deep learning datasets at scale on AWS

At this point, you must be thinking now I know how to build and test my data loader, and even put my data on FSx for Lustre to integrate with SageMaker training, but what if I need to do large-scale downloads or transformations ahead of time? How can I do those at a large scale, in a cost-effective and simple way?

While there are many different tools and perspectives for attacking this problem, my personal favorite is always to take the simplest, least expensive, and most scalable approach. To me, that's actually with **job parallelism** on SageMaker Training.

As it turns out, SageMaker Training is a very broad compute service offering you can use to run essentially any type of script. In particular, you can use it to run large CPU-based data transformation jobs in parallel. There's no upper limit on how many SageMaker Training jobs you can run, and we have customers who run *thousands of jobs a day* in order to train models for their unique business purposes. This might be training tiny models for advertising, personalized recommendations, pricing, or other enhancements.

For my Stable Diffusion case study, I actually used 18 concurrent SageMaker jobs to download all of my data! First, I used one large CPU job to download all of the Parquet files included in the Laion-5B dataset. Then, I looped through them, sending each Parquet file to its own job. It looked something like this:

```
for p_file in parquet_list[:18]:

    part_number = p_file.split('-')[1]

    output_dir = "s3://{}/data/part-{}/".format(bucket, part_number)

    if is_open(output_dir):

        est = get_estimator(part_number, p_file, output_dir)

        est.fit({"parquet":"s3://{}/meta/{}".format(bucket, p_file)}, wait=False)
```

Figure 6.13 – Use job parallelism to transform data at scale

See how I am actually running 18 different jobs? This way, you can easily track, manage, and assess each job. All of the results are sent back to S3 – in this case, by the tool itself, which writes to S3 on my behalf. Now I don't even need to use Spark! I can just run as many SageMaker jobs as I need to, using Python and its `multiprocessing` package, to execute as many tasks as I need.

```
140  if __name__ == "__main__":
141
142      args = parse_args()
143
144      print ('Train data dir is here: {}'.format(args.train_data_dir))
145
146      part_list = glob.glob("{}/part-*".format(args.train_data_dir))
147
148      print ('Found {} parts to work on, starting multiprocessing pool'.format(len(part_list)))
149
150      cpus = mp.cpu_count()
151
152      with Pool(cpus) as p:
153
154          if 'unzip' in args.function:
155              p.map(unzip_part, part_list)
156
157          if 'index' in args.function:
158              p.map(write_index, part_list)
159
160      # dataset = load_index(args)
161
162      cmd = 'cp {}/data_index.jsonl {}'.format(args.train_data_dir, args.model_dir)
163
164      os.system(cmd)
```

Figure 6.14 – A data processing script

How does `multiprocessing` with Python work, you ask? It's simple. The lynchpin is the critical `Pool.map()` process. First, you create the pool by providing it with the number of available CPUs. You can look that up using the `multiprocess.cpu_count()` method. Then you'll bring two objects to `map()`: first, a list of objects you want farmed out to all of the processes, and second, a function that you want executed on each object in that list. It's basically the concept of a `for` loop, but here, instead of using only one process, you're using as many processes as are available on the instance. That means if you are going from 2 CPUs up to 96 CPUs, you can run more than 10x faster.

It's a great idea to offload as much data transformation to CPUs as you can because CPUs are dirt cheap. In comparing the costs of my 192 GPUs per hour versus 18 CPU-based jobs, the CPU was about 13x cheaper than the GPUs!

As you also may have guessed, we have literally hundreds of other options for manipulating data on AWS. I won't go into detail on that here, but feel free to explore for yourself.

## Summary

At this point in the book, and in your project, you should have a fully functional data loader built, tested, and optimized on both your local notebook and your SageMaker training instances. You should have your entire dataset identified, downloaded, processed, and ready to run through your training loop. You should have done at least one full pass through your training loop with a tiny sample of your dataset – something as small as 100 samples would be fine. You should have identified how you want to send your large dataset to your SageMaker training instances, possibly by using FSx for Lustre, and you should have this built, tested, and operational. You should also know a few other ways to store and process data on AWS.

You should be very comfortable making architectural decisions that reduce your project costs, such as opting for CPU-based data downloading and processing, along with the Python `multiprocessing` package to easily farm your tasks out to all available CPUs. You should also be comfortable parallelizing jobs on SageMaker training, such that you can run different jobs at the same time, each working on different parts of your project.

Now that you've fully prepared your dataset, in the next chapter, we'll move on to the main event: training your model!

## References

Please go through the following content for more information on a few topics covered in the chapter.

1. *amazon-sagemaker-notebook-instance-lifecycle-config-samples*: `https://github.com/ aws-samples/amazon-sagemaker-notebook-instance-lifecycle- config-samples/blob/master/scripts/mount-fsx-lustre-file-system/ on-start.sh`

2. *Choose the best data source for your Amazon SageMaker training job*: `https://aws.amazon. com/blogs/machine-learning/choose-the-best-data-source-for-your- amazon-sagemaker-training-job/`

# Part 3: Train Your Model

In part 3, you'll learn how to train your large-scale language and vision model. You'll learn how to find the right hyperparameters, ensure that loss decreases, and troubleshoot ongoing performance issues.

This section has the following chapters:

- *Chapter 7, Finding the Right Hyperparameters*
- *Chapter 8, Large-Scale Training on SageMaker*
- *Chapter 9, Advanced Training Concepts*

# 7

# Finding the Right Hyperparameters

In this chapter, you'll dive into the key hyperparameters that govern performance for top vision and language models, such as batch size, learning rate, and more. First, we'll start with a quick overview of hyperparameter tuning for those who are new or need a light refresh, including key examples in vision and language. Then, we'll explore hyperparameter tuning in foundation models, both what is possible today and where trends might emerge. Finally, we'll learn how to do this on Amazon SageMaker, taking incremental steps in a cluster size and changing each hyperparameter as we do. In this chapter, we're going to cover the following main topics:

- Hyperparameters – batch size, learning rate, and more

- Tuning strategies

- Tuning for foundation models

- Scaling up as a function of world size with SageMaker

## Hyperparameters – batch size, learning rate, and more

**Hyperparameters** determine a huge majority of critical decision points in deep learning. They operate like an intermediary between you, your model, your dataset, and your overall compute environment. You'll pick up terms such as batch size, learning rate, number of attention heads, and more to balance your overall solution to the problem at hand, balance costs, and ensure optimal performance of your model during both training and inference.

**Batch size** tells your training algorithm literally how many objects from your dataset to pick up into memory for each training step. Basic physics tells us that if you pick up more objects than your GPU can hold in memory at a single time, you'll hit an `Out of Memory` error. A large batch size helps you step through your training loop quickly but runs the risk of failing to capture all the variation in your dataset if you do not run the optimizer frequently enough. This core trade-off is one you want to get familiar with and learn methods to solve. Hint, the entire next section is dedicated to a method called **hyperparameter tuning**.

**Learning rate** operates almost like a steering wheel for the entire learning process the gradient descent optimization. Literally, it's an amount you use that parameterizes how much to update your trainable weights. A small learning rate means you take small steps down the gradient, ideally down your loss curve, but it can slow down your job considerably. A large learning rate means you are taking large steps down the loss curve, which can speed up your job but runs the risk of getting stuck in what's called a **local minimum**, or a *small valley in the gradient descent function*. Basically, that means your model underfits; the loop will think it's completed because the optimizer indicates that loss has plateaued, but the model is just stuck in a small loss valley. As before, this introduces another core trade-off that hyperparameter tuning is well suited to help us solve. Learning rate schedulers are one step towards solving this problem, letting you pick a large enough value at the beginning of the loop and decreasing this throughout.

Let's look at a variety of important hyperparameters that determine performance across notable vision and language models.

## Key hyperparameters in vision and language

Let's look at a few key hyperparameters in vision and language:

- **Batch size** – The number of objects your model picks up into GPU memory during each training step. A high number speeds up the job, while a lower number can increase generalization performance. Gradient noise scales seem a promising avenue for predicting the largest possible batch size.

- **Learning rate** – A term used to determine how much the trainable weights should be updated during the gradient descent optimization process. A large number speeds up the job and may overfit, while a lower number can underfit and fail to adequately learn the training data. As mentioned previously, these are typically paired with schedulers.

- **Number of epochs** – The number of total passes to make through your entire dataset. A small number decreases the total runtime of your training job, while a large number can increase accuracy. However, setting this number too large can be wasteful and cause overfitting. In *Chapter 9*, we learn how to use the scaling laws to solve this.

- **Number of attention heads** – The total number of self-attention heads used in your model. This is a big determining factor in the overall size of your model in trainable parameters. When you see the 10x jump in size from GPT-2 to GPT-3, more often than not, it's due to both more attention heads and larger heads.

- **Sequence length** – The total number of tokens used as one object during the training loop. This is especially relevant in language models, where each step in the training loop uses some part of the sentence to predict another part. Tokens map, roughly speaking, to words. This means that sequence length can almost be generally interpreted as the number of words in each prediction step. This has a direct impact on both training and inference. For inference, it means this is the maximum number of words this model can use. For training, it can directly increase or decrease your GPU memory footprint.

There are countless more hyperparameters. You'll see hyperparameters that are specific to different SDKs, such as Hugging Face's `transformers` or `diffusers`, which let you define aspects of your training job such as your base model name, dataset name, data type, and more. SageMaker has hyperparameters for our distributed training libraries, such as optimizer state sharding, tensor parallelism, activation checkpointing and offloading, and more. In the SageMaker Training Job API, you can also define and bring any arbitrary hyperparameter you like.

## Tuning strategies

In some sense, hyperparameter tuning is the art and science of *guessing and checking at scale*. Using sophisticated algorithms and strategies, you can actually train *whole fleets of models* to test entire ranges of hyperparameters in a huge variety of configurations. Your *tuning strategy* will then help you find the best models in the end, eventually identifying critical hyperparameters to use at larger scales. I've seen hyperparameter tuning help customers get boosts in accuracy of anywhere from less than 1 all the way up to over 15 percentage points. If that's a direct translation into business returns, you can see why it's an attractive proposition.

There are many strategies and technical solutions for hyperparameter tuning. These are all similar in that you, as the end user, will need to pick hyperparameters and ranges for these that you'd like to test. Many hyperparameter tuning solutions will provide defaults for you as a starting point, in addition to relevant documentation. As you progress toward using your preferred hyperparameter tuning solution, I'd suggest you budget a healthy amount of time researching at least some of these hyperparameters in some detail. If you plan on interviewing for a data science position someday, then spend a great amount of time understanding these, and especially how they impact model performance.

Most hyperparameter tuning solutions will actually train anywhere from a few to a few hundred models for you, each with slightly different hyperparameter configurations. At the end of the tuning process, you should see an improvement in your preferred metric, such as a decrease in your loss or an increase in your accuracy. How do these solutions find and pick the optimal hyperparameters, you ask? Through a **tuning strategy**.

A tuning strategy is an optimization method that tests a variety of configurations and evaluates each based on a pre-defined performance metric. These vary along a few dimensions. Some of them are simply random guesses, others try to logically fill a space, some use basic machine learning, and some use extremely sophisticated machine learning algorithms. In addition to the search method, they will also vary in the timing of their search. Some tuning methods run all experiments at the same time, or concurrently, which is valuable because the overall job will complete more quickly. Others run sequentially, testing some configurations and running another set after these are completed. This is valuable because you may ultimately hit a higher accuracy, but it comes with the downside of a longer overall runtime. Let's look at some common hyperparameter tuning strategies, along with their trade-offs.

Here are some common hyperparameter tuning strategies:

- **Random search** – Just as it sounds, random search is a tuning strategy that will simply use randomness to evaluate your search space. For example, let's say you want to explore batch sizes from 2 to 26, and using random search, you indicate that you want a total of 4 jobs to be run. You'd probably have 4 jobs run at the same time, each with a randomly selected batch size, for example, 4, 7, 17, and 22. Your tuning solution should tell you which job gives you the best performance on your preferred metric.

- **Grid search** – In contrast to random search, grid search will establish an orderly set of experiments to run that balances your available search space. For example, using the same configuration as the previous on batch size, but using grid search, you might end up running 4 jobs at the same time with 8, 14, 20, and 26. Like last time, these jobs will run at the same time and give you the best-performing model.

- **Bayesian search** – Bayesian search flips this basic idea on its head in two ways:

  - First, it's a sequential tuning strategy. This means it runs a few jobs at the same time, then evaluates the results of them, and initiates another set of experiments to run.

  - Second, it's actually using a machine learning algorithm to select the hyperparameters. Commonly, this is a simple logistic regression; using the metadata of the model as an input, it predicts the values for the next hyperparameters to evaluate. We've had this available in Amazon SageMaker since at least 2018! For the record, SageMaker also has random and grid search.

- **Hyperband** – Presented by a *research team (1)* in 2018, the Hyperband strategy actually focuses on optimizing the random search. They developed an infinite-armed bandit to adaptively explore and select tuning configurations, using predefined preferences. This is very similar to reinforcement learning! At AWS, we've combined this with a massively parallel strategy known as **Asynchronous Successive Halving Algorithm** (**ASHA**) *(2)*, which exploits parallelism and aggressive early stopping. We've shown that these solutions together enable large-scale tuning, such as for vision and language models. Our *tests (3)* demonstrate a ~5x and ~4.5x speedup relative to random and Bayesian strategies, respectively.

As you may have noticed, I've essentially listed the search strategies from simple to complex. In your learning journey, you can consider that a good target path for yourself as well. Start with the easiest and most simple tuning strategies, then slowly build yourself up to ones that are more complex over time.

Another theme you may have already guessed by now is the critical need to *balance cost with accuracy gains*. Take a look at where and how your search strategy is running; are they using compute efficiently or inefficiently? Will they continue running jobs and experiments for you even after the gains have slowed down, or will they aggressively shut down your resources when the gains stop?

Lastly, it's helpful to know that when you have a full application built around your model, you will most likely want to integrate a tuning strategy in your retraining pipeline. Say you have a vision or language model deployed on SageMaker; when new data arrives, you trigger a pipeline that retrains your model. A great asset in that pipeline would be tuning your model to ensure you have the highest possible accuracy. More on that in *Chapter 14*!

For now, let's explore unique challenges and approaches for tuning hyperparameters in foundation models.

# Hyperparameter tuning for foundation models

Foundation models present some unique challenges for hyperparameter tuning. Let's try to understand them:

- **Model size** – Possibly the largest obstacle to tuning foundation models is their sheer size. Many of the classic tuning strategies we looked at previously *rely on training the model as many times as possible*. When simply holding one copy of the model in memory requires tens of accelerators, the economics around this approach fall apart.

- **Volume of downstream tasks** – As we've seen throughout the book, the sheer volume of candidate downstream tasks for foundation models is enormous. This makes hyperparameter tuning much more complex because the objective metrics for each of these tasks are unique. Picking the right downstream task itself could be a kind of tuning challenge!

- **Variety of hyperparameters** – At these scales, the relevant hyperparameters aren't just indicators of the training procedure. They are also about the distribution techniques, such as model and data parallel, as we learned about previously.

How should we think about overcoming these challenges? One approach is suggested here; basically, you can tune hyperparameters efficiently on a tiny sample of your dataset. This means you can do large-scale searches for hyperparameters using 1% of your data, and this helps you find the right settings at the start of your job.

Another approach, as we mentioned previously, is a much more efficient tuning strategy called **Hyberband**. Following this example post *(4)*, you can see how to integrate this with SageMaker Training, with an example for Cifar10.

Is that the end of the story? I don't think so. Today, so much of the foundation model development world relies on following work that others have done, including reusing their exact same hyperparameters or running very lightweight experiments on massive datasets and accelerator scales; it seems only natural to me that this will converge with hyperparameter tuning strategies someday. Also, given some of the parameter efficient fine-tuning strategies we'll learn about in Chapters 10 and 15, we may see hyperparameter tuning become even more relevant when adapting a model after the pretraining process. We will also look at strategies for *tuning inference requests* in *Chapter 13*.

Next, let's look at how we think about scaling up our tuning experiments to handle large models and datasets, in addition to working with hyperparameter tuning on SageMaker.

# Scaling up as a function of world size with SageMaker

In this section, we'll break down two critical concepts that you need to master hyperparameter tuning, especially in the context of distributed training. The first one is the concept of scaling, especially using hyperparameter tuning as a method to run smaller experiments before ultimately running your large training job. The second is using tips and tricks available on SageMaker for hyperparameter tuning generally.

## Tuning on a sample of your data and updating based on world size

As you've learned in this chapter, hyperparameter tuning is a great way to eke out performance gains, but it can require intensive compute that executes a large number of experiments. You might be wondering, *How do I easily apply this to my use case with a dataset size of at least a few hundred GB, and maybe a few TB or more?* The answer is just to start with a tiny sample!

The goal of tuning at a tiny fraction of your dataset is *to see how sensitive your model is to changes in its key hyperparameters.* At a 1% sample, you might be interested in core algorithmic settings such as the number of attention heads, variations in the optimizer or layer operations, sequence length, and any other critical settings in your overall training loop. If you see a big boost, that's a signal that you may want to pay more attention to this hyperparameter and either integrate tuning into your training job directly or simply add a check to determine what setting will give you the best performance at scale. You might also tune the batch size and learning rate, including its warm-up, to see which performs best.

As I hope you are thinking already, if you're tuning on only 1% of your entire dataset, then you'll only need a tiny fraction of your overall compute! That means you can and should plan on using very small instances for hyperparameter tuning, such as `ml.g5.12xlarge` or smaller. Once you're ready to move up to more instances, however, you'll want to update your key hyperparameters as a function of your overall world size.

Remember, the world size is just a phrase for counting all of the GPUs or accelerators available in your training cluster. If you have 2 instances with 8 GPUs each, that means your overall world size is 16 GPUs. Some of your hyperparameters should be updated every time you change your world size because they govern how your model interacts with the training environment. These are especially batch size and learning rate.

For example, in our previous 16 GPU example, let's say you used hyperparameter tuning to find a good per-device batch size of 22 and a learning rate of 5e-5. Next, maybe you want to move up to 4 instances, each with 8 GPUs, giving you a total world size of 32 GPUs. That jump from 16 to 32 is clearly a doubling, increasing the number of accelerators by a multiple of 2. We'll apply this same factor to the global batch size and learning rate, so they scale up to the same degree as the world size.

### Simple hyperparameter tuning scale-up example

Let's go through the examples as follows:

*Original*:

- Two instances, each with eight GPUS

- World size = 16

- Per device batch size = 22

- Learning rate = 5e-5

*Increased cluster size*:

- Four instances, each with eight GPUs

- World size = 32

- Per device batch size = 22

Notice that the *per-device* batch size won't necessarily change as you increase the world size. Depending on your script, however, make sure you know whether you are supplying the per-device or the global batch size. The global batch size will, of course, need to be changed!

*Learning rate = 5e-5 * 2 = 0.0001*

On top of updating the batch size and learning rate as you scale up in your overall world size, make sure you are *also considering the size of the model itself*. This might include adding more parameters, more attention heads, more layers, and so on. As we've seen, this is a strong indicator of ultimately getting a more accurate model. For example, in our public examples *(4)* of training large-scale GPT-2 models, we provide three different configurations of the model, with hyperparameters selected for each model size:

```
if model_config == "gpt2-30b":
    model_params = {
        "max_context_width": 512,
        "hidden_width": 7168,
        "num_layers": 48,
        "num_heads": 64,
        "tensor_parallel_degree": 8,
        "pipeline_parallel_degree": 1,
        "train_batch_size": 5,
        "val_batch_size": 5,
        "prescaled_batch": 0,
    }

elif model_config == "gpt2-xl":
    # 1.5B
    model_params = {
        "max_context_width": 512,
        "hidden_width": 1536,
        "num_layers": 48,
        "num_heads": 24,
        "tensor_parallel_degree": 4,
        "pipeline_parallel_degree": 1,
        "train_batch_size": 2,
        "val_batch_size": 4,
        "prescaled_batch": 0,
    }
elif model_config == "gpt2-small":
    model_params = {
        "max_context_width": 512,
        "hidden_width": 768,
        "num_layers": 12,
        "num_heads": 12,
        "tensor_parallel_degree": 4,
        "pipeline_parallel_degree": 1,
        "train_batch_size": 2,
        "val_batch_size": 4,
        "prescaled_batch": 0,
    }
```

Figure 7.1 – Model config parameters

You can see that for a model size of 30b parameters, we'd suggest setting the number of heads to 64, layers to 48, hidden width to 7168, and train batch size to 5.

However, for a much smaller model size of only 1.5b parameters, we set the number of heads to 24, hidden width to 1536, and a train batch size of 2. Why would a smaller model use a smaller batch size, you ask? Isn't it somewhat counterintuitive, since a smaller model should have a smaller GPU footprint, allowing you to increase batch size?

The answer to that question is yes, theoretically, a smaller model should have a *larger* batch size, but in this case, because we implement *significant model parallelism* on the large model, it actually counteracts this influence and has a net smaller GPU memory footprint.

The hidden width parameter, if you're curious, is simply the size of the inner layers in your neural networks. We call them hidden because they are inside the black box; one step after the input layer and one step before the output layer. This very logically follows from the overall model size; a larger model in parameter count should absolutely have a larger hidden width.

Lastly, let's take a quick look at hyperparameter tuning on SageMaker.

### Tuning with Amazon SageMaker

Using SageMaker for hyperparameter tuning is quite simple, and you have a few options. First, as always, you can simply add any tuning strategy directly inside your script and execute it on the training cluster directly. You might do this with grid search, simply bringing your own scripts in and running them.

As you scale, however, and especially as you build tuning into your retrain pipeline, you may want to eventually use our fully managed `HyperparameterTuner`. This is essentially an object that takes your training job, in the form of a prebuilt estimator, along with a few other specifications:

```
tuner = HyperparameterTuner(
    estimator,
    objective_metric_name,
    hyperparameter_ranges,
    metric_definitions,
    max_jobs=9,
    max_parallel_jobs=3,
    objective_type=objective_type,
)
```

Figure 7.2 – Defining the tuning object

You define your objective metric, your hyperparameters, and their ranges, along with the total number of jobs you'd like to run and the ones in parallel. These default settings will then use Bayesian optimization. In fact, in this example, they'd spin up a maximum of three instances at the same time, reusing them to run up to nine total jobs.

You might enhance this with early stopping, or with the **Hyperband** algorithm we learned about earlier. You can point to the strategy just by adding it as another argument to this function. *(5)*

In terms of the objective metric, you'll be happy to know that you can bring whatever you want. What we do for that is walk through the CloudWatch logs for your job and look for the metric definition. Honestly, I've found this to be the single hardest part of the process: matching your regex string exactly to what's coming out of your training job. In a PyTorch MNIST example, here's what this looks like:

```
objective_metric_name = "average test loss"
objective_type = "Minimize"
metric_definitions = [{"Name": "average test loss", "Regex": "Test set: Average loss: ([0-9\\.]+)"}]
```

Figure 7.3 – Defining a tuning metric for the job config

You can see we're asking you to write a regex string and supply that in this object. This then should directly match what is defined in the training script here:

```
logger.info(
    "Test set: Average loss: {:.4f}, Accuracy: {}/{} ({:.0f}%)\n".format(
        test_loss, correct, len(test_loader.dataset), 100.0 * correct / len(test_loader.dataset)
    )
)
```

Figure 7.4 – Defining a tuning metric in your training script

For good measure, here's a visual of the hyperparameter ranges so you can see how they're defined:

```
hyperparameter_ranges = {
    "lr": ContinuousParameter(0.001, 0.1),
    "batch-size": CategoricalParameter([32, 64, 128, 256, 512]),
}
```

Figure 7.5 – Defining hyperparameter ranges

We have another method I think is particularly well designed. It lets you run analytics on your tuning job by porting it into a pandas DataFrame! The notebook for this is here (6):

```
tuner = sagemaker.HyperparameterTuningJobAnalytics(tuning_job_name)

full_df = tuner.dataframe()
```

Figure 7.6 – Calling tuner.dataframe()

And that's a wrap! Let's quickly take a look at everything you learned in this chapter.

## Summary

In this chapter on hyperparameter tuning, you learned about what hyperparameters are, including batch size, learning rate, number of epochs, number of attention heads, sequence length, and more. You learned how to use hyperparameter tuning to improve the performance of your model, along with top strategies for doing so. You learned how to scale up your tuning, starting at 1% of your dataset, then modifying your key hyperparameters as a function of your overall GPU world size. Finally, you learned about key features for doing all of this on Amazon SageMaker.

In the next chapter, we'll learn about large-scale distributed training!

# References

1.  *Hyperband: A Novel Bandit-Based Approach to Hyperparameter Optimization*: `https://arxiv.org/pdf/1603.06560.pdf`

2.  *A SYSTEM FOR MASSIVELY PARALLEL HYPERPARAMETER TUNING*: `https://arxiv.org/pdf/1810.05934.pdf`

3.  *Amazon SageMaker Automatic Model Tuning now provides up to three times faster hyperparameter tuning with Hyperband*: `https://aws.amazon.com/blogs/machine-learning/amazon-sagemaker-automatic-model-tuning-now-provides-up-to-three-times-faster-hyperparameter-tuning-with-hyperband/`

4.  *amazon-sagemaker-examples*: `https://github.com/aws/amazon-sagemaker-examples/blob/main/training/distributed_training/pytorch/model_parallel/gpt2/smp-train-gpt-simple.ipynb`

5.  *HyperparameterTuner*: `https://sagemaker.readthedocs.io/en/stable/api/training/tuner.html`

6.  *amazon-sagemaker-examples*: `https://github.com/aws/amazon-sagemaker-examples/blob/main/hyperparameter_tuning/analyze_results/HPO_Analyze_TuningJob_Results.ipynb`

# 8

# Large-Scale Training on SageMaker

In this chapter, we will cover the key features and functionality available with Amazon SageMaker to run highly optimized distributed training. You'll learn how to optimize your script for SageMaker training, along with key usability features. You'll also learn about backend optimizations for distributed training with SageMaker, such as GPU health checks, resilient training, checkpointing, and script mode.

We are going to cover the following topics in this chapter:

- Optimizing your script for SageMaker training
- Top usability features for SageMaker training

## Optimizing your script for SageMaker training

So far in this book, you have learned quite a lot! We have covered everything from the foundations of pretraining to GPU optimization, picking the right use case, dataset and model preparation, parallelization basics, finding the right hyperparameters, and so on. The vast majority of this is that these are applicable in any compute environment you choose to apply them to. This chapter, however, is exclusively scoped to AWS and SageMaker especially. Why? So that you can master all the nuances included in at least one compute platform. Once you have learned how to become proficient in one compute platform, then you will be able to use that to work on any project you like! When, for various reasons, you need to transition onto another platform, you will at least have the basic concepts you need to know about to look for and consider the transition.

First, let us look at your scripts. The core of most SageMaker training scripts has at least three things:

- Package imports
- Argument parsing
- Function definitions and usage

Let's break these down next.

## Importing packages

As we've covered previously, you can install and access really any package you need. You have many different ways to make these accessible within SageMaker training. At a minimum, when you define your job, you can bring a `requirements.txt` file with the packages defined. SageMaker will then use `pip install` to install these on your training compute for you, making them available.

Alternatively, you can build a base container with all of these pre-installed. This is certainly the fastest option, since it saves time during the training process. Rather than using *pip install*, you can use a pre-built image with all of the packages available. Another option is to import your own Python packages, sending your entire project to the SageMaker training environment. Then, you can import whatever code you're working on.

## Argument parsing

An extremely common package we use in the SageMaker training environment is `argparse`. If you're not familiar with this, let me introduce you to it.

Once you've built a Python script, you might need to run it with different flags, settings, or arguments. Some of these might be with different hyperparameters, modes, or features that you want your script to run for you. The `argparse` package is a great way to do this in Python. First, in your script, you'll need to *explicitly add a line of code for each argument you want to use*. In SageMaker, you might start with something like this.

```
import argparse
import os

def parse_args():

    parser = argparse.ArgumentParser()

    # remember this environment variable needs to exactly match what you defined earlier
    parser.add_argument("--train_folder", type=str, default=os.environ["SM_CHANNEL_TRAIN"])

    args = parser.parse_args()

    return args
```

Figure 8.1 – A basic arg parsing function

As you can see in *Figure 8.1*, I'm simply importing `argparse`, creating the `parser` object, and then adding an argument called `train_folder`. This will default to looking up *my environment variable*, which, as you may remember, is how SageMaker training injects information into your environment. If you're curious, you can step through the CloudWatch logs for any of your SageMaker training jobs to see a list of all of the available environment variables. These will include all of the metadata for your job, all of your hyperparameters, and so on.

In this brief example, I'm pointing to my *train channel*. I created this by pointing to S3, or an optional FSx for Lustre, when I created my training job. That's my training data. First, I upload it to S3. Then, I point to it when I configure my job. SageMaker copies that onto my SageMaker training instance and loads it onto a local path. The local path is usually something like /opt/ml/input/data/train/. When you want to point to that local path on your training container, you call args.train_folder, or however you've defined it. To read the file, you can either list the name from the folder or pass the name as another argument.

My personal favorite way to keep my script clean and tidy is to wrap all of my arg parsing in a dedicated function. Then, this will neatly return the args object. Here's the full script.

```python
import argparse
import os

def parse_args():

    parser = argparse.ArgumentParser()

    # remember this environment variable needs to exactly match what you defined earlier
    parser.add_argument("--train_folder", type=str, default=os.environ["SM_CHANNEL_TRAIN"])

    args = parser.parse_args()

    return args

if __name__ == "__main__":

    print ('running your job!')

    args = parse_args()

    print ('train path looks like {}, now we will try an ls'.format(args.train_folder))

    cmd = 'ls {}'.format(args.train_folder)

    os.system(cmd)
```

Figure 8.2 – Invoking the arg parsing function in your main script

Another common argument you might pass is model_dir. You can point this to the SM_MODEL_DIR SM environment variable. SageMaker will write your model from the training container to S3 after the job is finished.

You can add any other hyperparameter you want, using the hyperparameters argument in the job config. Then, you can use these in your scripts. I've built arguments to point to things such as my data index, how to run my scripts, a path to checkpoint my model, and countless other arguments you may need for your project.

## Functions definition and usage

At the risk of stating the obvious here, you can write whatever software you want to write. You can copy directly to and from any accessible data source, spawn other jobs, initiate other cloud resources, or use open source packages – the possibilities are endless.

## Invoke your script with mpi

When you're using distributed training, SageMaker invokes your script with `mpi`. As you learned earlier, this is a core library useful to run distributed training. We'll use `mpirun` or `smddprun` to invoke your script. As you can see, we'll invoke your script with all of the relevant parameters.

```
Invoking script with the following command:

mpirun --host algo-2:8,algo-1:8 -np 16 --allow-run-as-root --display-map --tag-output -mca btl_tcp_if_include eth0 -mca oob_tcp_if_include eth0 -mca plm_rsh_no_tree_spawn 1 -
bind-to none -map-by slot -mca pml ob1 -mca btl ^openib -mca orte_abort_on_non_zero_status 1 -mca btl_vader_single_copy_mechanism none -x NCCL_MIN_NRINGS=4 -x
NCCL_SOCKET_IFNAME=eth0 -x NCCL_DEBUG=INFO -x LD_LIBRARY_PATH -x PATH -x LD_PRELOAD=/opt/conda/lib/python3.8/site-packages/gethostname.cpython-38-x86_64-linux-gnu.so -x
NCCL_DEBUG=WARN -x SMDEBUG_LOG_LEVEL=ERROR -x SMP_DISABLE_D2D=1 -x SMP_D2D_GPU_BUFFER_SIZE_BYTES=1 -x SMP_NCCL_THROTTLE_LIMIT=1 -x FI_EFA_USE_DEVICE_RDMA=1 -x FI_PROVIDER=efa -x
RDMAV_FORK_SAFE=1 -x FI_PROVIDER=efa -x FI_EFA_USE_DEVICE_RDMA=1 -x NCCL_PROTO=simple -x SM_HOSTS -x SM_NETWORK_INTERFACE_NAME -x SM_HPS -x SM_USER_ENTRY_POINT -x
SM_FRAMEWORK_PARAMS -x SM_RESOURCE_CONFIG -x SM_INPUT_DATA_CONFIG -x SM_OUTPUT_DATA_DIR -x SM_CHANNELS -x SM_CURRENT_HOST -x SM_CURRENT_INSTANCE_TYPE -x
SM_CURRENT_INSTANCE_GROUP -x SM_CURRENT_INSTANCE_GROUP_HOSTS -x SM_INSTANCE_GROUPS -x SM_INSTANCE_GROUPS_DICT -x SM_DISTRIBUTION_INSTANCE_GROUPS -x SM_IS_HETERO -x
SM_MODULE_NAME -x SM_LOG_LEVEL -x SM_FRAMEWORK_MODULE -x SM_INPUT_DIR -x SM_INPUT_CONFIG_DIR -x SM_OUTPUT_DIR -x SM_NUM_CPUS -x SM_NUM_GPUS -x SM_MODEL_DIR -x
SM_TRAINING_ENV -x SM_USER_ARGS -x SM_OUTPUT_INTERMEDIATE_DIR -x SM_CHANNEL_TEST -x SM_CHANNEL_TRAIN -x SM_HP_ACTIVATION_LOADING_HORIZON -x SM_HP_BF16 -x SM_HP_CHECKPOINT_FREQ -
x SM_HP_DELAYED_PARAM -x SM_HP_FP16 -x SM_HP_GRADIENT_ACCUMULATION -x SM_HP_HIDDEN_WIDTH -x SM_HP_LOGGING_FREQ -x SM_HP_LR -x SM_HP_LR-DECAY-STYLE -x SM_HP_LR_DECAY_ITERS -x
SM_HP_MAX_CONTEXT_WIDTH -x SM_HP_MAX_STEPS -x SM_HP_MIN_LR -x SM_HP_MP_PARAMETERS -x SM_HP_NUM_HEADS -x SM_HP_NUM_KEPT_CHECKPOINTS -x SM_HP_NUM_LAYERS -x
SM_HP_OFFLOAD_ACTIVATIONS -x SM_HP_SAVE_FINAL_FULL_MODEL -x SM_HP_SEED -x SM_HP_SHARDED_DATA_PARALLEL_DEGREE -x SM_HP_TRAIN_BATCH_SIZE -x SM_HP_USE_DISTRIBUTED_TRANSFORMER -x
SM_HP_VAL_BATCH_SIZE -x SM_HP_VALIDATION_FREQ -x SM_HP_WARMUP -x PYTHONPATH /opt/conda/bin/python3.8 -m mpi4py train_gpt_simple.py --activation_loading_horizon 4 --bf16 1 --
checkpoint_freq 200 --delayed_param 1 --fp16 0 --gradient_accumulation 1 --hidden_width 1536 --logging_freq 1 --lr 0.0002 --lr-decay-style linear --lr_decay_iters 125000 --
max_context_width 2048 --max_steps 100 --min_lr 1e-05 --mp_parameters
activation_loading_horizon=4,bf16=True,ddp=True,delayed_parameter_initialization=True,fp16=False,offload_activations=True,partitions=1,sharded_data_parallel_degree=2,skip_tracin
g=True --num_heads 24 --num_kept_checkpoints 5 --num_layers 48 --offload_activations 1 --save_final_full_model 0 --seed 12345 --sharded_data_parallel_degree 2 --train_batch_size
4 --use_distributed_transformer 1 --val_batch_size 4 --validation_freq 200 --warmup 0.01
```

Figure 8.3 – How SageMaker training invokes your script

This is from a very complex example, training tens of billions of parameters for GPT-2, but it shows you many of the available ways you can configure your distributed training cluster on SageMaker.

### Logging and CloudWatch

As you may be aware, you have many options for logging. print statements are a great way to debug, but as you grow, you may move to something more managed such as the `logging` package. Remember that all of these are sent to CloudWatch logs, so you can easily view and debug your scripts. Open up the training job view in the AWS console, scroll to the bottom, and click the *View logs*. This takes you to CloudWatch, giving you one log stream per node in your cluster, each called `algo`. Usually, the top log stream is the leader node, but all of the streams will try to connect to the leader, so just see which algo they are trying to connect to. The logs will start after your instances are online and the script has been invoked, so it may take a few minutes after the job starts to see these.

### Checkpointing

One last parameter to be aware of in your SageMaker training scripts is **checkpointing**. In SageMaker, this actually serves a different role than just the model path. The model path will be copied to S3 at the end of your training job, but your checkpoints *will be copied throughout*. This makes them a great candidate for in-job debugging, running TensorBoard *(2)*, and restarting from the latest checkpoint.

Implementing a restart from your checkpoint is an extremely efficient technique to learn and perfect. It's not hard – just look in S3 for the right path, configure your job, and then make sure you're looking in the right directory for your base model. For large-scale jobs, we recommend you checkpoint at least every 2–3 hours. This makes it easy for you to get through any hardware, software, networking, data, or other issues that will almost certainly arise throughout your training process.

For a detailed example of this, take a look at our GPT-2 training example at *(3)* in the *References* section. It implements a `load_partial` parameter that points to the S3 path you can provide for checkpointing.

### Configuring your job via the SageMaker estimator

While you do have multiple ways of running your SageMaker job, notably through the UI, the CLI, and `boto3`, probably the most popular way of doing this is through the Python SDK.

Here's an example of what this might look like:

```python
import sagemaker
from sagemaker.pytorch import PyTorch

sess = sagemaker.Session()
role = sagemaker.get_execution_role()

bucket = sess.default_bucket()

estimator = PyTorch(
    entry_point="test.py",
    base_job_name="lustre-test",
    role=role,
    image_uri = '<my_image_uri>',
    source_dir="fsx_scripts",
    # configures the SageMaker training resource, you can increase as you need
    instance_count=1,
    instance_type="ml.m5.large",
    py_version="py38",
    framework_version = '1.10',
    sagemaker_session=sess,
    debugger_hook_config=False,
    hyperparamers = {'my_param_name':'my_param_value'},
    distribution = {'my_distribution_configs':values},
    # enable warm pools for 60 minutes, useful for debugging
    keep_alive_period_in_seconds = 60 * 60,
    **kwargs
)

estimator.fit(inputs = data_channels, wait=False)
```

Figure 8.4 – Using the SageMaker estimator to run your remote training job

Note that we're pointing to a base image, actually through the `PyTorch` object. This points to a base AWS Deep Learning Container, defined by what framework version you specify. You can override this by pointing to `image_uri`, which will need to be a Docker container in Amazon ECS. In this estimator, you can also pass key parameters such as the following:

- `instance_count` and `instance_type` to configure your training resource.
- Your entry point script and its source directory. This is where SageMaker will look for `requirements.txt` and your main script to execute both of the files.
- Your hyperparameters – again, you define them based on what you need.
- Your distribution parameters. We'll cover them in the last section of this chapter.

Next, let's take a look at some interesting usability features for SageMaker training.

# Top usability features for SageMaker training

Now that you have some sense of how to integrate your scripts with SageMaker training, let's learn about a few key aspects of SageMaker that make it especially easy and fun to work with.

## Warm pools for rapid experimentation

Once your SageMaker job is online, it moves through the following phases:

- Initializing resources
- Downloading your data
- Downloading your training image
- Invoking your main script
- Uploading the model artifact to S3 on completion

You might be wondering, what happens if my job breaks and I need to update a few lines of code? Do I need to completely restart the entire cluster from scratch?

Fortunately for you, the answer is no! Definitely not. You can use managed warm pools. Just add one extra hyperparameter, `keep_alive_period_in_seconds`, and it'll keep your job online even after your script either fails or finishes completely. This is useful because, in many cases, that upfront job initialization actually is the largest bottleneck in your flow. It can take anywhere from a few minutes for smaller CPU-based instances to as much as 8 minutes or more for larger GPU-based instances to initialize.

On the upside, that wait time for GPU instances is ultimately saving you money and time because we're running GPU health checks on the backend to ensure you get only good news. On the downside, 8 minutes is a long time to wait between development iterations. This is particularly painful if you're updating something embarrassingly simple, such as a basic syntax error.

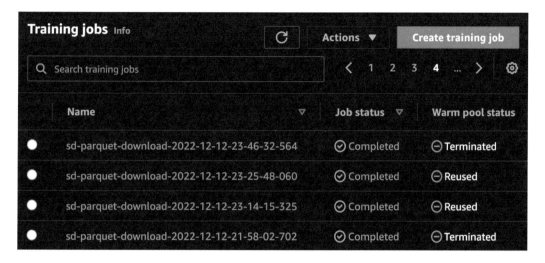

Figure 8.5 – Viewing your training jobs in the console

Managed warm pools solve this problem for you as follows:

1.  First, add that hyperparameter to your job configuration.

2.  Next, once the job finishes training, either successfully or with an error, the warm pool status should show **Available**.

3.  Afterward, when you submit another job with a matching image URI, instance type, and instance count, this will show the **In Use** status and then ultimately **Reused**, as shown in *Figure 8.5*.

While saving a few minutes through using managed warm pools may not seem like a huge gain, it truly adds up a scale. When you're working up against a deadline and every hour of the day counts, using warm pools may be the difference between hitting your deadline and not. It means that in a single hour, you can update your script easily hundreds of times, whereas before you may only have been able to do this up to about 10 times in an hour.

## SSM and SSH into training instances

Once your job is up and running successfully, especially a long-running job with lots of complex steps along the way, you can imagine how useful it would be to connect to the instance directly, view it, and run debug commands.

Fortunately, we have a solution for that – a group of our very own ML SAs built out a custom design pattern that helps you enable this in your own environments *(1)*. They listened closely to customers, iterated on requirements, and developed a very nice project.

You can follow the steps in the following repository to install this in your own SageMaker resources, allowing you to easily connect to running jobs and analyze them in flight.

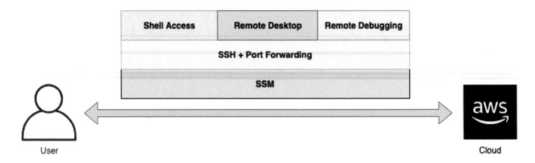

Figure 8.6 – SSH in SageMaker training jobs

From a systems architecture perspective, there are two key paths forward in evaluating this solution. On the one hand, you can use the fully-managed service, AWS Systems Manager. This is generally more secure than SSH but is a bit more limited in functionality. If all you need is to open up a terminal onto a remote instance, run some debug commands, and view the output in progress, this is probably the solution for you. Setting it up isn't too hard; you just need to configure the IAM and SSM resources accordingly. When used in combination with warm pools, this is really powerful!

On the other hand, you can also use SSH directly. SSH is generally less secure than SSM. This is because SSM uses a managed AWS service, while SSH opens up the possibility that any malicious user could connect to the nodes using port forwarding. This means that in an enterprise environment, in many cases you're better off starting with SSM. SSH will, however, let you update a local script and use port forwarding. This means if you want something to take your local script and send it to the remote training instance seamlessly, SSH is the way to go. However, given that you now have warm pools, it's questionable whether you'd need this. The SSH solution is really nice if your IDE supports remote connection points, such as VS Code or PyCharm.

## Track jobs and experiments to replicate results

One of my personal favorite features of SageMaker training is, honestly, its most basic – storing everything about your job and keeping it searchable by default! That's called the **metadata**. All the hyperparameters, input data locations, images, variables, and other information about your job are stored every time you submit them. This means you can easily track your jobs over time, logging in to view the CloudWatch logs, downloading the model from S3 whenever you need to, adding tags to specify other details, and so on.

Figure 8.7 – Viewing your training job metadata in the AWS console

All of this data is in your account for the long haul, without your paying for any of it. You also use SageMaker Search to find jobs with the highest accuracy from a given S3 path, an instance type or count, a hyperparameter, or any available value. Just recently we've launched a few new features that make using SageMaker Training much easier. One of them is a hosted TensorBoard (https://aws.amazon.com/about-aws/whats-new/2023/04/amazon-sagemaker-hosted-tensorboard/) which lets you easily track and compare experiments. The second is a new @remote decorator that lets you transition local functions to remote jobs very easily! (`https://aws.amazon.com/blogs/machine-learning/run-your-local-machine-learning-code-as-amazon-sagemaker-training-jobs-with-minimal-code-changes/?sc_channel=sm&sc_campaign=Machine_Learning&sc_publisher=LINKEDIN&sc_geo=GLOBAL&sc_outcome=awareness&sc_content=ml_services&trk=machine_learning&linkId=211795861`)

Now, let's close out the chapter by learning about backend optimizations!

### *Backend optimizations for distributed training with SageMaker*

You've learned how to update your training scripts for SageMaker, and you've taken a closer look at some of the ways SageMaker is pretty fun and friendly to work with. Let's finish by exploring ways that SageMaker optimizes the backend for large-scale distributed training.

As you have probably guessed, SageMaker can spin up anywhere from a few to a few thousand GPUs. This is due to the core service offering for training – the ability to turn on, orchestrate, and manage all of these GPUs on your behalf. You define this cluster when you define a training job, and as you learned earlier in this chapter, you use *mpi* to communicate between all of the nodes. You can store all of the hyperparameters and job metadata, stream all of your logs to CloudWatch, plug into your favorite operations tooling, ensure the nodes are healthy, connect to your data in S3, download and run your image, and so on. This *large-scale cluster orchestration* is completely elastic, easily flowing from one to hundreds of instances.

However, orchestrating this cluster is not especially useful, unless you have healthy GPUs. As you learned earlier in the book, writing software to successfully orchestrate all the tens of thousands of cores in a single GPU is no small task. Even when you have updated CUDA, drivers, and the latest deep learning frameworks, the bad news is that you may still get a bad GPU. Hardware fails, and GPU failures are incredibly common. As you scale up your training jobs to more GPUs, the odds of you getting a GPU failure even once in that massive pool of compute increases. This is why the *GPU health checks* that SageMaker brings to the table are incredibly useful! We can track down the latest GPU errors and have integrated checks for these in our job orchestrator. It means that when you get a node on SageMaker, it is much more likely to be healthy.

Even with extensive GPU health checks and large-scale job orchestration, it is still possible that your job will error out even before it starts. You might get something like an *insufficient capacity error*, indicating that there are simply not enough of your requested instance type in your requested region. You could also get an *internal service error*, unsurprisingly telling you that something went wrong at your end. For these and other cases, it is extremely useful to have **resilient training**. Adding this is simple – you just need to bring an extra parameter to your training job configuration. Set `max_retry_attempts` to your preference; personally, I just max it out at 30 every time I am running something with more than 8 instances.

While this is useful to get a job successfully started, I also have customers who *implement another job restart*. This might come into play when stepping through your mini-batches during your training loop. While the `bf16` data type has proven extremely useful to improve the stability of large-scale distributed GPU training, it is still not uncommon to see the loss of your model spontaneously spike, plateau, or drop. You might also see your total job throughput unexpectedly change. If any of these things happen, it's wise to trigger an emergency checkpoint, kill the job, and then start again from that same checkpoint and step number. A combination of a few extra functions in your training script and a Lambda function listening via the `EventBridge` would be a natural way to do this. For a recent summary of some best practices, take a look at the blog post *(4)* in the *References* section.

### Distributed training libraries – a model and data parallel

As you've learned previously, AWS has optimizations for distributed training. These are extremely effective methods to scale up to hundreds and thousands of GPUs on SageMaker. Let's take one more look at them in detail.

Remember that AlexNet only achieved groundbreaking results because it used multiple GPUs? Historically speaking, one of the earliest approaches to a multi-node deep learning process was called a **parameter server**. Parameter servers, as you can see in the following diagram, are a simple and effective way to orchestrate distributed gradient descent at scale. One node operates as the leader. It synchronizes gradients with the worker nodes, checking their health, and maintaining one globally consistent version of the model. Parameter servers can be somewhat slow, but they are actually more efficient in terms of the bandwidth they consume. Let's explore this visually.

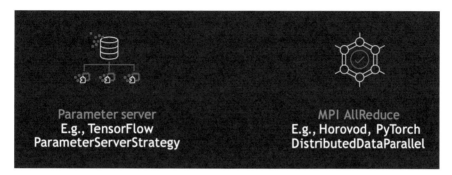

Figure 8.7 – Historical approaches to distributed gradient descent

This slowness, however, led to a slightly different approach. Ring-based topologies used the `AllReduce` algorithm under the hood to communicate between all nodes, collecting the average of the gradients and distributing the result to each of the nodes. This is the same basic approach common in Horovod and PyTorch DistributedDataParallel, popularized by their increase in speed over their older cousin.

However, `AllReduce` as a basic collective does *not* perform well at scale. Every additional node increases the bandwidth consumed during the `AllReduce` step. This means that your scaling efficiency gets worse as you add more instances, ultimately leading to poor utilization of your instances and, thus, your compute budget.

To counter this negative impact, AWS developed *custom collectives for data parallel*. These are the single best way to get the highest performance on the AWS Cloud. This was introduced as **SageMaker Distributed Data Parallel** (**SMDDP**) *(5)*, available as an SDK, in your container, and for any supported SageMaker job. Use SMDDP to ensure your large-scale GPU jobs are running as quickly and efficiently as possible, using them as the backend for any supported distributed software. SMDDP also integrates with Amazon's Elastic Fabric Adapter, a low-jitter low-latency communication enhancement on AWS. Generally, SMDDP makes it easy for you to point to it from deep learning frameworks, setting it as your distributed backend.

Fortunately for you, as of the December 2022 release, this is now also available in the *model parallel* family. Now, you can set a `ddp` backend in the `smp_options` object, with `ddp_dist_backend:auto`. When this new backend option is combined with the *sharded data parallel* configuration we discussed in *Chapter 5*, this gives you another 30% boost!

Now, let's close out the chapter with a quick recap.

## Summary

In this chapter, we learned about the key features of Amazon SageMaker for large-scale distributed training. We looked at how to optimize your script, from importing packages to parsing arguments, writing code, invoking your script with `mpi`, writing to CloudWatch logs, checkpointing, working with the SM estimator, and so on. We covered key usability features to make SageMaker more fun and friendly to work with, such as warm pools for rapid experimentation, SSM and SSH in training instances, and tracking jobs. Finally, we learned about backend optimizations for distributed training, such as SMDDP collectives, using it both standalone and in combination with the model parallel package.

In the next chapter, we'll explore even more advanced topics in distributed training!

## References

Please go through the following content for more information on a few topics covered in the chapter:

1. *aws-sample/sagemaker-ssh-helper*: `https://github.com/aws-samples/sagemaker-ssh-helper`

2. *Use TensorBoard in Amazon SageMaker Studio*: `https://docs.aws.amazon.com/sagemaker/latest/dg/studio-tensorboard.html`

3. *aws/amazon-sagemaker-examples*: `https://github.com/aws/amazon-sagemaker-examples/blob/main/training/distributed_training/pytorch/model_parallel/gpt2/train_gpt_simple.py`

4. *Training large language models on Amazon SageMaker: Best practices*: `https://aws.amazon.com/blogs/machine-learning/training-large-language-models-on-amazon-sagemaker-best-practices/`

5. *Introduction to SageMaker's Distributed Data Parallel Library*: `https://docs.aws.amazon.com/sagemaker/latest/dg/data-parallel-intro.html`

# 9

# Advanced Training Concepts

In this chapter, we will cover advanced training concepts at scale, such as evaluating throughput, calculating model **teraFLOPS** (**TFLOPS**) per device, compiling, and using the scaling laws to determine the right length of training time. In the last chapter, you learned about how to do large-scale training on SageMaker, in general terms. In this chapter, you'll learn about particularly complex and sophisticated techniques you can use to drive down the overall cost of your job. This lower cost directly translates to higher model performance because you can train for longer on the same budget.

We will cover the following topics in this chapter:

- Evaluating and improving throughput with model TFLOPS
- Using FlashAttention to speed up your training runs
- Speeding up your jobs with compilation
- Amazon SageMaker Training Compiler and Neo
- Running compiled models on Amazon's Trainium and Inferentia custom hardware
- Solving for an optimal training time

## Evaluating and improving throughput

As we've previously covered in the book, total job throughput is an important metric to track. On the one hand, you want to keep a batch size small enough to ensure your model is trained appropriately. On the other hand, you want to max out your overall job performance to get the most possibly accurate model you can. We learned in *Chapter 7* how to use hyperparameter tuning to solve both of those. We also covered other tips and tricks for reducing your **graphics processing unit** (**GPU**) memory footprint in *Chapter 5* and *Chapter 8*. Now, let's close out a few more gaps in this area.

First, it's important to consider how you measure throughput in general terms. You have probably used some logging packages in PyTorch that handily report iterations per second during the training loop. Obviously, this is extremely useful in clocking your training speed, but how would you take into account the size of the model? What if you wanted to compare your speed with others to see whether you're in the same ballpark?

To solve this problem, many research teams calculate an aggregate term that combines both indicators for the model's size with operations completed. Commonly, this is called **model TFLOPS**. These calculations will vary based on individual team preferences, but we'll explore the setup from a recent Chinchilla *(11)* paper that just won a **Neural Information Processing Systems (NeurIPS)** best paper award. You'll find this phrase is common in evaluating large-scale distributed training systems.

## Calculating model TFLOPS

You've heard of **floating operations per second (FLOPS)**. This is a simple way of presenting how many computations a given machine can perform. Higher is better because this means your machine can complete more tasks given the same amount of time. **TFLOPS** is an easier way of comparing performance for distributed training solutions.

In Chinchilla, the authors have a clean way of computing model TFLOPS. First, let's consider that the performance of the forward pass and the backward pass is different. The backward pass is actually two times the compute costs of the forward pass because we need to both compute the gradients and update the weights and parameters. So, the model TFLOPS would then be the following:

$$model_{TFLOPS} = forward\_pass + 2 \cdot forward\_pass$$

Simple enough? Now let's unpack that term.

$$forward\_pass$$
$$= embeddings + num\_layers$$
$$\cdot (total\_attention + dense\_block) + \text{logits}$$

In *Appendix F* of their paper, they define the rest of their terminology in detail. Another much more simple but slightly less precise way of computing your total model TFLOPS is simply $C=6 \cdot D \cdot N$, where $N$ is the number of parameters in your model. Chinchilla actually found no significant difference between this computation and theirs presented in the preceding formula.

As you read through these metrics, consider that each term relates to a part of your neural network, specifically scoping how large it is. When you combine these with the number of tokens processed per second, you get a realistic metric for the efficiency of your overall training loop. This efficiency metric then becomes a single common denominator you can use to compare your experiments at runtime.

Remember that in *Chapter 3*, you learned how to think about your overall project as a series of experiments? While the accuracy of your project should no doubt be a key performance indicator, I would strongly recommend including an efficiency indicator as well. This helps ensure that you're making the best use of your compute budget, which is relevant for the initial training runs, subsequent retraining, inference, monitoring, and overall project maintenance.

For example, you might consider the following experiment schedule:

| Phase | Model type | Model size | Datase size | Compute size | Compute efficiency | Experiment run-time |
|---|---|---|---|---|---|---|
| One – small-scale testing | Generic pretrained | Base | 5–30 GBs | 1–4 less expensive GPUs | Low | One full pass through a small data sample |
| Two – increase the dataset | Semi-custom | A few billion parameters | 100 GBs–TBs | Tens to hundreds of better GPUs | Medium | A few steps or epochs |
| Three – increase model (and data) | Very custom | Tens of billions of parameters | TBs | Hundreds to thousands of high-performance GPUs | High | A few steps or epochs |
| Four – maximize compute budget | Fully custom | Tens to hundreds of billions of parameters | TBs–PBs | Thousands or more high-performance GPUs | State of the art | Train to optimal period |

Figure 9.1 – Suggested phase of experiments for training foundation models at scale

Let me be explicitly clear about this table; I do not under any circumstances expect every person to follow this exactly. There are countless nuances in novel training regimes, dataset sizes, models, GPU performance, modeling results, compute budget, and perspectives for a single table to encompass all of them. Some teams will never hit models over 1 billion parameters and still build something the world adores, such as Stable Diffusion! But I guarantee you that the lab staged its build across multiple phases that eventually culminated in a massive run. You want to learn how to increase the scope of your projects from very doable to very impressive. It's up to you how to do that appropriately for the problem you're solving at hand.

Now let's look at a few more methods you can use to boost your training efficiency. Next up is Flash Attention!

# Using Flash Attention to speed up your training runs

In earlier chapters, we learned about the core Transformer model, with its underlying self-attention mechanism that serves as the basis for most state-of-the-art models across vision, language, and generative use cases today. While Transformer models are easily parallelizable, they aren't particularly good at optimizing for different memory speeds within modern GPUs. This becomes a problem when they materialize the Transformer in the slowest part of the GPU due to a naïve implementation. As you can imagine, that leaves performance gains on the table.

A Stanford-led research team realized that they could improve this and developed a novel implementation of the Transformer architecture. Simply put, it's an extremely clever way to handle a quadratic nested for-loop. Let's take a closer look.

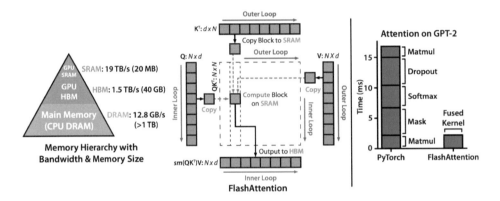

Figure 9.2 – From FlashAttention by Tri Dao et al, 2022 *(1)*

This visual from the paper demonstrates three key concepts. On the left-hand side, we see a simple pyramid showing the three common types of compute available on most GPU servers. At the base, we have a lot of CPUs with more than 1 TB available of main memory. However, this peaks at 12.8 GB/s bandwidth. Next, we have the slower part of the GPU, with much less memory but much more bandwidth, only 40 GB of GPU HMB but up to 1.5 TBs. Finally, we have the fastest part of the GPU, with only 20 MB of memory but up to 19 TBs of bandwidth. Obviously, 19 TBs is more than 10 times faster than 1.5 TBs! This shows you right away that moving as much of the compute to the **static random-access memory (SRAM)** can save you a lot of time.

However, you'll notice that this 10 times is in bandwidth, not necessarily throughput. While pure throughput means efficiently processing a large volume of data, bandwidth here helps optimize **input/ output (I/O)**. In this case, it refers to how data is passed between different data structures in this overall computer architecture. This is why it's the bandwidth metric we're most interested in; bandwidth controls the volume of data we can pass to or from a given compute. This means that when we have an I/O intensive process, such as the quadratic nested for-loop used in self-attention heads, pushing as much of the data to the part with the highest bandwidth is a way to increase the overall speed.

What types of gains does this give us? In the far right-hand side of the visual, you can see that this new *fused kernel*, provided by FlashAttention, finishes in the amount of time it takes just one of the five operations to complete in a naïve PyTorch implementation. While a naïve implementation needs about 17 seconds to finish all the **Matrix multiplication** (**Matmul**), Masking, Softmax, Dropout, and finally Matmul, the FlashAttention fused kernel can run all of these in around seconds!

FlashAttention hasn't yet been upstreamed into PyTorch directly, although I would be shocked if that didn't happen in the next 12 months. For the time being, you can use an open source implementation available here *(2)*. The authors show that this leads to a 3–5 times speedup for **generative pre-trained transformer** (**GPT**) models over the Hugging Face options, reaching up to 189 TFLOPS on each NVIDIA A100 GPU. While that may not sound like a big jump at smaller scales, once you've hit hundreds to thousands of GPUs, that can equal massive savings! Support for FlashAttention is available in the SageMaker Model Parallel library as of December 2022 *(3)*.

Now let's look at another advanced training concept to help speed up your training runs: compilation.

## Speeding up your jobs with compilation

Remember that in *Chapter 4*, we learned about some basic concepts in GPU systems architecture. We covered the foundational **Compute Unified Device Architecture** (**CUDA**) software framework that lets you run normal Python code on GPUs. We talked about managed containers and deep learning frameworks, such as PyTorch and TensorFlow, which are already tested and proven to run nicely on the AWS cloud. The problem with most neural network implementations is that they aren't particularly optimized for GPUs. This is where compilation comes in; you can use it to eke out an extra two-times jump in speed for the same model!

In the context of compilers for deep learning, we're mostly interested in **accelerated linear algebra** (**XLA**). This is a project Google originally developed for TensorFlow, which has since merged into the *Jax* framework. PyTorch developers will be happy to know that major compilation techniques have been upstreamed into PyTorch 2.0. You can now compile any arbitrary PyTorch function with the new `torch.compile` method.

Before we get into any examples of using compilation, let's first try to understand what it is and why it's useful. Imagine you have two vectors (remember, think "lists"), both of size 1000. One of them is filled with zeros, and the other is filled with ones. Now imagine that you have a basic operation to apply to both of these vectors: addition. You want to add these two vectors to produce a third vector with a length of 1000, which is simply the direct sum of each item in both of the original vectors.

A naïve way of doing this would be to walk through both lists, compute the sum, and add it to the new list. But what if you knew ahead of time that one of these vectors was zero? Wouldn't you want to then skip the addition operation altogether? If you did, it could save you a lot of time!

This jump is possible as a result of an intermediate representation. As presented in a 2020 survey *(4)*, deep learning compilers profile the graph that is your neural network. First, a frontend compiler computes a more optimal version of your graph, such as fusing operators, simplifying the algebraic expressions, performing static memory planning, and many more techniques. Next, a backend compiler computes this again for specific hardware, lower-level representations, memory allocation, custom kernels, and more. This then generates the new code that is consumed by the accelerator.

Now let's learn how to add compilation to your scripts!

## Integrating compilation into your PyTorch scripts

From the launch PyTorch documentation here *(5)*, you'll see that there are three major ways to use compilation in your own PyTorch code. First, you can use any PyTorch built-in functions such as `torch.sin` or `torch.cos`, and then pass these into `torch.compile`. This uses a variety of the techniques we discussed previously to compile your function based on the available GPUs. Alternatively, you can add a decorator to your PyTorch function, simply `@torch.compile`, which provides the same functionality. Both of these features are also available for the `torch.nn.Module` base object, which means you should be able to use them for any of your PyTorch models!

If you're thinking these speedups with compilation seem useful, but I don't want to re-write my model code to use them, this next section will be extremely interesting for you! Let's look at managed compilation features on AWS – SageMaker Training Compiler and SageMaker Neo.

# Amazon SageMaker Training Compiler and Neo

If you use Hugging Face language models today, such as BERT, GPT, RoBERTa, AlBERT, DistiliBERT, or hundreds of others, then you are in luck! Without much work, you can easily speed up the run-time of your jobs by up to 50%. This is because of **SageMaker Training Compiler** (**SMTC**). As we learned earlier, compilation generally has the potential to increase the speed of your training. With SMTC, we provide a managed compilation feature within SageMaker training to easily enable this for your own models and scripts.

As you can see in the visual provided, enabling this is quite simple. Here we use the Hugging Face AWS-managed deep learning container and simply add `TrainingCompilerConfig()`. If you're using a model with the Hugging Face `Trainer` API, this will automatically trigger Training Compiler:

```
from sagemaker.huggingface import HuggingFace
from sagemaker.huggingface import TrainingCompilerConfig

pytorch_estimator = HuggingFace(entry_point='train.py',
                                instance_count=1,
                                instance_type='ml.p3.2xlarge',
                                transformers_version='4.11.0',
                                pytorch_version='1.9.0',
                                compiler_config=TrainingCompilerConfig(),
                                hyperparameters = {'epochs': 20,
                                                   'batch-size': 64,
                                                   'learning-rate': 0.1}
                                )

pytorch_estimator.fit({'train': 's3://my/path/to/my/training/data',
                       'test': 's3://my/path/to/my/test/data'})
```

Figure 9.3 – Configure SageMaker Training Compiler

How does it work? SMTC uses a variety of compilation methods on three different levels: compilations for the graph, the data flow, and the backend. The graph-level optimizations include operator fusion, memory planning, and algebraic simplifications. The data flow-level optimizations include layout transformation and common sub-expression elimination. Backend optimizations include memory latency hiding and loop-oriented optimizations. This accelerates the training process by up to 50%, and the resultant model is the same as if SMTC had not been applied. For example, when fine-tuning Hugging Face's GPT-2 model, SMTC reduced the training time from nearly 3 hours to just 90 minutes!

## Best practices for compilation

When working with compilers, you'll want to ensure that you are updating your hyperparameters accordingly. This is because the net effect of a compiler is that it reduces the GPU memory footprint of the model. For example, without compiling, your model might consume a solid 10 GB of GPU memory. After compilation, you might get that down to 5 GB! This opens up more space for you to pack in objects in your batch size. As we learned earlier in the book, this directly increases your GPU utilization and, thus, your overall project efficiency. Just be careful not to over-increase batch size, which then makes it harder to converge. You'll also want to increase your learning rate at the same pace.

As you might be anticipating, there are clear times when compilation is expected to be quite useful. There are also times when compilation could be a waste of time. This is because most compilers *take some time to run their compilation process* before executing your code. That means that, in contrast to normal Python code execution, the compiler will run its subprocess ahead of time to produce a more optimized version of your model. Once this is produced, your code will run in earnest.

This ahead-of-time compilation process introduces the key tradeoff for evaluating the impact of compilation as a whole. The longer your model training period, the larger the boost from the compilation. This means if you're using a large number of epochs, or if your dataset is quite large, then compilation should be a useful way to save compute costs. Personally, I'd say if your model runs for anything longer than 30 or 40 minutes, try to find a way to drive that down with compilation.

Alternatively, if you have a frequent retraining pipeline or job, one that runs on a semi-frequent schedule, try to use compilation to drive down that time. Some of my customers retrain their models every day, every week, or even every few hours or minutes. We'll dive into this and other topics about operations in *Chapter 14*.

Now, let's learn how using PyTorch compilation enables us to easily use Amazon's custom hardware for machine learning: Trainium and Inferentia!

# Running compiled models on Amazon's Trainium and Inferentia custom hardware

So far in this book, most of the accelerators we evaluated have been GPUs designed and built by NVIDIA. As we learned earlier, NVIDIA's excellent software enables the lion's share of deep learning frameworks to run nicely on those same GPUs, which ends up being a primary deciding factor in using GPUs. We also learned earlier how those same GPUs are also available on AWS, notably through our machine learning service, Amazon SageMaker.

However, as you have no doubt realized by this point, the price tag of those same GPUs can be high! Even though AWS has generous enterprise discount programs, such as using reserved instances to save up to 75% *(6)*, you would still benefit from learning about alternatives. Basic economics tells us that when supply increases, such as through alternative accelerators, while demand stays constant, the price drops! This is exactly what we're thrilled to provide customers: our custom accelerators for machine learning – Trainium and Inferentia. As you might have guessed, Trainium is dedicated to training machine learning models, while Inferentia does the same for hosting. As of this writing, these are available on EC2 and SageMaker as Inf1 and Trn1 instances.

Fortunately for those of you who made it through the previous section on compilation, many models compiled with XLA are supported by Trainium and Inferentia! This means that if you are already using XLA compilation, either through PyTorch or TensorFlow, you are well on your way to a successful migration onto Trainium and Inferentia. A word of caution, however, is that not every model and operation is supported by these yet. Expect some friction as you develop and test. The AWS Neuron **software development kit** (**SDK**) is a great way to test compatibility *(7)*.

There are two reasons to evaluate our custom accelerators:

- First, it's a new type of hardware. This is particularly valuable for you scientists out there because you could quite literally be the first person to use a certain type of model on this hardware in the world. This may actually increase your odds of publication and recognition because you could develop a truly novel insight based on how this model performs.

- Second, as with all of our new instances on AWS, the price-performance ratio should be substantially better than it was previously.

What is a price-performance ratio? Consider each task you need to complete. In the case of Inferentia, that would be model inference requests completed. For Trainium, that would be steps through your training loop. Then consider the cost for each task to be completed. Now you have your ratio! Our Trn1 instances offer up to 50% cost-to-train savings over comparable GPU instances, and Amazon Search reduced their inference costs by 85% with Inferentia *(8)*.

Now that we've looked at Trainium and Inferentia at a very high level, let's explore how to solve for an optimal training time using the scaling laws.

## Solving for an optimal training time

Time is an interesting construct in training large vision and language models. On the one hand, you might consider it a hyperparameter, simply the number of epochs. On the other hand, you might consider it a facet of your training data, its total number of tokens or images. You might also consider it a fixed input to your project, your total compute budget. Most research teams I work with use their intuition and good judgment to use a combination of all of these.

As we learned earlier in the book, the proposed *scaling laws* provide an interesting theoretical tool you can use to predict the performance of your model. Their original author, Kaplan et al. *(9)*, actually suggested that optimal usage of a given compute budget should stop "significantly before convergence." They proposed this because of their proposed insight into large language models being more "sample efficient" than smaller ones.

However, 2022 saw these original laws being turn on their head. In this visual, you can see the theoretical predictions determined by a new set of scaling laws from **Chinchilla**:

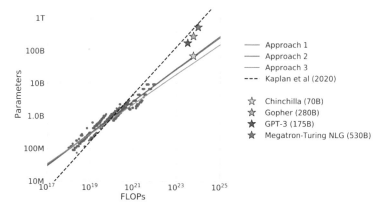

Figure 9.4 – Improved performance from Hoffman et al., 2022 *(10)*

Here Hoffman et al. make the elegant proposal that *training data and model sizes should be increased linearly*. That is to say, if you double the size of the model, you should double the size of the training data. I appreciate this natural symmetry and find it quite intuitive. Happily, these predictions were validated by extensive empirical evidence across no less than 400 models, 150 downstream tasks, and 6 domains, including language modeling, reading comprehension, question answering, common sense reasoning, and more. Per the authors, "Chinchilla uniformly and significantly outperforms **Gopher (280 B)**, **GPT-3 (175 B)**, **Jurassic-1 (178 B)**, and **Megatron-Turing NLG (530B)** on a large range of downstream evaluation tasks." This implies that these models are undertrained, actually needing much larger datasets to validate their parameter size.

Using these equations and a massive set of experimental results, the authors suggest the following set of values for parameters, FLOPS, and tokens:

| Parameters | FLOPs | FLOPs (in *Gopher* unit) | Tokens |
|---|---|---|---|
| 400 Million | 1.92e+19 | 1/29, 968 | 8.0 Billion |
| 1 Billion | 1.21e+20 | 1/4, 761 | 20.2 Billion |
| 10 Billion | 1.23e+22 | 1/46 | 205.1 Billion |
| 67 Billion | 5.76e+23 | 1 | 1.5 Trillion |
| 175 Billion | 3.85e+24 | 6.7 | 3.7 Trillion |
| 280 Billion | 9.90e+24 | 17.2 | 5.9 Trillion |
| 520 Billion | 3.43e+25 | 59.5 | 11.0 Trillion |
| 1 Trillion | 1.27e+26 | 221.3 | 21.2 Trillion |
| 10 Trillion | 1.30e+28 | 22515.9 | 216.2 Trillion |

Figure 9.5 – Suggested FLOPS and tokens per model size

Remember that when we look at this FLOPS value, we need to consider the following:

1.  What value do I expect this model to bring to my organization?

2.  From this, what total compute budget can I plan for?

3.  How large is my training data?

4.  What size of a model should I use based on this?

5.  How efficient are my training loop and distributed system? Said another way, how many TFLOPS per GPU am I able to eke out?

6.  How many GPUs can I get from my cloud provider?

7.  How long will I need to run my entire training loop to train to convergence?

The answers to questions (*1*), (*2*), (*3*), and (*5*) can only come from you. The answers to questions (*4*) and (*7*) are functional derivatives of the previous answers. The answer to question (*6*), I would say is halfway between a functional derivative from the answer to (*1*), and a simple fact of the market at that point in time. If there's a global supply chain issue for electronics, then accessing GPUs will be hard.

Whew, you made it through the advanced chapter! Now let's do a quick concept recap, and then we'll move into *Part Four: Evaluate your model*.

## Summary

In this chapter, we covered some advanced concepts in training large-scale vision and language models. First, you learned how to evaluate and improve throughput by computing model TFLOPS per GPU, and using this as one of a number of metrics to compare experimental results. You learned about FlashAttention, and how its I/O-aware optimized quadratic for-loop speeds up the Transformer self-attention mechanism by as much as 3–5 times. You learned about compilation using methods built into PyTorch natively and those managed by AWS. You also learned about a few different types of compilation methods. You learned to update your hyperparameters for compilation, in addition to cases where the compilation is expected to provide a boost (or not).

You also learned about how to use compilers to run on Amazon's custom hardware for machine learning, Trainium, and Inferentia. Lastly, we used the scaling laws to solve for an optimal train time.

In the next chapter, you'll learn how to fine-tune your model and compare it with open source alternatives.

## References

1. FlashAttention: Fast and Memory-Efficient Exact Attention with IO-Awareness: `https://arxiv.org/pdf/2205.14135.pdf`

2. HazyResearch/flash-attention: `https://github.com/HazyResearch/flash-attention`

3. New performance improvements in Amazon SageMaker model parallel library: `https://aws.amazon.com/blogs/machine-learning/new-performance-improvements-in-amazon-sagemaker-model-parallel-library/`

4. The Deep Learning Compiler: A Comprehensive Survey: `https://arxiv.org/pdf/2002.03794.pdf`

5. TORCH.COMPILE TUTORIAL: `https://pytorch.org/tutorials/intermediate/torch_compile_tutorial.html`

6. Enterprise Customers: `https://aws.amazon.com/pricing/enterprise/`

7. Welcome to AWS Neuron: `https://awsdocs-neuron.readthedocs-hosted.com/en/latest/`

8.  How Amazon Search reduced ML inference costs by 85% with AWS Inferentia: `https://aws.amazon.com/blogs/machine-learning/how-amazon-search-reduced-ml-inference-costs-by-85-with-aws-inferentia/`

9.  Scaling Laws for Neural Language Models: `https://arxiv.org/abs/2001.08361`

10. Training Compute-Optimal Large Language Models: `https://arxiv.org/pdf/2203.15556.pdf`

11. Training Compute-Optimal Large Language Models: `https://openreview.net/pdf?id=iBBcRUlOAPR`

# Part 4: Evaluate Your Model

In part 4, you'll learn how to evaluate your model. You'll use the scaling laws to identify the shortest possible training time, fine-tune your model to compare with public benchmarks, and identify and mitigate bias.

This section has the following chapters:

- *Chapter 10, Fine-Tuning and Evaluating*
- *Chapter 11, Detecting, Mitigating, and Monitoring Bias*
- *Chapter 12, How to Deploy Your Model*

# 10

# Fine-Tuning and Evaluating

In this chapter, you'll learn how to fine-tune your model on use case-specific datasets, comparing its performance to that of off-the-shelf public models. You should be able to see a quantitative and qualitative boost from your pretraining regime. You'll dive into some examples involving language, text, and everything in between. You'll also learn how to think about and design a human-in-the-loop evaluation system, including the same RLHF that makes ChatGPT tick! This chapter focuses on updating the trainable weights of the model. For techniques that mimic learning but don't update the weights, such as prompt tuning and standard retrieval augmented generation, see *Chapter 13* on prompt engineering.

We are going to cover the following topics in this chapter:

- Fine-tuning for language, text, and everything in between
- LLM fine-tuning breakdown – instruction fine-tuning, parameter efficient fine-tuning, and reinforcement learning with human feedback
- Vision fine-tuning
- Evaluating foundation models in vision, language, and joint tasks

## Fine-tuning for language, text, and everything in between

At this point in the book, we've already covered a lot of ground. We've focused primarily on the pretraining aspect, looking at everything from finding the right use cases and datasets to defining your loss functions, preparing your models and datasets, defining progressively larger experiments, parallelization basics, working with GPUs, finding the right hyperparameters, advanced concepts, and more! Here, we'll explore how to make your models even more targeted to a specific application: **fine-tuning**.

Presumably, if you are embarking on a large-scale training project, you might have one of the following goals:

- You might be pretraining your own foundation model
- You might be designing a novel method for autonomous vehicles

- You might be classifying and segmenting 3D data, such as in real estate or manufacturing

- You might be training a large text classification model or designing a novel image-text generation model

- You might be building a text-to-music generator, or working on a completely new jointly trained modality, as yet undiscovered by the machine learning community

- You might be training a large language model to solve general-purpose search and qquestion and answering for the entire world, or for specific communities, languages, organizations, and purposes

All these use cases have something in common; they use one large-scale model that achieves general-purpose intelligence through learning patterns in extreme-scale datasets and model sizes. In many cases, however, *these models only become extraordinarily useful when fine-tuned to solve a specific problem*. This is not to say that you cannot simply deploy one of them and use specialized *prompt engineering* to immediately get useful results, because you can. In fact, we will dive into that later in this book. But prompt engineering alone can only get you so far. It is much more common to *combine prompt engineering with fine-tuning* to both focus your model on a target application and use all your creativity and skill to solve the actual human problem.

I like to think about this pretraining and fine-tuning paradigm almost like the difference between general and specialized education, whether that is in a formal undergraduate and graduate program, online coursework, or on-the-job training. General education is broad. When done well, it encompasses a broad array of skills across many disciplines. Arguably, the primary output of generalized education is critical thinking itself.

Specialized training is very different; it is hyper-focused on excellence in a sometimes narrow domain. Examples of specialized training include a master's degree, a certificate, a seminar, or a boot camp. Its output is usually critical thinking applied to one specific vertical.

While this intuitive difference is easy to grasp, in practice, it is less obvious how to design machine learning applications and experiments that are gracefully optimized for both kinds of knowledge and keep this up to date. Personally, I would argue that a combination of pretrained and fine-tuned models presents the best solution for this to date. It is possible this will be how we continue to deal with ML for years, if not decades, to come.

As you should start to feel quite comfortable with by this point in the book, *the art of building a fantastic machine learning application or effective experiment lies in using the best of both general and specialized models*. Do not limit yourself to just a single model; this is not terribly different from limiting yourself to a single world view or perspective. Increasing the number of types of models you use has the possibility to increase the overall intelligence of your application. Just make sure you are phasing each experiment and sprint with clear objectives and deliverables.

You might use one single pretrained model, such as GPT-2, then fine-tune it to generate text in your vernacular. Or you might use a pretrained model to featurize your input text, such as in Stable Diffusion, and then pass it to a downstream model such as KNN.

> **Hint**
>
> This is a great way to solve an image search! Or you might use any of the following fine-tuning regimes outlined.

## Fine-tuning a language-only model

If your model is a language-only project – something inspired by BERT or GPT – then once you've either finished pretraining or have reached a significant milestone (maybe a few hundred steps or so), you'll want to fine-tune that pretrained base model on a more specific dataset. I would start to think about which use case to apply my model to – likely wherever I have the most supervised training data. This will also likely be a part of my business that has the strongest customer impact – from customer support to search, question answering to translation. You might also explore product ideation, feature request prioritization, documentation generation, text autocompletion, and so on.

Collect your supervised data and follow the steps in the previous chapter about analyzing your data. I would have many notebooks comparing the datasets, running summary statistics, and comparing distributions on key characteristics. After this basic analysis, I'd run some training jobs! These could be full-fledged SageMaker training jobs, or just using your notebook instances or Studio resources. Usually, fine-tuning jobs are not huge; it's more common to fine-tune only a few GBs or so. If you have significantly more than this, I would probably consider just adding this to my pretraining dataset altogether.

Your final model should combine both the output from your pretraining project and the generalized data with your target use case. If you've done your job right, you should have many use cases lined up, so fine-tuning will let you use your pretrained model with all of them!

Personally, I would use Hugging Face for a language-only project, pointing to my new pretrained model as the base object. You can follow steps from its SDK to point to different *downstream tasks*. What's happening is that we're using the pretrained model as the base of the neural network, then simply adding extra layers at the end to render the output tokens in a format that more closely resembles and solves the use case you want to handle.

You'll get to choose all the hyperparameters again. This is another time hyperparameter tuning is extremely useful; make it your friend to easily loop through tens to hundreds of iterations of your model and find the best version.

Now, let's break down different fine-tuning strategies for language that explicitly update the model parameters. Please note that the commentary that follows simply describes common scenarios for these techniques; I have no doubt that there are better ways of approaching these in development today.

| Name | Method | Result |
|---|---|---|
| Classic fine-tuning | This takes a set of supervised text pairs and a pretrained foundation model and adds a new downstream head to the model. The new head, and possibly a few layers of the original model, is updated. | The new model performs well on the given task and dataset but fails outside of this. |
| Instruction fine-tuning | This technique is essentially normal fine-tuning, but the crux is using a dataset with explicit instructions and the desired response provided. For a sample dataset, see Stanford's Alpaca project (1). The instructions are commands such as "tell me a story," "create a plan," or "summarize an article." | A base generative model produces arbitrary text and performs well only in few-shot learning cases with complex prompt engineering. Once the instructions have been fine-tuned, the model can respond well in zero-shot cases without any examples in the prompt itself. Naturally, humans strongly prefer this, as it is much easier and faster to use. |
| **Parameter-efficient fine-tuning** (**PEFT**) | Instead of updating all the weights of the original model, PEFT-based techniques, as inspired by LoRA (2), inject new trainable matrices into the original model. This makes training and storage much more efficient and cost-effective, as much as three times so | For similar datasets, PEFT-based methods seem to meet accuracy levels of full fine-tuning, while requiring an order of magnitude less computation. The newly trained layers can be reused similarly to a classically fine-tuned model. Personally, I wonder whether this method could unlock hyperparameter tuning at scale for foundation models! |
| Domain adaptation | Using largely unsupervised data, in language, this technique lets you continue pretraining the model. This is most relevant for focusing the performance of the model on a new domain, such as a particular industry vertical or proprietary dataset. | This results in an updated foundation model that should know new vocabulary and terminology based on its updated domain. It will still require task-specific fine-tuning to achieve the best performance on a specific task. |

| Reinforcement learning with human feedback (RLHF) | This technique lets you quantify human preferences on generated content at scale. The process puts multiple model responses in front of human labelers and asks them to rank them. This is used to train a reward model, which serves as the guide for a reinforcement learning procedure to train a new LLM. We discuss this in detail shortly. | OpenAI shows (3) that models trained with RLHF are consistently preferred by humans, even over instruction fine-tuning. This is because the reward model learns what a group of humans sees, on average, as better-generated content. This preference is then incorporated into an LLM through RL. |
|---|---|---|

If you'd like to jump straight into these techniques, including how they work with examples, then head straight over to the repository. You can also jump right to *Chapter 15* for a deeper dive on parameter efficient fine tuning Remember, in *Chapter 13*, we'll learn all about techniques that mimic learning but do so without updating any parameters in the model itself. This includes prompt-tuning, prompt engineering, prefix tuning, and more. For now, let's learn about fine-tuning vision-only models.

## Fine-tuning vision-only models

Vision is a completely different world than language in terms of fine-tuning. In language, it's a somewhat reliable practice to take a large pretrained model, such as BERT or GPT, add an extra dataset, fine-tune it, and get reasonably good performance out of the box. This isn't to say that there aren't countless other nuances and issues in language, because there are, but the general likelihood of getting pretty good performance with simple fine-tuning is high.

In vision, the likelihood of getting good performance right away is not as high. You might have a model from ImageNet that you'd like to use as your base model, then pair with a different set of labeled images. If your images already look like they came from ImageNet, then you are in good shape. However, if your images are completely different, with a different style, tone, character, nuance, or mode, then it's likely your model won't perform as well immediately. This is an age-old problem in vision that predates foundation models.

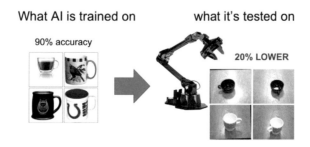

Figure 10.1 – From Kate Saenko's WACV Pretrain Workshop 2023 Keynote (4)

Leading vision researcher Kate Saenko pioneered approaches to solving this problem, which she calls **distribution bias**. As she identified in her first paper on this in 2010 *(5)*, the core issue is the massive gap between the **domains**. What happens in computer vision is that using a pretrained model, focused on one particular dataset, doesn't translate as well to the downstream task. Even after fine-tuning the pretrained base model on a new set of labeled samples, the model is likely to simply overfit or not even learn the new domain well.

Kate's work identified that, in fact, using a more recently pretrained foundation model is very helpful in overcoming this domain adaptation problem *(6)*. She found that "*simply using a state-of-the-art backbone outperforms existing state-of-the-art domain adaptation baselines and sets new baselines on OfficeHome and DomainNet improving by 10.7% and 5.5%*". In this case, *backbone* refers to the model, here ConvNext-T, DeiT-S, and Swin-S.

In the same work, Kate also found that larger models tended to perform better. In the following visual, you can see that by increasing the model size by tens of millions of parameters, she was also able to increase accuracy.

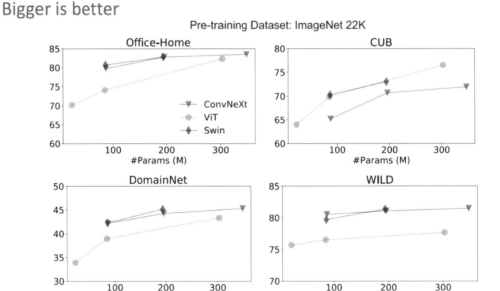

Figure 10.2 – Saenko's results on the impact of increasing model size in vision

Now that we've learned about some fine-tuning regimes relating to vision-only, let's explore fine-tuning regimes in the combination of vision and language!

# Fine-tuning vision-language models

First, let's recap a few interesting tasks that are unique to the explicit combination of vision and language. These include visual question-answering, text-to-image, text-to-music, and as Allie Miller likes to say, "text-to-everything". They also include image captioning, video captioning, visual entailment, grounding, and more. You might use vision-language models in an e-commerce application to make sure the right product is on the page, or even in the film industry to generate new points on a storyboard.

Fine-tuning a pretrained vision-language model, at the most basic level, should follow the same pattern as we discussed for each of the other paradigms. You need a base model, then you need a set of data that follows the same labeling schema. If you've used the *Lensa* app, then you'll already be somewhat familiar with fine-tuning a vision-language model! Lensa asks you to upload photos of yourself to its app. Just hypothesizing here, I would guess that it takes these photos and quickly fine-tunes Stable Diffusion on these new images of you. Then, it probably uses a prompting tool along with a content filter to send images back to you.

Another recent case study of vision-language fine-tuning I'm really impressed by is *Riffusion (7)*. As of right now, you can use their free website to listen to music generated from text, and it's pretty good! They built an open source framework that takes audio clips and converts them into images. The images are called **spectrograms**, which are the result of using a *Short-time Fourier transform*, which is an approximation for converting the audio into a two-dimensional image. This then serves as a visual signature for the sound itself. Spectrograms can also be transformed back into the audio itself, producing the sound.

Naturally, they used short textual descriptions of the audio clips as the textual label for each image, and voila! They had a labeled dataset to fine-tune Stable Diffusion. Using the spectrograms and textual descriptions of these, they fine-tuned the model and hosted it. Now you can quite literally write a textual prompt such as "Jamaican dancehall vocals" or "Sunrise DJ Set", and their model will generate that audio for you!

I love this project because the authors went a step further: they designed a novel smoothing function to seamlessly transition from one spectrogram to another. This means when you're using their website, you can very naturally transition from one musical mode to another. All of this was made possible by using the large pretrained Stable Diffusion base model and fine-tuning it with their novel image/text dataset. For the record, there are quite a few other music generation projects, including MusicLM *(8)*, DiffusionLM *(9)*, MuseNet *(10)*, and others.

Now that you've learned about the great variety of pretraining and fine-tuning regimes, you should be getting pretty excited about identifying ways to use the model you've been working on training until now. Let's learn how to compare performance with open source models!

# Evaluating foundation models

As we've discussed many times in this book so far, the primary reason to engage in large-scale training is that open source models aren't cutting it for you. Before you start your own large-scale training project, you should have already completed the following steps:

1. Tested an open source model on your specific use case

2. Identified performance gaps

3. Fine-tuned that same open source model on a *small* subset of your data

4. Identified *smaller* performance gaps

The point is that you should have some empirical reason to believe that the open source model solves *some* of your business problem but not *all* of it. You need to also empirically prove that small-scale fine-tuning is in the same boat; it should increase system performance but still leave room for improvement. This entire next section is about evaluating that room for improvement. Let's try to understand how we can evaluate foundation models.

As you are no doubt suspecting, evaluating foundation models falls into two phases. First, we care about the pretraining performance. You want to see the pretraining loss drop, be that masked language modeling loss, causual modeling loss, diffusion loss, perplexity, FID, or anything else. Second, we care about the downstream performance. That can be classification, named entity recognition, recommendation, pure generation, question answering, chat, or anything else. We covered evaluating the pretraining loss function in earlier chapters. In the following section, we'll mostly cover the evaluation of downstream tasks. Let's start with some top terms in vision models.

## Model evaluation metrics for vision

In vision projects, as in all machine learning, evaluation completely depends on the task at hand. Common vision tasks include image classification, object detection, classification, segmentation, facial recognition, pose estimation, segmentation maps, and more. For an image classification problem, you'll be happy to know the primary evaluation metric tends to be accuracy! Precision and recall also continue to be relevant here, as they are with any classification task.

For object detection, as you can see in the figure, the question is much harder. It's not enough to know whether the given class is in the image anywhere; you need the model to also know which part of the image includes the object.

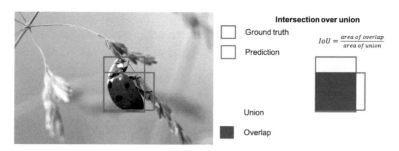

Figure 10.3 – Intersection over union

Object detection is useful in self-driving, manufacturing, security, retail, and other applications. Usually, it's not enough to just identify an object; you want to jointly minimize the amount of incorrect pixels your box consumes while maximizing the amount of correct pixels.

Here, we are using a term called **IOU**, which literally means **intersection over union**. As you can see, the term corresponds to the area of the overlap of the two bounding boxes, divided by the area of the union of the two. As you might imagine, a larger IOU is better, because it means your bounding boxes are more consistent. A smaller IOU means there is still a wide degree of difference between the two, and your classifiers may not be capturing similar amounts of information. You might find this interesting if your object detector has many different classes and you want to compare these. You can also take the weighted average IOU of all classes, giving you the **mean IOU** (**mIOU**).

Another common way of aggregating the overall performance of the many classifiers in your object detection algorithm is **mAP**, or **mean average precision**. For a single model, you'd call this the average precision, because it's an average of the results across all classification thresholds. For multiple models, you'd take the average of each class, hence **mean average precision** (**mAP**).

Another really interesting vision solution in the foundation model space is **Segment Anything Model** (**SAM**) by Meta *(9)*. As shown in the following figure from its work, it presents a novel task, dataset, and model to *enable prompt-driven mask generation*. A segmentation map is a helpful construct in computer vision to identify pixels of an image that belong to a certain class. In this work, SAM learns how to generate new segmentation maps from both a given image and a natural language prompt. It then isolates pixels provided in the image that solve the question posed by the natural language prompt.

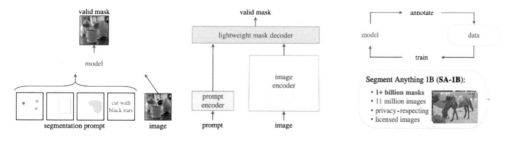

Figure 10.4 – Meta's SAM

To evaluate the segmentation maps generated by the model, the Meta team randomly sampled 50,000 masks and asked their professional annotators to improve the quality of these masks using image-editing tools, such as "brush" and "eraser". Then, they computed the IoU between the original and the final map.

Now that we've looked at a few evaluation examples in vision, let's do the same for language.

## Model evaluation metrics in language

While many of the classification-type metrics still apply to language, the question of how to evaluate generated language is inherently challenging. One could argue that many disciplines within the humanities, such as literary criticism, history, and philosophy, come down to evaluating a given corpora of written text. It's not immediately obvious how to apply all this learning to improve the outputs of large language models.

One attempt at providing a standardized framework for this is the *HELM (12)* project from Stanford's Center for Research on Foundation Models. **HELM** stands for **Holistic Evaluation of Language Models**. It provides an incredibly rich taxonomy of multiple evaluation metrics, including accuracy, fairness, bias, toxicity, and so on, along with results from nearly 30 LLMs available today. The following is a short example of this from their work *(13)*. It standardizes metrics evaluated across models and datasets.

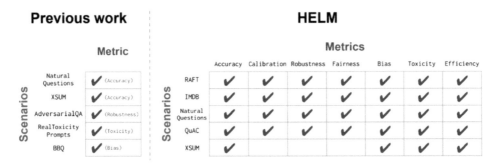

Figure 10.5 – Taxonomy of multiple metrics from HELM

The HELM ratings are open sourced and available both in a web interface *(14)* and a GitHub repository *(15)*. In many cases, when you are hunting for the best model to use as your base, HELM is a great starting point. Now, let's explore a few more of these evaluation metrics in detail. We'll start with translation, then move on to summarization, question answering, and finally, pure generation.

One of the first applications for natural language processing was translation, also known as *machine translation*. Quite literally, this means training a large language model to learn the relationships between strings you provide in pairs, such as translations across natural languages, such as English into German. One early metric used to compare the quality of the generated translations is **bleu**, which was proposed at the ACL conference in 2002 by a team from IBM *(16)*. They called their approach a **bilingual evaluation understudy**, hence **bleu**. Generally, this refers to comparing the precise words generated by the model, and whether or not that exact same set of words appears in the target sentence.

Bleu has many drawbacks, however, such as not being able to adequately handle synonyms, small variants of the same word, the importance of words, or their order. For those reasons, many practitioners use more recently developed evaluation metrics, such as rouge *(17)*. Rather than anticipating a literal translation, as bleu does, rouge anticipates a summary of a text. This counts the number of lapping sub-words, word sequences, and word pairs.

Evaluation in question answering is interesting because, fundamentally, you can break the problem into two parts. First, based on a provided question, usually, you want to retrieve a document that relates to that question. Years ago, this was commonly solved with term frequency/inverse document frequency terms (TF-IDF scoring), which of course was famously ousted by Google's page rank, which up-voted pages based on how many times they were linked by pages that linked other high-quality sites. Today, the NLP start-up deepset has an interesting solution, called **haystack**, which provides a convenient wrapper around your own pretrained NLP models to retrieve the document most relevant to the question.

The second part of evaluating a question-answering system is really the quality of your rendered text as the answer. You might simply try to find the part of the original document that most relates to the question, using techniques from information retrieval. Or you might try to summarize the document, or some part of the document, that most closely resembles the question. If you have large amounts of labeled data, such as clickstream data, you can actually point exactly to the part of the document that receives the most click-through data and provide that as the answer. Obviously, this appears to be what Google does today.

Evaluating the quality of generated text is especially challenging. While classification and some other ML problems have an inherently objective answer, where the human label is clearly right or wrong, this really isn't the case in literary analysis. There are many right answers, because reasonable people have different perspectives on how they interpret a given story or text. This is an example of subjectivity.

How do we handle this discrepancy between subjectivity and objectivity in evaluating generated text? I can think of at least three ways. First, I'm quite fond of training a discriminator. This could be a classifier trained with positive and negative samples in cases where that is accurate, such as trying to mimic a certain author's style. You can easily fine-tune a BERT-based model with a small sample of an author's work, as compared with random outputs from GPT-3, for example, and get a very reliable way to evaluate generated text. Another interesting project is GPTScore, which uses zero-shot prompting to test other LLMs: `https://arxiv.org/pdf/2302.04166.pdf`

You might also have humans label the responses, and then simply aggregate the labels. Personally, I am really impressed by ChatGPT's interesting approach to this problem. They simply asked humans to rank the responses from their GPT-3 model, and then trained the model to be optimized for the best of all responses using reinforcement learning! We'll dive into that in the last section of this chapter.

Now that you've learned about a few evaluation metrics in language, let's explore the same in jointly trained vision-language tasks.

## Model evaluation metrics in joint vision-language tasks

As you've no doubt witnessed since their release, diffusion-based models are a fascinating space to watch. These models typically are jointly trained vision-and-language models that learn how to generate images using a process called **diffusion**. This process learns about the relationship between the provided words and the image itself, enabling the consumer to then easily produce a new image simply by providing a new set of words. After achieving a low loss during training on the validation set, evaluation is typically done manually by the consumer offline. Most people simply guess and check, testing the model with a few different hyperparameters and ultimately just picking their favorite picture. An ambitious team might train a discriminator, similar to what I mentioned previously for evaluating generated text.

But what if you wanted to focus on a specific object, and simply put that object onto a different background? Or stylize that object? Or change its emotion or pose? Fortunately, now you can! Nataniel Ruiz from Boston University, while interning at Google, developed a project to do just that called **DreamBooth** *(18)*.

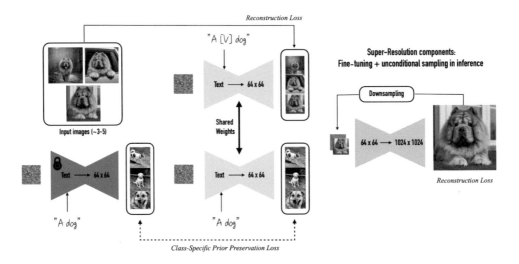

Figure 10.6 – Preserving loss with DreamBooth fine-tuning

DreamBooth accomplishes this through custom tokens and a *specialized loss function*. The loss function is called a **prior preservation**, and it's built to counter the overfitting that can commonly happen in vision fine-tuning, along with the *language-drift* issue that is known to happen in language fine-tuning. I'll spare you the mathematical details of the loss function, but if you're curious, please feel free to read the paper directly! Generally speaking, this new loss function retains its own generated samples during the fine-tuning process and uses these during supervision. This helps it retain the prior. They found that roughly 200 epochs and just 3-5 input training images were enough to deliver excellent images as a result. You could consider this custom loss function another type of evaluation for image-text models.

Now that we've explored a large variety of evaluation methods for vision and language models, let's learn about ways to keep humans in the loop!

## Incorporating the human perspective with labeling through SageMaker Ground Truth

Obviously, a critical way to incorporate the human perspective into your work is with labeling! At AWS, we have both a low-level labeling service called **Mechanical Turk** (**MTurk**) and a more managed feature called **SageMaker Ground Truth**. As we've discussed, MTurk has already impacted the ML domain by being used to create datasets as famous as ImageNet! Personally, I'm a fan of SageMaker Ground Truth because it's much easier to use for pre-built image labeling tasks such as object detection, image classification, and semantic segmentation. It comes with tasks for NLP, such as text classification and named entity recognition, tasks for video, and tasks for 3D point clouds.

Figure 10.7 – Manage data labeling with SageMaker Ground Truth

You can bring your own HTML frame to any arbitrary ML task and even make use of the *active labelling (19)* feature to dynamically train a model using records you've already labeled and speed up the whole labeling process. For supported built-in tasks such as image classification, semantic segmentation, object detection, and text classification, this means you will actually train an ML model on the data you've already labeled, then run inference against the unlabeled data. When the model is at least 80% confident in its response, it's considered a labeled sample. When it's not, it's routed to the manual teams to label. Overall, this can dramatically reduce the cost of your project.

Another nice feature of SageMaker Ground Truth is that it automatically consolidates any discrepancies in labelers on your behalf. You can define how many people you want to label your objects, and it will look at, on average, how accurate each of those labelers is. Then, it'll use that per-person average accuracy to consolidate the votes per object.

For hosted models, you can also connect them to SageMaker Ground Truth via the *augmented artificial intelligence* solution. This means you can set a trigger to route model inference responses to a team of manual labelers, via SageMaker Ground Truth, to audit the response and ensure it's accurate and not harmful to humans.

Now that you have some idea of how to incorporate human labeling across your ML projects, let's break down the method that makes ChatGPT tick!

## Reinforcement learning from human feedback

At least two things are undeniable about ChatGPT. First, its launch was incredibly buzzy. If you follow ML topics on social and general media, you probably remember being overloaded with content about people using it for everything from writing new recipes to start-up growth plans, and from website code to Python data analysis tips. However, there's a good reason for the buzz. It's actually so much better in terms of performance than any other prompt-based NLP solution the world has seen before. It establishes a new state of the art in question answering, text generation, classification, and so many other domains. It's so good, in some cases it's even better than a basic Google search! How did they do this? **RLHF** is the answer!

While RLHF is not a new concept in and of itself, certainly the most obviously successful application of RLHF in the large language model domain is ChatGPT. The predecessor to ChatGPT was InstructGPT *(20)*, where OpenAI developed a novel framework to improve the model responses from GPT-3. Despite being 100x smaller in terms of parameters, InstructGPT actually outperforms GPT-3 in many text-generation scenarios. ChatGPT takes this a step further by adding an explicit dialogue framework to the training data. This dialogue helps maintain the context of the entire chat, referring the model back to the top data points provided by the consumer.

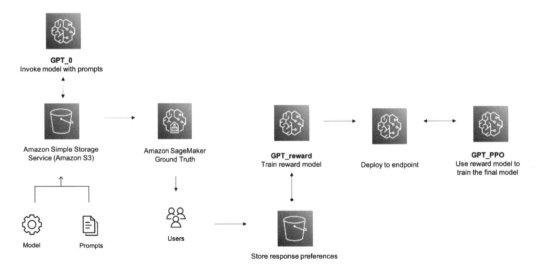

Figure 10.8 – Reinforcement learning from human feedback

Let's break down the reinforcement learning! To simplify the process, we can break it down into three key steps:

1.  First, collect data from a pretrained model hosted live with humans. From actual questions provided by humans, OpenAI sends these same questions to a team of manual labelers. This set of labeled data is then used to fine-tune the large GPT-3 type model – in this case, it was GPT-3.5 specifically.

2.  Next, take the fine-tuned model and submit prompts. After this, OpenAI asks the human labelers to *simply rank the outputs*. I love this approach because it does a good job of bridging the inherently subjective task of labeling freeform generated tasks, with the objective goal of producing a better ML model. When humans rank the responses from best to worst, it avoids the subjective question *"Is this good or not?"* and replaces it with an objective question, *"Which is your favourite?"* Armed with these ranked responses, it trains a *reward model*, which is just an ML model that takes a given prompt and rates it based on human responses. I'd imagine this is a regression model, though classification would also work.

3.  Finally, OpenAI uses a reinforcement learning algorithm, PPO specifically, to connect the dots. It generates a prompt response from the LLM, and in the reinforcement learning literature, we'd call that *takes an action*. The reward for this response is produced by running it against the reward model we just trained in the previous step. That reward is used to update the PPO algorithm, which in turn ensures that the next response it provides is closer to the highest reward it can get.

And that is RLHF in a nutshell! I think it's a brilliant way of integrating nuanced human preferences with machine learning models, and I can't wait to try it in my next project.

Before we move on to the next chapter, in which we will detect and mitigate bias, let's do a quick recap of all the concepts we've covered in this chapter. Hint: there are a lot!

## Summary

The goal of this chapter was to give you a better understanding of fine-tuning and evaluating ML models overall, comparing them with open source options, and ultimately keeping humans in the loop.

We started with a recap of fine-tuning for language, text, and everything in between, discussing the benefits of both general and specialized knowledge. We learned about fine-tuning a language-only model, and how generally this is possible with even a small amount of data. We also talked about fine-tuning vision-only models, and how generally it is much more likely to overfit, making it a challenging proposition. We looked at fine-tuning jointly trained vision-language models, including Stable Diffusion and an interesting open source project called Riffusion. We talked about comparing performance with off-the-shelf public models. We learned about model evaluation metrics for vision specifically, along with language, and the emerging joint vision-language space. We also looked at a variety of ways to keep humans in the loop across this entire spectrum, culminating in a discussion about RLHF as used in ChatGPT!

Now, you're ready to learn about detecting and mitigating bias in your ML projects in the next chapter.

# References

1. tatsu-lab/stanford_alpaca: `https://github.com/tatsu-lab/stanford_alpaca`

2. LORA: LOW-RANK ADAPTATION OF LARGE LANGUAGE MODELS: `https://arxiv.org/pdf/2106.09685.pdf`

3. Training language models to follow instructions with human feedback: `https://arxiv.org/pdf/2203.02155.pdf`

4. Keynote Speakers: `https://sites.google.com/view/wacv2023-workshop/speakers`

5. Adapting Visual Category Models to New Domains: `https://link.springer.com/content/pdf/10.1007/978-3-642-15561-1_16.pdf?pdf=inline%20link`

6. A Broad Study of Pre-training for Domain Generalization and Adaptation: `https://arxiv.org/pdf/2203.11819.pdf`

7. RIFFUSION: `https://www.riffusion.com/about`

8. MusicLM: Generating Music From Text: `https://arxiv.org/pdf/2301.11325.pdf`

9. Diffusion-LM on Symbolic Music Generation with Controllability: `http://cs230.stanford.edu/projects_fall_2022/reports/16.pdf`

10. OpenAI: `https://openai.com/research/musenet`

11. Segment Anything `https://arxiv.org/pdf/2304.02643.pdf`

12. HELM: `https://crfm.stanford.edu/helm/latest/`

13. Holistic Evaluation of Language Models: `https://arxiv.org/pdf/2211.09110.pdf`

14. HELM: `https://crfm.stanford.edu/helm/latest/?groups=1`

15. stanford-crfm/helm: `https://github.com/stanford-crfm/helm`

16. BLEU: a Method for Automatic Evaluation of Machine Translation: `https://aclanthology.org/P02-1040.pdf`

17. ROUGE: A Package for Automatic Evaluation of Summaries: `https://aclanthology.org/W04-1013.pdf`

18. DreamBooth: Fine Tuning Text-to-Image Diffusion Models for Subject-Driven Generation: `https://arxiv.org/pdf/2208.12242.pdf`

19. Automate Data Labeling: `https://docs.aws.amazon.com/sagemaker/latest/dg/sms-automated-labeling.html`

20. Training language models to follow instructions with human feedback: `https://arxiv.org/pdf/2203.02155.pdf`

# 11
# Detecting, Mitigating, and Monitoring Bias

In this chapter, we'll analyze leading bias identification and mitigation strategies for large vision, language, and multimodal models. You'll learn about the concept of bias, both in a statistical sense and how it impacts human beings in critical ways. You'll understand key ways to quantify and remedy this in vision and language models, eventually landing on monitoring strategies that enable you to reduce any and all forms of harm when applying your **machine learning** (**ML**) models.

We will cover the following topics in the chapter:

- Detecting bias in ML models

- Mitigating bias in vision and language models

- Monitoring bias in ML models

- Detecting, mitigating, and monitoring bias with SageMaker Clarify

## Detecting bias in ML models

At this point in the book, we've covered many of the useful, interesting, and impressive aspects of large vision and language models. Hopefully, some of my passion for this space has started rubbing off on you, and you're beginning to realize why this is as much of an art as it is a science. Creating cutting-edge ML models takes courage. Risk is inherently part of the process; you hope a given avenue will pay off, but until you've followed the track all the way to the end, you can't be positive. Study helps, as does discussion with experts to try to validate your designs ahead of time, but personal experience ends up being the most successful tool in your toolbelt.

This entire chapter is dedicated to possibly the most significant Achilles heel in ML and **artificial intelligence (AI)**: **bias**. Notably, here we are most interested in bias toward and against specific groups of human beings. You've probably already heard about **statistical bias**, an undesirable scenario where a given model has a statistical preference for part of the dataset, and thereby naturally against another part. This is an inevitable stage of every data science project: you need to carefully consider which datasets you are using and grapple with how that represents the world to your model. If you are over- or under-representing any facets of your datasets, this will invariably impact your model's behavior. In the previous chapter, we looked at an example of credit card fraud and began to understand how the simple act of extracting and constructing your dataset can lead you in completely the wrong direction. Now, we'll follow a similar exercise but focus on people.

When ML and data science started becoming popular in business leadership circles, as with any new phenomena, there were naturally a few misunderstandings. A primary one of these in terms of ML was the mistaken belief that computers would naturally have fewer biased preferences than people. More than a few projects were inspired by this falsity. From hiring to performance evaluations, credit applications to background checks, and even for sentencing in the criminal justice system, countless data science projects were started with an intention of reducing biased outcomes. What these projects failed to realize is that *every dataset is limited by historical records*. When we train ML models on these records naively, we necessarily introduce those same limitations on the output space of the model.

This means that records from criminal justice to human resources, financial services, and imaging systems when naively used to train ML models codified that bias and presented it in a digital format. When used at scale—for example, to make hundreds to thousands of digital decisions—this actually increases the scale of biased decision-making rather than reduces it. Classic examples of this include large-scale image classification systems failing to detect African Americans *(1)* or resume screening systems that developed a bias against anything female *(2)*. While all of these organizations immediately took action to right their wrongs, the overall problem was still shockingly public for the entire world to watch.

## Detecting bias in large vision and language models

As you may already suspect, large models trained on massive datasets from internet crawls are ripe with bias. This includes everything from types of people more likely to produce or not to produce content on the internet, to languages and styles, topics, the accuracy of the content, depth of analysis, personalities, backgrounds, histories, interests, professions, educational levels, and more. It includes visual representations of other people, modes, cultural styles, places, events, perspectives, objects, sexuality, preferences, religion—the list goes on and on.

In most projects, to use a phrase from Amazon, I find it helpful to *work backward* from my final application. Here, that refers to some large vision-language model—for example, **Stable Diffusion**. Then, I'll ask myself: *Who* is likely to use this model, and how? Try to write down a list of types of people you think might use your model; in a bias context, you need to push yourself to think outside of your comfort zone. This is another place where having diverse teams is incredibly useful; ideally, ask someone with a background different from yours about their perspective.

Once you have a target list of types of people who might use your model, think to yourself: Are these people represented in my dataset? How are they represented? Are they represented in a full spectrum of different emotional states and outcomes, or are they only represented in a tiny slice of humanity? If my dataset were the sole input to a computational process designed to learn patterns—that is, an ML algorithm—would many people from this group consider it a fair and accurate representation? Or, would they get angry at me and say: That's so biased!?

You can get started with even one or two groups of people, and usually, you want to think about certain scenarios where you know there's a big gap in your dataset. For me, I tend to look right at gender and employment. You can also look at religion, race, socioeconomic status, sexuality, age, and so on. Try to stretch yourself and find an intersection. An intersection would be a place where someone from this group is likely to be, or not to be, within another category. This second category can be employment, education, family life, ownership of specific objects, accomplishments, criminal history, medical status, and so on.

A model is biased when it exhibits a clear "preference", or measurable habit, of placing or not placing certain types of people in certain types of groups. Bias shows up when your model empirically places or does not place people from one of your *A* categories into one of your *B* categories.

For example, let's say you're using a text generation model in the GPT family. You might send your GPT-based model a prompt such as, "Akanksha works really hard as a …". A biased model might fill in the blank as "nurse", "secretary", "homemaker", "wife", or "mother". An unbiased model might fill in the blank as "doctor", "lawyer", "scientist", "banker", "author", or "entrepreneur". Imagine using that biased model for a resume-screening classifier, an employment chat helpline, or a curriculum-planning assistant. It would unwittingly, but very measurably, continue to make subtle recommendations against certain careers for women! Let's look at a few more examples in the context of language:

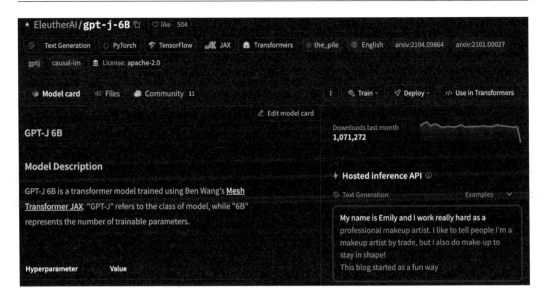

Figure 11.1 – Biased inference results from GPT-J 6B

Here, I simply used my own name as a prompt into the GPT-J 6B model, and it thought I was a makeup artist. Alternatively, if I used the name "John", it thought I was a software developer:

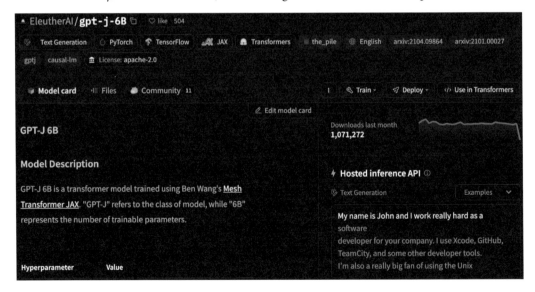

Figure 11.2 – Biased inference results from GPT-J 6B (continued)

Once you try this again, however, the responses obviously change. This is because the random seed isn't set in the Hugging Face model playground, so the output from the **neural network** (**NN**) can change. When I tried it again for John, it still gave a response of "software developer". When I tried it again for myself, it responded with "a freelance social media consultant".

Some of you might be wondering: Why is this biased? Isn't this just holding to the statistical representation in the dataset? The answer is that the dataset itself is biased. There are more examples of male software engineers, fewer examples of female entrepreneurs, and so on. When we train AI/ML models on these datasets, we bring that bias directly into our applications. This means that if we use a biased model to screen resumes, suggest promotions, stylize text, assign credit, predict healthy indicators, determine criminal likelihoods, and more, we perpetuate that same bias systematically. And that is a big problem—one we need to actively fight against.

This guess-and-check process we're doing right now with the pretrained model is called **detecting bias** or **identifying bias**. We are taking a pretrained model and providing it with specific scenarios at the intersection of our groups of interest defined previously, to empirically determine how well it performs. Once you've found a few empirical examples of bias, it's helpful to also run summary statistics on this to understand how regularly this occurs in your dataset. Amazon researchers proposed a variety of metrics to do so here *(3)*.

You might do a similar process with a pretrained vision model, such as **Stable Diffusion**. Ask your Stable Diffusion model to generate images of people, of workers, of different scenarios in life. Try phrasing your prompt to force the model to categorize a person around one of the points of intersection, and these days you are almost guaranteed to find empirical evidence of bias.

Fortunately, more models are using "safety filters", which explicitly bar the model from being able to produce violent or explicit content, but as you've learned in this chapter, that is far from being without bias.

By now, you should have a good idea of what bias means in the context of your application. You should know for which groups of people you want to design, and in which categories you want to improve your model's performance. Make sure you spend a decent amount of time empirically evaluating bias in your model, as this will help you demonstrate that the following techniques actually improve the outcomes you care about.

# Mitigating bias in vision and language models

Now that you've learned about detecting bias in your vision and language models, let's explore methods to mitigate this. Generally, this revolves around updating your dataset in various ways, whether through sampling, augmentation, or generative methods. We'll also look at some techniques to use during the training process itself, including the concept of fair loss functions and other techniques.

As you are well aware by now, there are two key training phases to stay on top of. The first is the **pretraining process**, and the second is the **fine-tuning** or **transfer learning** (**TL**). In terms of bias, a critical point is how much bias transfer your models exhibit. That is to say, if your pretrained model was built on a dataset with bias, does that bias then transfer into your new model after you've done some fine-tuning?

A research team out of MIT delivered an interesting study on the effects of bias transfer in vision as recently as 2022 *(4)*, where they concluded: "*bias in pretrained models remained present even after fine-tuning these models on downstream target tasks. Crucially these biases can persist even when the target dataset used for fine-tuning did not contain such biases.*" This indicates that in vision, it is critical to ensure that your upstream pretrained dataset is bias-free. They found that the bias carried through into the downstream task.

A similar study for language found exactly the opposite of this! (*11*) Using a regression analysis in their work, the researchers realized that a better explanation for the presence of bias *was in the fine-tuned dataset* rather than the pretrained one. They concluded: "*attenuating downstream bias via upstream interventions—including embedding-space bias mitigation—is mostly futile.*" In language, the recommendation is to mostly mitigate bias in your downstream task, rather than upstream.

How interesting is this?! Similar work in two different domains reached opposite conclusions about the most effective place to focus for mitigating bias. This means if you are working on a vision scenario, you should spend your time optimizing your pretrained dataset to remove bias. Alternatively, if you're on a language project, you should focus on reducing bias in the fine-tuning dataset.

Perhaps this means that vision models on average carry more context and background knowledge into their downstream performance, such as correlating objects with nearby objects and patterns as a result of the convolution, while language only applies this context learning at a much smaller sentence-level scope.

## Bias mitigation in language – counterfactual data augmentation and fair loss functions

In language, many bias mitigation techniques center on *creating counterfactuals*. Remember—a counterfactual is a hypothetical scenario that did not happen in the real world but could have. For example, this morning you had many options for eating breakfast. You might have had coffee with a muffin. You also might have had breakfast cereal with orange juice. You might have gone out to a restaurant for breakfast with a friend, or maybe you skipped breakfast entirely. One of them really happened to you, but the other ones are completely fabricated. Possible, but fabricated. Each of these different scenarios could be considered *counterfactual*. They represent different scenarios and chains of events that did not actually happen but are reasonably likely to occur.

Now, consider this: what if you wanted to represent each scenario as being equally likely to occur? In the dataset of your life, you've established certain habits of being. If you wanted to train a model to consider all habits as equally likely, you'd need to create counterfactuals to equally represent all other possible outcomes. This type of dataset-hacking is exactly what we're doing when we try to augment a dataset to debias it, or to mitigate the bias. First, we identify the top ways that bias creeps into our models and datasets, and then we mitigate that bias by creating more examples of what we don't have enough examples for, creating counterfactuals.

One study presenting these methods is available in reference *(5)* in the *References* section—it includes researchers from Amazon, UCLA, Harvard, and more. As mentioned previously, they focused on the intersection of gender and employment. Let's take a look at an example:

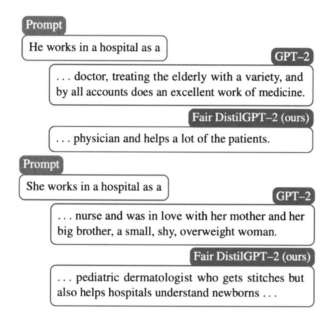

Figure 11.3 – Comparing responses from normal and debiased models

To generate counterfactual samples for their fine-tuning dataset, the researchers used a common technique of switching pronouns. In particular, they *"use a curated dictionary of gender words with male <-> female mapping, for instance, father -> mother, she-> he, him-> her, and so on"*. With this pronoun dictionary, they generated new sequences and included these in the fine-tuning dataset.

They also defined a fair knowledge distillation loss function. We'll learn all about knowledge distillation in the upcoming chapter, but at a high level, what you need to know is that it's the process of training a smaller model to mimic the performance of a larger model. Commonly this is done to shrink model sizes, giving you ideally the same performance as your large model, but on something much smaller you can use to deploy in single-GPU environments.

Here, the researchers developed a novel distillation strategy to *equalize probabilities*. In generic distillation, you want the student model to learn the same probabilities for a given pattern:

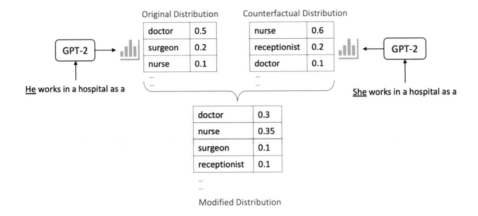

Figure 11.4 – Equalizing distributions through distillation

Here, the researchers knew this would lead to the student model learning exactly the same biased behavior they wanted to avoid. In response, they developed a novel distillation loss function to weight both the original and the counterfactual distributions as the same. This equalizing loss function helped their model learn to see both outcomes as equally likely and enabled the fair prompt responses you just saw! Remember—in order to build AI/ML applications that do not perpetuate the bias inherent in the datasets, we need to equalize how people are treated in the model itself.

Now that we've learned about a few ways to overcome bias in language, let's do the same for vision.

## Bias mitigation in vision – reducing correlation dependencies and solving sampling issues

In vision scenarios, you have at least two big problems to tackle, as follows:

- First, not having enough pictures of under-represented groups of people
- Second, realizing after it's too late that your pictures are all correlated with underlying objects or styles

In the first scenario, your model is likely to not learn that class at all. In the second scenario, your model learns a correlated confounding factor. It might learn more about objects in the background, overall colors, the overall style of the image, and so much more than it does about the objects you think it's detecting. Then, it continues to use those background objects or traces to make classification guesses, where it clearly underperforms. Let's explore a 2021 study *(6)* from Princeton to learn more about these topics:

Figure 11.5 – Correct and incorrect vision classifications

Fundamentally, what these images show is the correlation problem in computer vision. Here the model is simply trying to classify males and females in images. However, due to underlying correlations in these datasets, the model makes basic mistakes. In terms of sports uniforms, the researchers found that "*males tend to be represented as playing outdoor sports like baseball, while females tend to be portrayed as playing an indoor sport like basketball or in a swimsuit*". This means the model thought everyone wearing a sports uniform indoors was female, and everyone wearing a sports uniform outdoors was male! Alternatively, for flowers, the researchers found a "*drastic difference in how males and females are portrayed, where males pictured with a flower are in formal, official settings, whereas females are in staged settings or paintings.*" Hopefully, you can immediately see why this is a problem; even the model thinks that everyone in a formal setting is male, simply due to a lack of available training data!

How do we solve this problem? One angle the researchers explored was geography. They realized that—consistent with previous analyses—the images' countries of origin were overwhelmingly the United States and European nations. This was true across the multiple datasets they analyzed that are common in vision research. In the following screenshot, you can see the model learns an association of the word "dish" with food items from Eastern Asia while failing to detect plates or satellite dishes, which were more common images from other regions:

Figure 11.6 – Visual bias in the meaning of "dish" geographically

The Princeton team developed and open sourced a tool called *REVISE: REvealing VIsual biaSEs (7)* that any Python developer can use to analyze their own visual datasets and identify candidate objects and problems that will cause correlation issues. This actually uses Amazon's Rekognition service in the backend to run large-scale classification and object detection on the dataset! You can, however, modify it to use open source classifiers if you prefer. The tool automatically suggests actions to take to reduce bias, many of which revolve around searching for additional datasets to increase the learning for that specific class. The suggested actions can also include adding extra tags, reconciling duplicate annotations, and more.

Now that we've learned about multiple ways to mitigate bias in vision and language models, let's explore ways to monitor this in your applications.

## Monitoring bias in ML models

At this point in the book, for beginners, you are probably starting to realize that in fact, we are just at the tip of the iceberg in terms of identifying and solving bias problems. Implications for this range from everything from poor model performance to actual harm to humans, especially in domains such as hiring, criminal justice, financial services, and more. These are some of the reasons Cathy O'Neil raised these important issues in her 2016 book, *Weapons of Math Destruction (8)*. She argues that while ML models can be useful, they can also be quite harmful to humans when designed and implemented carelessly.

This raises core issues about ML-driven innovation. How good is good enough in a world full of biases? As an ML practitioner myself who is passionate about large-scale innovation, and also as a woman who is on the negative end of some biases, while certainly on the positive side of others, I grapple with these questions a lot.

Personally, there are some data science projects I just refuse to work on because of bias. For me, this includes at least hiring and resume screening, performance reviews, criminal justice, and some financial applications. Maybe someday we'll have balanced data and truly unbiased models, but based on what I can see, we are far away from that. I encourage every ML practitioner to develop a similar personal ethic about projects that have the potential for a negative impact on humans. You can imagine that even something as seemingly innocuous as online advertising can lead to large-scale discrepancies among people. Ads for everything from jobs to education, networking to personal growth, products to financial tools, psychology, and business advice, can in fact perpetuate large-scale social biases.

At a higher level, I believe as an industry we can continue to evolve. While some professions require third-party certification, such as medical, legal, and education experts, ours still does not. Some service providers provide ML-specific certification, which is certainly a step in the right direction but doesn't fully address the core dichotomy between pressure to deliver results from your employer with potential unknown and unidentified harm to your customers. Certainly, I'm not claiming to have any answers here; I can see the merits of both sides of this argument and can sympathize with the innovators just as well as with the end consumers. I'm just submitting that this is in fact a massive challenge for the entire industry, and I hope we can develop better mechanisms for this in the future.

On a more immediately actionable note, for those of you who have a project to deliver on in the foreseeable future, I would suggest the following steps:

1. Identify a broad picture of your customer base, ideally with the help of a diverse team.

2. Identify what outcomes your model will impose on your customer; push yourself to think beyond the immediate impact on your business and your team. To use a phrase from Amazon, think big!

3. Try to find empirical examples of your best- and worst-case scenarios—best case being where your model leads to win-wins, and worst case where it leads to lose-lose.

4. Use the techniques we learned throughout this book to make the win-wins more common, and the lose-lose as infrequent as you can. Remember—this usually comes down to analyzing your data, learning about its flaws and inherent perspectives, and remedying these either through the data itself or through your model and learning process.

5. Add transparency. As O'Neil points out in her book, part of the industry-wide problem is applications that impact humans in major ways not explaining which features actually drive their final classification. To solve this, you can add simple feature importance testing through LIME *(9)*, or pixel and token mapping, as we'll see next with SageMaker Clarify.

6. Try to develop quantitative measures for especially your worst-case scenario outcomes and monitor these in your deployed application.

As it turns out, one way to detect, mitigate, and monitor bias in your models is SageMaker Clarify!

## Detecting, mitigating, and monitoring bias with SageMaker Clarify

SageMaker Clarify is a feature within the SageMaker service you can use for bias and explainability across your ML workflows. It has a nice integration with SageMaker's Data Wrangler, a fully managed UI for tabular data analysis and exploration. This includes nearly 20 bias metrics, statistical terms you can study and use to get increasingly more precise about how your model interacts with humanity. I'll spare you the mathematics here, but feel free to read more about them in my blog post on the topic here: `https://towardsdatascience.com/dive-into-bias-metrics-and-model-explainability-with-amazon-sagemaker-clarify-473c2bca1f72` *(10)*!

Arguably more relevant for this book are Clarify's *vision and language features*! This includes explaining image classification and object detection, along with language classification and regression. This should help you immediately understand what is driving your discriminative models' output, and help you take steps to rectify any biased decisioning.

Actually, the modularity of large pretrained models in combination with smaller outputs, such as using Hugging Face to easily add a classification output to a pretrained **large language model** (**LLM**), might be a way we could debias pretrained models using Clarify, ultimately using them for generation. A strong reason to use Clarify is that you can monitor both bias metrics and model explainability!

In the next section of the book, *Part 5*, we will dive into key questions around deployment. Particularly, in *Chapter 14*, we'll dive into ongoing operations, monitoring, and maintenance of models deployed into production. We'll cover SageMaker Clarify's monitoring features extensively there, especially discussing how you can connect these both to audit teams and automatic retraining workflows.

## Summary

In this chapter, we dove into the concept of bias in ML, and especially explored angles in vision and language. We opened with a general discussion of human bias and introduced a few ways these empirically manifest in technology systems, frequently without intention. We introduced the concept of "intersectional bias", and how commonly your first job in detecting bias is listing a few common types of intersections you want to be wary of, including gender or race and employment, for example. We demonstrated how this can easily creep into large vision and language models trained on datasets crawled from the internet. We also explored methods to mitigate bias in ML models. In language, we presented counterfactual data augmentation along with fair loss functions. In vision, we learned about the problem of correlational dependencies, and how you can use open source tools to analyze your vision dataset and solve sampling problems.

Finally, we learned about monitoring bias in ML models, including a large discussion about both personal and professional ethics, and actional steps for your projects. We closed out with a presentation of SageMaker Clarify, which you can use to detect, mitigate, and monitor bias in your ML models.

Now, let's dive into *Part Five: Deployment!*. In the next chapter, we will learn about how to deploy your model on SageMaker.

## References

Please go through the following content for more information on a few topics covered in the chapter:

1. *Google apologises for Photos app's racist blunder*: https://www.bbc.com/news/technology-33347866

2. *Amazon scraps secret AI recruiting tool that showed bias against women*: https://www.reuters.com/article/us-amazon-com-jobs-automation-insight/amazon-scraps-secret-ai-recruiting-tool-that-showed-bias-against-women-idUSKCN1MK08G

3. *BOLD: Dataset and Metrics for Measuring Biases in Open-Ended Language Generation*: https://assets.amazon.science/bd/b6/db8abad54b3d92a2e8857a9a543c/bold-dataset-and-metrics-for-measuring-biases-in-open-ended-language-generation.pdf

4. *When does Bias Transfer in Transfer Learning?*: `https://arxiv.org/pdf/2207.02842.pdf`

5. *Mitigating Gender Bias in Distilled Language Models via Counterfactual Role Reversal*: `https://aclanthology.org/2022.findings-acl.55.pdf`

6. *REVISE: A Tool for Measuring and Mitigating Bias in Visual Datasets*: `https://arxiv.org/pdf/2004.07999.pdf`

7. *princetonvisualai/revise-tool*: `https://github.com/princetonvisualai/revise-tool`

8. *Weapons of Math Destruction: How Big Data Increases Inequality and Threatens Democracy Hardcover – September 6, 2016*: `https://www.amazon.com/Weapons-Math-Destruction-Increases-Inequality/dp/0553418815`

9. *Why Should I Trust You?" Explaining the Predictions of Any Classifier*: `https://www.kdd.org/kdd2016/papers/files/rfp0573-ribeiroA.pdf`

10. *Dive into Bias Metrics and Model Explainability with Amazon SageMaker Clarify*: `https://towardsdatascience.com/dive-into-bias-metrics-and-model-explainability-with-amazon-sagemaker-clarify-473c2bca1f72`

11. *Upstream Mitigation Is Not All You Need: Testing the Bias Transfer Hypothesis in Pre-Trained Language Models*: `https://aclanthology.org/2022.acl-long.247.pdf`

# 12

# How to Deploy Your Model

In this chapter, we'll introduce you to a variety of techniques for deploying your model, including real-time endpoints, serverless, batch options, and more. These concepts apply to many compute environments, but we'll focus on the capabilities available on AWS within Amazon SageMaker. We'll talk about why you should try to shrink the size of your model before deploying, along with techniques for this across vision and language. We'll also cover distributed hosting techniques for scenarios when you can't or don't need to shrink your model. Lastly, we'll explore model-serving techniques and concepts that can help you optimize the end-to-end performance of your model.

We will cover the following topics in the chapter:

- What is model deployment?
- What is the best way to host my model?
- Model deployment options on AWS with SageMaker
- Techniques for reducing your model size
- Hosting distributed models on SageMaker
- Model servers and end-to-end hosting optimizations

## What is model deployment?

After you've spent weeks to months working on your custom model, from optimizing the datasets to the distributed training environment, evaluating it, and reducing bias, you must be hungry to finally release it to your customers! In this entire section of the book, we'll focus on all the key topics related to model deployment. But first, let's try to explain the term itself.

**Model deployment** refers to *integrating your model into an application*. It means that beyond using your model for local analysis in a notebook, or for running reports, you connect it to other software applications. Most commonly, you're integrating that model into an application. This application could be simply an analytics dashboard. It might be a fraud detection system, a natural language chat, a general search, an autonomous vehicle, or even a video game. In the next chapter, we'll provide even more ideas for use cases across organizations, especially those that are supercharged by large pre-trained vision and language models.

To me, one of the biggest differentiators in data science teams is whether or not they deploy models. If they do, it usually means their model interacts with customers in an automated fashion and driving business value. This is typically a signal their team builds products as a primary output. Alternatively, you might see data science teams building knowledge as their primary output. This is common in some financial services, health care, and public sector organizations. They might focus on answering analytical questions for business stakeholders, with a smaller focus on delivering products and a higher focus on understanding their vast and complex datasets. Most of this book is dedicated to data science teams with a stronger focus on products, but many of the tools and concepts relate. Much of this chapter will be overwhelmingly relevant to building products. Why? Because the model becomes part of the product. Deployment is the step where this happens.

It is common for data science teams to offload model deployment to engineering. This is usually so that the data scientists and applied scientists can focus on the core research and development, while engineering can focus on optimizing the application end to end. Some teams include both data science and platform engineering, and some people are just insatiably curious about the entire flow! In *Chapter 14*, we'll dive into the operations questions, today known as MLOps, that will help you develop people, processes, and technology to streamline deployments. This usually includes model monitoring, auditing, automatic retraining, tuning, and more.

Most of the deployment patterns we'll focus on in this book explicitly keep the model in the cloud. This is to streamline your end-to-end operations. However, some applications can't afford the extra latency of a round-trip hop to the cloud, no matter how low we drive this down. These include autonomous vehicles, video game execution, mobile phone deployments, low-internet connectivity scenarios, robotics, and more. These applications usually integrate the model artifact and inference scripts into the SDK builds directly. This is only possible, however, if the model is small enough to fit on the target deployment device. This is relevant for Meta's smaller LLaMA models *(1)*, Stable Diffusion, and other single-GPU models. This means that the same model reduction techniques we'll cover later in this chapter are relevant for both cloud and on-device deployments.

In 2021, I led a team at AWS to deliver a 35-page whitepaper on **Hybrid Machine Learning**. This is available online for free right here: `https://docs.aws.amazon.com/pdfs/whitepapers/latest/hybrid-machine-learning/hybrid-machine-learning.pdf` *(2)*. It includes prescriptive guidance for and the advantages and disadvantages of each architecture. Similar to this book, many of the concepts apply to a variety of compute environments but offer deep technical information for working on AWS.

Now that you have a better idea of the concept of model deployment, let's explore your available options!

# What is the best way to host my model?

As you probably expected, the answer to this question completely depends on the application you're building. To begin, most customers start with one big question: do you need responses from your model in a real-time or synchronous manner? This would be the case for searches, recommendations, chat, and other applications. Most real-time model deployments use a *hosted endpoint*, which is an instance that stays on in the cloud to interact with requests. This is usually contrasted with its opposite: *batch*. Batch jobs take your model and inference data, spin up compute clusters to execute the inference script on all of the requested data, and spin back down. The key difference between real-time deployments and batch jobs is the amount of waiting time between new data and model inference requests. With real-time deployments, you're getting the fastest possible model responses and paying more for the premium. With batch jobs, you won't get a model response until the job has been completed. You'll wait several minutes for the response but pay much less.

Let's explore the real-time endpoints in more detail first, then we'll unpack batch and even more options. For those of you who are already familiar with hosting on SageMaker and would like to jump straight to questions about how to host foundation models, please feel free to go ahead straight to the following sections.

One of our earliest features on Amazon SageMaker was our real-time endpoints. These are fully managed APIs that host your model and your scripts. As you can see in the following figure, when specified, they run on multiple instances across availability zones. They can be auto-scaled by SageMaker, spinning up and down based on customer traffic. SageMaker manages a load balancer to send traffic to them, all front-ended by the endpoint itself, which interacts with the request traffic.

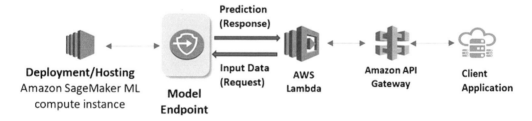

Figure 12.1 – Example architecture pointing to a SageMaker endpoint

The endpoint then interacts with an interface, for example, a Lambda function or simply an API gateway. The gateway then interacts with the client application directly. For example, you might be hosting a web application on premises, such as searching for airline flights. Based on the customer's preferences and flight history, you'd want to use a recommendation algorithm. Your data science team might analyze that data in another account, training models and optimizing the ROI of that model. Once they've found a reasonably performant artifact, they can load it onto a SageMaker endpoint using their own scripts, packages, and objects. You might then promote that artifact into your production account, running penetration and security tests. After deployment, this new endpoint can interact with API requests. The website hosting team can then simply point to your new API hosted in the cloud, while your data science team updates and monitors the model independently.

We'll cover many more of these architectural best practices in the upcoming chapters, but for now, let's look at some of the model deployment options already available in your AWS accounts.

## Model deployment options on AWS with SageMaker

The following terms are some of the model deployment options already available in your AWS accounts:

- **Real-time endpoints**: As mentioned earlier, real-time endpoints are always-on fully managed compute resources available through SageMaker. You bring your model and inference scripts; we bring the entire RESTful API for you. This includes the ability to spin up with increasing traffic and spin down with decreasing traffic. This impacts your costs because you are paying per instance per minute. Real-time endpoints come with many more features, such as the ability to run on GPUs, distributed hosting, multi-model endpoints, asynchronous endpoints, and more. Currently, they have a max payload size of 6 megabytes and a max request runtime of 60 seconds.

- **Batch transform and scheduled notebooks**: There are two big alternatives to real-time endpoints:

  - **Batch transform jobs**

  - **Scheduled notebook jobs**

  With **batch transform** on SageMaker, you start in a similar place as the real-time endpoint, with a trained model and an inference script, but you also point to a dataset known at runtime. This means you will start a batch transform job pointing to a known dataset. You will also identify the compute resources you need for this job. SageMaker will spin up these resources, invoke your model against your data on them, store the inference responses in S3, and spin the compute resources down.

  A similar service is a *notebook job*. Instead of taking a pre-trained model artifact, this takes a whole notebook as the starting point. You might use notebook jobs when you want to run a set of Python functions or data analysis steps, creating multiple graphs and charts as the result of your analysis. You can write your notebook in SageMaker Studio and simply create a scheduled notebook job without writing any code!

- **Asynchronous endpoints**: If you expect to host large models, or if you plan to have a lot of computations in your inference script, then it is likely the inference request will not be complete within 60 seconds. When this is the case, you may want to consider asynchronous endpoints. These can give you up to 15 minutes of runtime and come with managed queues to handle all your requests. You will have a max payload size of 1 GB, giving you a significant uplift from the payload limit of 6 MB on real-time endpoints. Asynchronous endpoints are great for document processing, such as entity recognition and extraction.

- **Multi-model endpoints**: When using real-time endpoints, you have the extra option of hosting *more than one model* on your endpoint. This itself comes in three varieties. First, you can use one container hosted on the endpoint with limitless models in S3. This is great for solving use cases involving thousands of models, such as training small linear models for every customer in your database. You store as many models as you want in S3, so long as they use the same hosting image, and you send the name of the model to the SageMaker multi-model endpoint. We will load that model from S3 for you and move it into RAM, responding to the request. This is then cached for future traffic and sent back to S3 when no longer needed.

  Another simpler option is *storing multiple containers on one endpoint*. In this pattern, you will create multiple containers, such as one using XGBoost, another using PyTorch, another using `pandas`, and so on. Your endpoint can host all of these, so long as it is large enough, and you can determine which container to use on request.

  Finally, you can also use what is called a **serial inference pipeline**. This also uses multiple containers, but each is invoked one after the other, similar to a pipeline. You might use this for feature preprocessing, such as running an LDA or a VAE, and then invoke it against your model.

- **Serverless endpoints**: Another option for hosting your models on SageMaker is a serverless endpoint. This is great for CPU-based models, such as KNNs or logistic regressions, when you are expecting intermittent traffic. This might include long periods without any inference requests, with a sudden burst of traffic. Serverless options are very cost-effective, so if you are able to meet your latency goals on serverless, then this tends to be a great choice. Given that Lambda functions can now hold up to 10 GB of memory (*3*), you might be able to shrink an already small foundation model down to those runtime requirements. The CPU-based runtime will be challenging, but if a slower response time doesn't block you, serverless may be an option.

There are so many other aspects of hosting on SageMaker. You can monitor your models, enable auto-scaling, explain them, validate models safely, apply shadow tests, catalog models in a registry, enable A/B testing, audit them, and more. We'll dive into these topics and more in *Chapter 14*. For now, let's learn about methods for reducing the size of our models for inference.

# Why should I shrink my model, and how?

After learning all about how the power of large models can boost your accuracy, you may be wondering, why would I ever consider shrinking my model? The reality is that large models can be very slow to respond to inference requests and expensive to deploy. This is especially true for language and vision applications, including everything from visual searching to dialogue, image-to-music generation, open-domain question-answering, and more. While this isn't necessarily an issue for training, because the only person waiting for your model to finish is you, it becomes a massive bottleneck in hosting when you are trying to keep your customers happy. As has been well studied, in digital experiences, every millisecond counts. Customers very strictly prefer fast, simple, and efficient interfaces online. This is why we have a variety of techniques in the industry to speed up your model inference without introducing drops in accuracy. Here, we'll cover three key techniques for this: compilation, knowledge distillation, and quantization.

## Model compilation

As we learned earlier, **compilation** is a technique you can use for GPU-based deep learning models. Depending on the operator support in your compiler, you may be able to compile a pre-trained model for your preferred target devices. AWS has a managed feature for this, SageMaker Neo, which runs a compilation job to transform your artifact for a specified environment. This works for deployments both in the cloud and on-device. While Neo can decrease the size of your model by up to 10 times, there's no guarantee it will work for any arbitrary neural network, so proceed with caution.

## Knowledge distillation

**Knowledge distillation** is a fascinating technique that uses a larger model, called a teacher model, to impact the performance of a smaller model, called a student model. Through gradient descent, specifically a KL divergence that computes the difference between two distributions, we can teach the student model to mimic the behavior of the teacher model. A very logical use for this is after large-scale pretraining! Scaling up the size of the model to match the size of your data, for example, with the scaling laws, helps you maximize all your potential for accuracy and computational intelligence. After this, however, you can use knowledge distillation to optimize that model for performance in production. Depending on the gap in model sizes between your teacher and student, you could easily boost inference runtime by 10 times or more, while losing only a few points on accuracy. Here's a visual rendition of knowledge distillation, as presented by Jianping Gou (3) et al. in their 2021 survey on the domain.

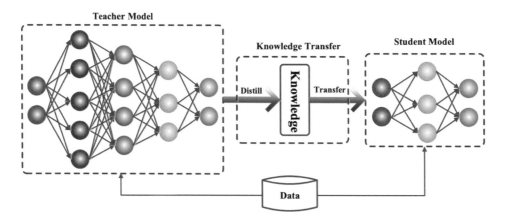

Figure 12.2 – Knowledge transfer through distillation

While the teacher model and the student model receive the same datasets, we *transfer knowledge* to the student by comparing the probabilities that both of them generate. Then, we simply update the student to minimize the difference between them!

Knowledge distillation is also useful in other applications, including machine translation and **reinforcement learning from human feedback** (**RLHF**). Pro tip: RLHF is one key underlying technology behind ChatGPT! We learned more about that in *Chapter 10*. Distillation is also responsible for DistiliBert *(4)*, a model presented by the Hugging Face team in 2019.

## Quantization

**Quantization** is another technique to reduce the runtime of your model. In this case, rather than strictly reducing the memory footprint of your model, which both compilation and distillation do, we refactor your network to use a lower precision data type. Here, data type refers to bit representations, usually ranging from a high of FP32 and dropping down to FP16 or even INT8. Integers are easier to represent computationally, so the literal storage required to hold them is smaller. However, floats are obviously more expressive, given that they can point to quite literally an infinite range of numbers between integers. Converting data representation, as you do with quantization, is useful, because when you convert your data types from floats in training into integers in hosting, the overall memory consumption drops. Instructions for how to do this vary across frameworks, with details about doing so in PyTorch right here *(5)* and NVIDIA's TensorRT here *(6)*. Quantization does have trade-offs. Make sure you test a quantized model robustly before deploying it, so you know how it impacts both speed and accuracy.

Now that you've learned a few ways to reduce the footprint of your model, let's cover techniques you can use when this isn't an option for you: distributed model hosting!

# Hosting distributed models on SageMaker

In *Chapter 5*, we covered distribution fundamentals, where you learned how to think about splitting up your model and datasets across multiple GPUs. The good news is that you can use this same logic to host the model. In this case, you'll be more interested in model parallel, placing layers and tensors on multiple GPU partitions. You won't actually need a data parallel framework, because we're not using backpropagation. We're only running a forward pass through the network and getting inference results. There's no gradient descent or weight updating involved.

When would you use distributed model hosting? To integrate extremely large models into your applications! Generally, this is scoped to large language models. It's rare to see vision models stretch beyond single GPUs. Remember, in *Chapter 4*, *Containers and Accelerators on the Cloud*, we learned about different sizes of GPU memory. This is just as relevant for hosting as it is for training. One simple way of estimating the GB size of your model is to just read the footprint when it's stored on disk. While the size will vary slightly as the object moves from disk to memory, the overall disk footprint is still a good estimate.

For extremely large models in the GPT-3 range of 175B parameters, it's not uncommon for the model to require at least 350 GB of storage! In this case study *(7)* for hosting large models on SageMaker, we show hosting a model of this size on one p4d instance, using only 8 A100s. That's one `ml.p4d.24xlarge` instance, which on public SageMaker pricing, is about $37 per hour! Granted, while this is a fraction of the cost of training, which can easily be 10 times or more for extremely large foundation models, it's still painful to see this on your bill.

On top of the massive cost of this cluster, you're also introducing the extra latency cost to your customer. Imagine running any process across 8 GPUs. Even with pipeline and tensor parallelism, that is still not going to be particularly fast.

Now, let's learn about a few key underlying technologies that bring all of this together. Then, we'll look at a few examples of hosting models at the 6B and 175B scales.

### Large model hosting containers on SageMaker

Just as we learned about in training foundation models, it all comes down to the base container and the relevant packages you're using to accomplish your goal. For hosting large models on SageMaker, we provide dedicated deep learning containers for this explicit purpose. These are open sourced on GitHub *(8)*, so you can easily view and build on top of them.

The large model inference containers package and provide two key technologies for you: DJLServing and DeepSpeed. The **Deep Java Library** (**DJL**) *(9)* was originally built for Java developers to build ML models and applications. They built a universal model-serving solution that is programming language-agnostic, providing a single common denominator to serve models across frameworks such as TensorFlow, ONNX, TensorRT, and Python. They also natively support multi-GPU hosting, through MPI and socket connections. This makes it an attractive proposition for distributed hosting!

The second key technology provided in the AWS large model hosting container is DeepSpeed. Notably, DeepSpeed is helpful because it shards your tensors across multiple GPUs, and it finds the best partitioning strategies for this automatically. As my colleagues discuss in this blog post *(10)*, DeepSpeed evaluates both inference latency and cost in determining the optimal sharding regime.

For hands-on examples of this in detail, feel free to look at our 6B GPT-J notebook: `https://github.com/aws/amazon-sagemaker-examples/blob/main/inference/generativeai/deepspeed/GPT-J-6B_DJLServing_with_PySDK.ipynb`.

The smaller example is a good starting point because it gives you very simple, practical, and less expensive content for hosting models across multiple GPUs. Once you've tested this, then you can upgrade to a much larger example of hosting 175B parameters with this BLOOM notebook: `https://github.com/aws/amazon-sagemaker-examples/blob/main/inference/nlp/realtime/llm/bloom_176b/djl_deepspeed_deploy.ipynb`.

Now that we've walked through a few options for distributed hosting, let's close out the chapter with a quick discussion on model servers and optimizing the end-to-end hosting experience.

# Model servers and end-to-end hosting optimizations

You might be wondering: if SageMaker is hosting my model artifact and my inference script, how do I convert that into a real-time service that can respond to live traffic? The answer is model servers! For those of you who aren't particularly interested in learning how to convert your model inference response into a RESTful interface, you'll be happy to know this is largely abstracted on SageMaker for easy and fast prototyping. However, if you'd like to optimize your inference stack to deliver state-of-the-art model responses, read on.

There are five key types of latency to trim down as you are improving your model hosting response. Here's how we can summarize them:

- **Container latency**: This refers to the time overhead involved in entering and exiting one of your containers. As we learned earlier, on SageMaker, you might host a variety of containers in a *serial inference pipeline*. This is pictured here. Container latency is the time to invoke and exit one of your containers.

- **Model latency**: This includes the invocation and exit time of all containers on the endpoint. As you can see below in *Figure 12.13*, the latency for an individual container may be much smaller than the entire latency for the model.

- **Overhead latency**: This refers to the time for SageMaker to route your request, receive the request from the client, and return it, minus the model's latency.

- **End-to-end latency**. This is primarily calculated from the perspective of the client. It is impacted by the client's requesting bandwidth, the connection to the cloud, any processing in front of SageMaker, the overhead latency, and the model's latency.

Let's look at all these pieces together:

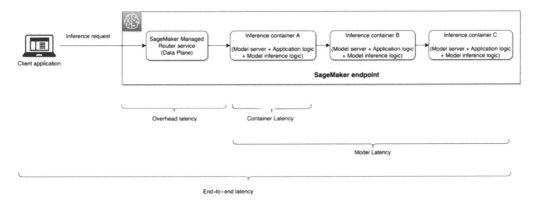

Figure 12.3 – End-to-end model latency on SageMaker

As a consumer of this service, you have a few optimization techniques you can deploy. First, and this is true for any application on AWS, *push the application to where your customers are!* A major reason to use AWS is that we have the single largest global infrastructure of any CSP. We have more regions, at higher availability designs, than any other cloud on the planet. Make this your asset when you push your application to a geographic region or point of presence that is closest to your customers. This will immediately reduce the amount of time it takes for their request to hit the cloud because it will have fewer miles to travel on the network.

My colleagues at AWS delivered a spectacular blog post on *optimizing the container* for your SageMaker hosting workloads. In particular, they explored NVIDIA's Triton, an open source project that delivers ultra-low latency model inference results, as in, single-digit milliseconds.

For more details about Triton, in addition to end-to-end optimizations for SageMaker hosting, See their blog post on the topic here: `https://aws.amazon.com/blogs/machine-learning/achieve-hyperscale-performance-for-model-serving-using-nvidia-triton-inference-server-on-amazon-sagemaker/` *(11)*.

Lastly, I'd like to also call out SageMaker's **inference recommender** *(12)*, which you can use to help you pick the right instance type, count, and configurations based on your expected traffic. In fact, my team used the inference recommender to run their tests on Triton!

Now that you have a much better understanding of what model servers are and how you can use them to optimize your end-to-end hosting performance, let's close out the chapter with an overall recap.

## Summary

We defined model deployment as integrating your model into a client application. We talked about the characteristics of data science teams that may commonly deploy their own models, versus those who may specialize in more general analysis. We introduced a variety of use cases where model deployment is a critical part of the entire application. While noting a variety of hybrid architectures, we focused explicitly on deployments in the cloud. We learned about some of the best ways to host your models, including options on SageMaker such as real-time endpoints, batch transform and notebook jobs, asynchronous endpoints, multi-model endpoints, serverless endpoints, and more. We learned about options for reducing the size of your model, from compilation to distillation and quantization. We covered distributed model hosting and closed out with a review of model servers and end-to-end hosting optimization tips on SageMaker.

Next up, we'll dive into a set of techniques you can use to interact with foundation models to eke out the best performance: prompt engineering!

# References

1. *LLaMA: Open and Efficient Foundation Language Models*: `https://arxiv.org/pdf/2302.13971.pdf`

2. *Lambda quotas*: `https://docs.aws.amazon.com/lambda/latest/dg/gettingstarted-limits.html`

3. *Knowledge Distillation: A Survey*: `https://arxiv.org/pdf/2006.05525.pdf`

4. *DistilBERT, a distilled version of BERT: smaller, faster, cheaper and lighter*: `https://arxiv.org/pdf/1910.01108.pdf`

5. *QUANTIZATION*: `https://pytorch.org/docs/stable/quantization.html`

6. *Achieve hyperscale performance for model serving using NVIDIA Triton Inference Server on Amazon SageMaker*: `https://aws.amazon.com/blogs/machine-learning/achieve-hyperscale-performance-for-model-serving-using-nvidia-triton-inference-server-on-amazon-sagemaker/`

7. *Deploy BLOOM-176B and OPT-30B on Amazon SageMaker with large model inference Deep Learning Containers and DeepSpeed*: `https://aws.amazon.com/blogs/machine-learning/deploy-bloom-176b-and-opt-30b-on-amazon-sagemaker-with-large-model-inference-deep-learning-containers-and-deepspeed/`

8. *Large Model Inference Containers*: `https://github.com/aws/deep-learning-containers/blob/master/available_images.md#large-model-inference-containers`

9. *Deep Java Library*: `https://djl.ai/`

10. *Deploy large models on Amazon SageMaker using DJLServing and DeepSpeed model parallel inference*: `https://aws.amazon.com/blogs/machine-learning/deploy-large-models-on-amazon-sagemaker-using-djlserving-and-deepspeed-model-parallel-inference/`

11. *Achieve hyperscale performance for model serving using NVIDIA Triton Inference Server on Amazon SageMaker*: `https://aws.amazon.com/blogs/machine-learning/achieve-hyperscale-performance-for-model-serving-using-nvidia-triton-inference-server-on-amazon-sagemaker/`

12. *Amazon SageMaker Inference Recommender*: `https://docs.aws.amazon.com/sagemaker/latest/dg/inference-recommender.html`

# Part 5: Deploy Your Model

In part 5, you'll learn how to deploy your model. You'll use techniques such as distillation, quantization, and compilation to reduce your model's overall footprint. You'll identify top use cases to scale your model across organizations, and learn about ongoing operations, monitoring, and maintenance.

This section has the following chapters:

- *Chapter 13, Prompt Engineering*
- *Chapter 14, MLOps for Vision and Language*
- *Chapter 15, Future Trends in Pretraining Foundation Models*

# 13
# Prompt Engineering

In this chapter, we'll dive into a special set of techniques called prompt engineering. You'll learn about this technique at a high level, including how it is similar to and different from other learning-based topics covered throughout this book. We'll explore examples across vision and language and dive into key terms and success metrics. In particular, this chapter covers all of the tips and tricks for improving performance *without updating the model weights*. This means we'll be mimicking the learning process, without necessarily changing any of the model parameters. This includes some advanced techniques such as prompt and prefix tuning. We will cover the following topics in this chapter:

- Prompt engineering – the art of getting more with less

- From few- to zero-shot learning

- Tips and tricks for text-to-image prompting

- Best practices for image-to-image prompting

- Prompting large language models

- Advanced techniques – prompt and prefix tuning

## Prompt engineering – the art of getting more with less

At this point in the book, and in your project, you should have a lot invested in your new foundation model. From compute costs to datasets, custom code, and research papers you've read, you might have spent a solid 50-100 hours or more of your own time eking out performance gains. Kudos to you! It's a great life to live.

After you've done this, however, and especially after you've learned how to build a complete application around your model, it's time to maximize your model's performance on inference. In the last chapter, we learned about multiple ways to optimize your model's runtime, from compilation to quantization and distillation to distribution, and each of these is helpful in speeding up your inference results.

This entire chapter, however, is dedicated to getting the most accurate response you can. Here, I use the word "accurate" heuristically to indicate any type of model *quality* or *evaluation* metric. As you learned in the previous chapter on evaluation, accuracy itself is a misleading term and frequently not your best pick for an evaluation metric. Please see *Chapter 10* for more details

Prompt engineering includes a set of techniques related to picking the best input to the model for inference. Inference refers to getting a result out of your model without updating the weights; think of it like just the forward pass without any backpropagation. This is interesting because it's how you can get *predictions* out of your model. When you deploy your model, you're deploying it for inference.

Prompt engineering includes a huge swath of techniques. It includes things such as *zero- and few-shot learning*, where we send multiple examples to the model and ask it to complete the logical sequence. It includes picking the right hyperparameters. It includes a lot of guessing and checking, testing your model results and figuring out the best techniques for it.

For those of you who are hosting a generative AI model for end consumers outside of your direct team, you might even consider standing up a client to handle prompt engineering for you. This seems to be somewhat common in model playgrounds, where not all the parameters and model invocation are directly exposed. As an app developer, you can and should modify the prompts your customer is sending to your models to ensure they get the best performance they can. This might include adding extra terms to the invocation, updating the hyperparameters, and rephrasing the request.

Let's explore prompt engineering in more detail and its related skill, few-shot learning.

## From few- to zero-shot learning

As you'll remember, a key model we've been referring back to is **GPT-3, Generative Pretrained Transformers**. The paper that gave us the third version of this is called *Language models are few shot learners. (1)* Why? Because the primary goal of the paper was to develop a model capable of performing well without extensive fine-tuning. This is an advantage because it means you can use one model to cover a much broader array of use cases without needing to develop custom code or curate custom datasets. Said another way, the unit economics are much stronger for zero-shot learning than they are for fine-tuning. In a fine-tuning world, you need to work harder for your base model to solve a use case. This is in contrast to a few-shot world, where it's easier to solve additional use cases from your base model. This makes the few-shot model more valuable because the fine-tuning model becomes too expensive at scale. While in practice fine-tuning solves problems more robustly than few-shot learning, it makes the entire practice of prompt engineering very attractive. Let's look at a few examples in the following screenshot.

The three settings we explore for in-context learning

Traditional fine-tuning (not used for GPT-3)

**Zero-shot**

The model predicts the answer given only a natural language description of the task. No gradient updates are performed.

```
1   Translate English to French:        ←── task description
2   cheese =>                            ←── prompt
```

**One-shot**

In addition to the task description, the model sees a single example of the task. No gradient updates are performed.

```
1   Translate English to French:        ←── task description
2   sea otter => loutre de mer          ←── example
3   cheese =>                           ←── prompt
```

**Few-shot**

In addition to the task description, the model sees a few examples of the task. No gradient updates are performed.

```
1   Translate English to French:        ←── task description
2   sea otter => loutre de mer          ←── examples
3   peppermint => menthe poivrée        ←─
4   plush girafe => girafe peluche      ←─
5   cheese =>                           ←── prompt
```

**Fine-tuning**

The model is trained via repeated gradient updates using a large corpus of example tasks.

```
1   sea otter => loutre de mer          ←── example #1
                    ↓
              gradient update
                    ↓
1   peppermint => menthe poivrée        ←── example #2
                    ↓
              gradient update
                    ↓
                   • • •
                    ↓
1   plush giraffe => girafe peluche     ←── example #N
              gradient update

1   cheese =>                           ←── prompt
```

Figure 13.1 – Few-shot learning examples from the GPT-3 paper

On the left-hand side, we see different options for inputs to the model on inference. In the paper, they use the phrase "in-context learning," referring to the fact that in the dataset, there can be samples of a task definition and examples. These repeated samples help the model learn both the name and the example of the learning. Here, the name of the task, or the task description, is **Translate English to French**. Then, we see examples of this, such as **sea otter -> loutre de mer**. When you provide the name of the task to GPT-3, along with a few samples, it is then able to respond quite well.

We call this **few-shot learning**. This is because we're providing a few examples to the model, notably more than one and less than a full dataset. I struggle with using the word "learn" here, because technically, the model's weights and parameters aren't being updated. The model isn't changing at all, so arguably we shouldn't even use the word "learn." On the other hand, providing these examples as input ahead of time clearly improves the performance of the model, so from an output-alone perspective perhaps we could use the word "learn." In any case, this is the standard terminology.

A similar example would then be **zero-shot learning**, where we provide no examples to the model of how we expect it to complete its task, and hope it performs well. This is ideal for open-domain question-answering, such as ChatGPT. However, as many people have discovered, a model that performs well in a zero-shot learning scenario can also be shown to perform well in a few-shot or even single-shot example. All of these are useful techniques to understand large models.

As we saw in *Figure 13.1*, a natural comparison with this type of learning is fine-tuning. In a fine-tuning approach, as we learned in *Chapter 10*, we use the pretrained model as a base and train it again using a larger dataset sample. Usually, this dataset sample will be supervised, but it is possible to use unsupervised fine-tuning when necessary. In a language scenario, this supervision might be classification, question answering, or summarization. In vision, you might see new image and text pairs across any number of use cases: fashion, e-commerce, image design, marketing, media and entertainment, manufacturing, product design, and so on.

The most common progression would entail the following:

1.    First, try zero-shot learning with your model. Does it work perfectly out of the box on every use case and edge scenario? Likely, it does in a few very narrow cases but can use some help elsewhere.

2.    Next, try single- and few-shot learning.

If you give it a few examples of what you are looking for, does it figure it out? Can it follow the prompts you provide and get a good response? If all else fails, move on to fine-tuning. Go collect a dataset more specific to the use case you want to enhance your model in and train it there. Interestingly, fine-tuning seems to be much more successful in language-only scenarios. In vision, fine-tuning very easily overfits or falls into *catastrophic forgetting*, where the model loses its ability to hold onto the images and objects provided in the base dataset. You may be better off exploring an image-to-image approach, which follows later.

Now, let's learn a few best practices for prompt engineering across vision and language.

## Text-to-image prompt engineering tips

As we mentioned earlier in the book, Stable Diffusion is a great model you can use to interact with via natural language and produce new images. The beauty, fun, and simplicity of Stable Diffusion-based models are that you can be endlessly creative in designing your prompt. In this example, I made up a provocative title for a work of art. I asked the model to imagine what an image would look like if it were created by Ansel Adams, a famous American photographer from the mid-twentieth century known for his black-and-white photographs of the natural world. Here was the full prompt: *"Closed is open" by Ansel Adams, high resolution, black and white, award winning. Guidance (20)*. Let's take a closer look.

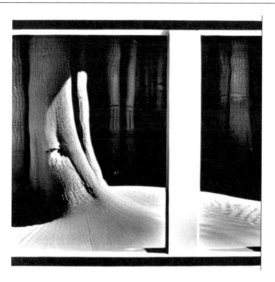

Figure 13.2 – An image generated by Stable Diffusion

In the following list, you'll find a few helpful tips to improve your Stable Diffusion results:

- **Add any of the following words to your prompt**: *Award-winning, high resolution, trending on <your favorite site here>, in the style of <your favorite artist here>, 400 high dpi*, and so on. There are thousands of examples of great photos and their corresponding prompts online; a great site is `lexica.art`. Starting from what works is always a great path. If you're passionate about vision, you can easily spend hours of time just pouring through these and finding good examples. For a faster route, that same site lets you search for words as a prompt and renders the images. It's a quick way to get started with prompting your model.

- **Add negative prompts**: Stable Diffusion offers a negative prompt option, which lets you provide words to the model that it will explicitly not use. Common examples of this are hands, human, oversaturated, poorly drawn, and disfigured.

- **Upscaling**: While most prompting with Stable Diffusion results in smaller images, such as size 512x512, you can use another technique, called upscaling, to render that same image into a much larger, higher quality image, of size 1,024x1,024 or even more. Upscaling is a great step you can use to get the best quality Stable Diffusion models today, both on SageMaker *(2)* and through Hugging Face directly. *(3)* We'll dive into this in a bit more detail in the upcoming section on image-to-image.

- **Precision and detail**: When you provide longer prompts to Stable Diffusion, such as including more terms in your prompt and being extremely descriptive about the types and styles of objects you'd like it to generate, you actually increase your odds of the response being good. Be careful about the words you use in the prompt. As we learned earlier in *Chapter 11* on bias, most large models are trained on the backbone of the internet. With Stable Diffusion, for better or for worse, this means you want to use language that is common online. This means that punctuation and casing actually aren't as important, and you can be really creative and spontaneous with how you're describing what you want to see.

- **Order**: Interestingly, the order of your words matters in prompting Stable Diffusion. If you want to make some part of your prompt more impactful, such as *dark* or *beautiful*, move that to the front of your prompt. If it's too strong, move it to the back.

- **Hyperparameters**: These are also relevant in language-only models, but let's call out a few that are especially relevant to Stable Diffusion.

---

**Key hyperparameters for Stable Diffusion prompt engineering**

1. **Guidance**: The technical term here is *classifier-free guidance*, and it refers to a mode in Stable Diffusion that lets the model pay more (higher guidance) or less (lower guidance) attention to your prompt. This ranges from 0 up to 20. A lower guidance term means the model is optimizing less for your prompt, and a higher term means it's entirely focused on your prompt. For example, in my image in the style of Ansel Adams above, I just updated the guidance term from 8 to 20. In an earlier version of the same image, I set guidance to 8. This produced rolling and gentle shadows. However, when I updated `guidance=20` on the second image, the model captures the stark contrast and shadow fades that characterized Adams' work. In addition, we get a new style, almost like M. C. Escher, where the tree seems to turn into the floor.

2. **Seed**: This refers to an integer you can set to baseline your diffusion process. Setting the seed can have a big impact on your model response. Especially if my prompt isn't very good, I like to start with the seed hyperparameter and try a few random starts. Seed impacts high-level image attributes such as style, size of objects, and coloration. If your prompt is strong, you may not need to experiment heavily here, but it's a good starting point.

3. **Width and height**: These are straightforward; they're just the pixel dimensions of your output image! You can use them to change the scope of your result, and hence the type of picture the model generates. If you want a perfectly square image, use 512x512. If you want a portrait orientation, use 512x768. For a landscape orientation, use 768x512. Remember you can use the upscaling process we'll learn about shortly to increase the resolution on the image, so start with smaller dimensions first.

4. **Steps**: This refers to the number of denoising steps the model will take as it generates your new image, and most people start with `steps` set to `50`. Increasing this number will also increase the processing time. To get great results, personally, I like to scale this against guidance. If you plan on using a very high guidance term (~16), such as with a killer prompt, then I wouldn't set inference steps to anything over 50. This looks like it overfits, and the results are just plain bad. However, if your guidance scale is lower, closer to 8, then increasing the number of steps can get you a better result.

---

There are many more hyperparameters to explore for Stable Diffusion and other text-to-image diffusion models. For now, let's explore techniques around image-to-image!

# Image-to-image prompt engineering tips

A fascinating trend in generative AI, especially when prompting the model, is *image-to-image*. This covers a broad array of techniques that let you bring an image when you invoke the model. The response will then incorporate your source image into the response, letting you more concretely determine what response the model will provide. This is incredibly helpful for increasing the resolution of the images, adding a mask, or even introducing objects to then seamlessly format into the output image in any context.

These core capabilities are possible through a technique introduced in early 2022 *(4)*, called **Stochastic Differential Equations Edit** (**SDEdit**), which uses stochastic differential equations to make image synthesis and editing a lot easier. While it sounds a bit intimidating, it's actually very intuitive. It lets you add a source image to your pretrained diffusion model and use that base image as inspiration. How? Through iteratively adding and removing noise in a variety of ways until the final result meets your preferred criteria. SDEdit improved on its predecessor, GAN-based methods, by up to 98% on realism and 91% on human satisfaction scores.

Let's explore the ways we can use this enhanced image-to-image technique while prompting with your diffusion models!

## Upscaling

As mentioned earlier, this is a simple and fast way to increase the resolution of your images. When prompting the model, you can enhance a low-resolution image along with other parameters to increase quality. You have a built-in option for this with SageMaker JumpStart *(5)*, and you also have a full upscaling pipeline available through Hugging Face directly.*(6)* This can take another textual prompt in addition to the source image.

## Masking

Another interesting technique when prompting diffusion models is **masking**. A mask is simply a set of pixels that covers a given area in a photo: mountains, cars, humans, dogs, and any other type of object present in the images. How do you find a pixel map? These days, honestly, an easy way might be to start with Meta's new **Segment Anything Model** *(SAM)*. *(7)* You can upload an image and ask the model to generate a pixel map for anything in that image.

Once you have a mask, you can send it to a Stable Diffusion image to generate a new image inside of the mask. Classic examples of this are changing the styles of clothing that people seem to be wearing. You can extract the area of a photo with clothing using either SAM or open source CV tools, render the mask, and then send the mask to Stable Diffusion. It will generate a new image, combining the original with a newly generated twist to fill in the area of the mask.

For a nice and simple end-to-end example of this, check out one I just found on GitHub! *(8)*

## Prompting for object-to-image with DreamBooth

Unlike the previous methods we looked at in the previous sections, DreamBooth *(9)* does not use the underlying SDEdit method. Instead, it uses a handful of input images and runs a type of fine-tuning process, combined with textual guidance, to place the source object from all of the input images into the target scene generated by the model. The technique uses two loss functions, one to preserve the previous class learned by the pretrained model and another to reconstruct the new object into the final image.

This means arguably, it's not a prompting technique; it's closer to a fine-tuning technique. However, I'm including it here because I find the intention more similar to masking than to creating a net-new model, but that is actually the outcome. Let's take a closer look at the DreamBooth loss function.

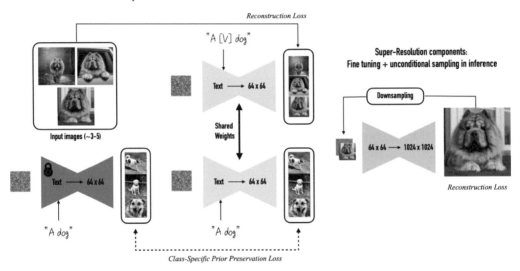

Figure 13.3 - Dreambooth prior-preserving loss function

DreamBooth is a great open source solution you can use to take any object you like and place it onto any background of your choice! Next, let's learn about some techniques you can use to improve your prompts for language models.

## Prompting large language models

I've said this before: I am a huge fan and big advocate of Hugging Face. I've learned a lot about **natural language processing** (**NLP**) from and with them, so I'd be remiss if I didn't call out their book as a great source for prompt engineering tips and techniques. *(10)* Most of those practices center around picking the right hyperparameters for your model, with each type of model offering slightly different results.

However, I would argue that the rise of ChatGPT has now almost completely thrown that out of consideration. In today's world, the extremely accurate performance of OpenAI's model raises the bar for all NLP developers, pushing us to deliver comparable results. For better or worse, there is no going back. Let's try to understand how to prompt our **large language models** (**LLMs**)! We'll start with instruction fine-tuning.

## Instruction fine-tuning

First, it's helpful to really understand the difference between a model that has been *instruction fine-tuned* and one that has not. As we learned in *Chapter 10* on fine-tuning, instruction fine-tuning refers to a supervised fine-tuning step that uses instructions provided to the model, such as "Tell me the difference between a mimosa and a samosa," and pairs these with an answer, something such as "While a mimosa is an alcoholic drink combining champagne with orange juice, a samosa is an Indian pastry filled with either vegetables or meat, and commonly with a potato filling." The model then explicitly learns what it means to follow instructions.

This matters for prompting LLMs because it will completely change your prompting style. If you're working with an LLM that has already been instruction fine-tuned, you can jump right into zero-shot performance and immediately have it execute tasks for you seamlessly. If not, you will probably need to add some examples to your prompt, that is, few-shot learning, to encourage it to respond in the way you want it to.

Once you've sorted out this key difference, it's helpful to also spend some time trying out the model of your choice. They have nuances; some of them look for different tokens and separators, while others respond well to keywords and phrases. You want to get to know and test your LLM, and prompt engineering is a great way to do that. Another style to learn is *chain-of-thought prompting*.

## Chain-of-thought prompting

Even if you are working with a model that performs well in zero-shot cases, such as one that has received instruction fine-tuning, as we discussed previously, you may still come across use cases where you need to add some examples in the prompt to get the desired output. A great example of this is chain-of-thought prompting. Chain-of-thought prompting refers to prompting the model *to demonstrate how it arrives at an answer*. This is extremely valuable in scenarios where explainability is critical, such as explaining why an LLM makes stylistic updates or classification decisions. Imagine you are using LLMs in legal scenarios, for example, and you'd like the LLM to update the language in a legal document. When you prompt it as follows, instead of simply providing the answer, the model can explain step by step how it came to a given conclusion. This logical clarity helps most users have more trust in the system, helping them understand and trust that the suggestions made by the model are valid.

It also in many cases helps with accuracy! This is because most LLMs are inherently auto-regressive; they're very good at predicting which word is most likely to come next in a given string. When you prompt them into a chain of thought, you're pushing them to generate thought by thought, keeping them closer to the truth. Let's take a closer look at this visually, using the following graphic from the original paper. *(11)*

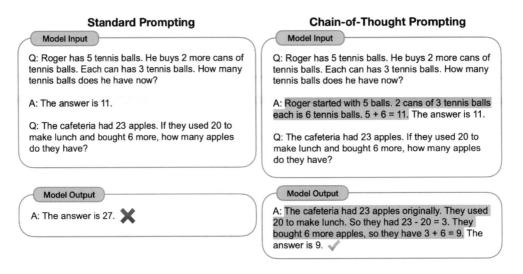

Figure 13.4 – Chain-of-thought prompting

As you can see, on the left-hand side, we're still doing some few-shot learning, but the answer provided in the prompt is simple. It only answers the question, full-stop. On the right-hand side, however, we prompt the model by providing an answer that *rephrases the question*. Now, the answer starts with re-generating a quick summary of the information provided in the question, then taking exactly one logical leap to output the correct answer. You can see that the model on the left-hand side fails to answer correctly, while the one on the right is correct. Actually, the model itself is the same, but the only difference here is the prompt.

For a model that has been instruction fine-tuned, you can also trigger a chain-of-thought performance with a statement such as "walk me through step by step how to...".

## Summarization

This is possibly the most common LLM scenario I see today: summarizing call transcripts, documents, and more. Summarization is now very easy with top LLMs. Simply paste as much of your document into the LLM as you can, based on the model's context length, and add *Summarize:* at the bottom of the prompt. Some models will vary; you can also add *TL;DR, in summary:*, or any similar variant.

Will they all work perfectly? No way. Will they catch absolutely everything? Absolutely not. Will they occasionally hallucinate? Without a doubt. How do we mitigate that? Fine-tuning, extensive validation, entity recognition, and auditing.

## Defending against prompt injections and jailbreaking

One technique to consider in prompting your model is *how sensitive it is to jailbreaking*. As we learned in *Chapter 11* on detecting and mitigating bias, jailbreaking refers to malicious users prompting your model to engage in harmful behavior. This might be like asking your model to tell a rude joke about certain groups of people, asking it for instructions about theft, or asking its opinion about certain politicians or social groups. Please anticipate that in every LLM application, at least some of your users will try to jailbreak your model to see whether they can trick it into behaving poorly. A parallel method is **prompt injection**, where users can maliciously trick your model into responding with IP from your dataset, from your prompt set, or anything else from your instruction list.

How can you defend against this? One way is with supervised fine-tuning. Anthropic maintains a large dataset of red-teamed data, available on Hugging Face here. *(12)* Please proceed with caution; the words used in this dataset are extremely graphic and may be triggering to some readers. Personally, I find it hard to study even a few lines of this dataset. As a supervised fine-tuning technique, or even, as suggested by Anthropic, as a reinforcement learning with human feedback technique, you can fine-tune your model to reject anything that looks malicious or harmful.

On top of this, you can *add classifiers to your application ingest*. This means as your app is taking in new questions from your users, you can easily add extra machine learning models to detect any malicious or odd behavior in these questions and circumvent the answer. This gives you a lot of control over how your app responds.

Now that we've learned about some basic techniques for prompting LLMs, let's look at a few advanced techniques!

## Advanced techniques – prefix and prompt tuning

You might be wondering; isn't there some sophisticated way to use optimization techniques and find the right prompt, without even updating the model parameters? The answer is yes, there are many ways of doing this. First, let's try to understand **prefix tuning**.

### Prefix tuning

This technique was proposed *(13)* by a pair of Stanford researchers in 2021 specifically for text generation. The core idea, as you can see in the following diagram from their paper, is that instead of producing a net-new model for each downstream task, a less resource-intensive option is to create a simple vector for each task itself, called the prefix.

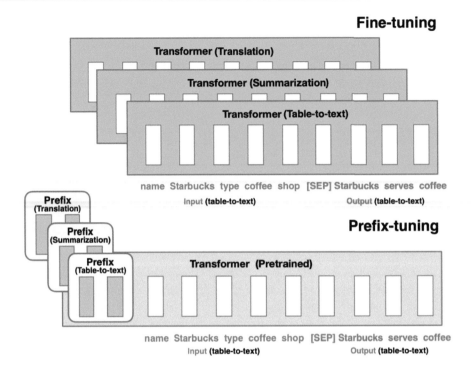

Figure 13.5 – Prefix tuning

The core idea here is that instead of fine-tuning the entire pretrained transformer for each downstream task, let's try to update just a single vector for that task. Then, we don't need to store all of the model weights; we can just store that vector!

Arguably, this technique is similar to one we briefly touched on in *Chapter 10, Fine-Tuning and Evaluating*. This technique injects trainable weights into an LLM, letting us learn just the new parameters rather than updating the entire model itself. I find prefix tuning interesting because we're not really touching the model architecture at all; we're just learning this basic object right at the start.

Why should you learn about this? Because, as the Stanford team shows, this method uses only 0.1% of the parameters of the full model yet gives performance comparable to fine-tuning the entire model.

How can you get started with prefix tuning? Using the new library from our friends at Hugging Face! They're building an open source library to make all kinds of parameter-efficient fine-tuning available here: `https://github.com/huggingface/peft`. Prefix tuning is certainly available.

Fortunately, the example for general PEFT, coming from the inimitable Phill Schmid, seems quite accessible here. *(14)* With some specialized data preprocessing and custom model configs, you too can add this to your scripts.

Now, let's look at prompt tuning.

## Prompt tuning

As we've seen, finding the right prompt is quite challenging. Usually, they are built on discrete words in human natural language and can require a fair amount of manual iteration to trick the model into providing the expected answer. In Google's 2021 ACL paper *(15)* introducing this concept, they proposed "soft prompts" that are learnable through backpropagation. Thankfully, this incorporates the signal from any number of labeled examples, simplifying the prefix-tuning approach proposed previously.

With prompt tuning, we freeze the entire pretrained model but allow an extra *k* tunable tokens per each downstream task to be added to the input text. These are then considered soft tokens, or signals learned by the model to recognize each downstream task. You can see this in the diagram from their paper shown here.

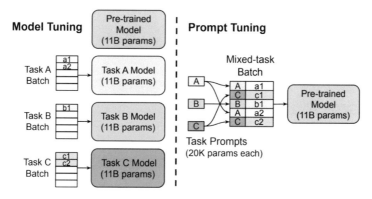

Figure 13.6 – Prompt tuning

Similar to prefix tuning, using prompt tuning, we still freeze the foundation model weights. We are also still adding some new, learnable items to the input dataset mixed with a variety of downstream task data samples. The key difference is that instead of learning full blocks for the model, we learn new, machine-readable tokens. That means the tokens themselves should change after the gradient updating, signaling something the model recognizes as basically a trigger for that type of downstream task. If you are working on scenarios where parameter-efficient fine-tuning isn't an option, such as where the model is completely obscured to you, then prefix or prompt tuning maybe be a good option to explore. Both techniques are available in the relevant Hugging Face library, `peft`.

Now, let's close out the chapter with a quick summary.

## Summary

In this chapter, we introduced the concept of prompt engineering. I'd define that as everything that ekes out accuracy gains from your model without updating the weights of the model itself. Said another way, this is the art of getting more with less. We walked through few-shot learning, where you send a few examples of your desired inference results to the model, to zero-shot learning, where you hope to get a response from the model without any prior information. Needless to say, consumers tend to strongly prefer zero-shot learning. We covered a few tips and tricks for prompting text-to-image models, especially how to get good performance out of the open source Stable Diffusion. We learned about image-to-image prompting, where you can pass images to your diffusion-based models to produce a new image using an intersection. We also learned about prompting LLMs, including the implications of instruction fine-tuning, chain-of-thought prompting, summarization, and defending against prompt injections and jailbreaking. Finally, we introduced a few advanced techniques, including prompt and prefix tuning.

Now, let's get started on *Chapter 14*, which is on MLOps for vision and LLMs!

# References

Please go through the following content for more information on some topics covered in the chapter:

1.  Language Models are Few-Shot Learners: https://arxiv.org/pdf/2005.14165.pdf

2.  Upscale images with Stable Diffusion in Amazon SageMaker JumpStart: https://aws.amazon.com/blogs/machine-learning/upscale-images-with-stable-diffusion-in-amazon-sagemaker-jumpstart/

3.  stabilityai/stable-diffusion-x4-upscaler Copied: https://huggingface.co/stabilityai/stable-diffusion-x4-upscaler

4.  SDEDIT: GUIDED IMAGE SYNTHESIS AND EDITING WITH STOCHASTIC DIFFERENTIAL EQUATIONS: https://arxiv.org/pdf/2108.01073.pdf

5.  Upscale images with Stable Diffusion in Amazon SageMaker JumpStart: https://aws.amazon.com/blogs/machine-learning/upscale-images-with-stable-diffusion-in-amazon-sagemaker-jumpstart/

6.  Hugging Face: https://huggingface.co/stabilityai/stable-diffusion-x4-upscaler

7.  Segment Anything: https://arxiv.org/pdf/2304.02643.pdf

8.  amrrs/stable-diffusion-prompt-inpainting: https://github.com/amrrs/stable-diffusion-prompt-inpainting/blob/main/Prompt_based_Image_In_Painting_powered_by_ClipSeg.ipynb

9.  DreamBooth: Fine Tuning Text-to-Image Diffusion Models for Subject-Driven Generation: https://arxiv.org/pdf/2208.12242.pdf

10. nlp-with-transformers/website: https://github.com/nlp-with-transformers/website

11. Chain-of-Thought Prompting Elicits Reasoning in Large Language Models: https://arxiv.org/pdf/2201.11903.pdf

12. Hugging Face: `https://huggingface.co/datasets/Anthropic/hh-rlhf`

13. Prefix-Tuning: Optimizing Continuous Prompts for Generation: `https://arxiv.org/pdf/2101.00190.pdf`

14. huggingface/notebooks: `https://github.com/huggingface/notebooks/blob/main/sagemaker/24_train_bloom_peft_lora/scripts/run_clm.py`

15. The Power of Scale for Parameter-Efficient Prompt Tuning: `https://aclanthology.org/2021.emnlp-main.243.pdf`

16. `https://arxiv.org/pdf/1902.00751.pdhttps://arxiv.org/pdf/1902.00751.pd`

# 14

# MLOps for Vision and Language

In this chapter, we'll introduce the core concepts of operations and orchestration for machine learning, also known as MLOps. This includes building pipelines, continuous integration and deployment, promotion through environments, and more. We'll explore options for monitoring and human-in-the-loop auditing of model predictions. We'll also identify unique ways to support large vision and language models in your MLOps pipelines.

We'll be covering the following topics in the chapter:

- What is MLOps?
- Continuous integration and continuous deployment
- Model monitoring and human-in-the-loop
- MLOps for foundation models
- AWS offerings for MLOps

## What is MLOps?

We've covered such a huge amount of content in this book that it's almost inconceivable. From the absolute foundations of pretraining, we've worked through use cases, datasets, models, GPU optimizations, distribution basis, optimizations, hyperparameters, working with SageMaker, fine-tuning, bias detection and mitigation, hosting your model, and prompt engineering. Now, we come to the art and science of *tying it all together*.

**MLOps** stands for **machine learning operations**. Broadly speaking, it includes a whole set of technologies, people, and processes that your organization can adopt to streamline your machine learning workflows. In the last few chapters, you learned about building RESTful APIs to host your model, along with tips to improve your prompt engineering. Here, we'll focus on *building a deployment workflow* to integrate this model into your application.

Personally, I find the pipeline aspect of MLOps the most poignant. A **pipeline** is a set of steps you can build to orchestrate your machine learning workflow. This can include everything from automatically retraining your model, hyperparameter tuning, auditing, and monitoring, application testing and integration, and promotion to more secure environments, drift and bias detection, and adversarial hardening.

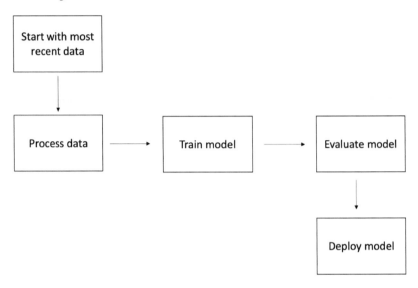

Figure 14.1 – Pipelines for machine learning operations

Pipelines are tools you can build using any number of software options. If you're using SageMaker-native tooling and you don't already have an orchestration stack, you might start by looking at **SageMaker Pipelines**. Alternatively, if you're already using an orchestration stack, such as AirFlow, KubeFlow, Ray, MLFlow, or StepFunctions, you might continue using those and simply point to SageMaker APIs for your machine learning workflows.

The core component of a pipeline is a *step*. A step might be something such as **data preprocessing**, **model training**, **model evaluation**, a **manual review**, **model deployment**, and so on. A basic pipeline will flow through a number of steps that you define. Pipelines usually start with a **trigger**, some event that delivers a notification system to the pipeline. Your trigger could be an upload to S3, a commit to your repository, a time of day, an update on your dataset, or a customer event. Usually, you'll see one trigger kicking off the entire pipeline, with each step initiated after the previous one completes.

Let's move on to the common MLOps pipelines.

## Common MLOps pipelines

Let's examine a few of the most common pipelines in machine learning:

- **Model deployment pipeline**: Here, the core task is to point to your pretrained model artifacts, notably your inference script and the model itself, and put these into whichever deployment option you select. You might use **SageMaker RealTime Endpoints** for product recommendation, or **asynchronous endpoints** to host large language models. You might have a variety of images through the **multi-container endpoint**, or even with the **multi-model endpoint**. In any case, the most basic pipeline steps might look something like this:

    I.      Update a model artifact.

    II.     Create a new endpoint

    III.    Test the endpoint.

    IV.     If the test is successful, set production traffic to the endpoint. If the test fails, notify the development team.

- **Model retraining pipeline**: A model retraining pipeline is useful for use cases where you need to retrain a model regularly. This might be every time you have new data, which can be as often as every few hours, or as irregular as every month. For a simple case, such as rerunning a report or notebook, you might use SageMaker's *notebook job* feature, launched in December 2022, to run a notebook on a schedule. A pipeline, however, would be useful if you wanted to trigger this retraining based on updated data. Alternatively, if the model or dataset were large and needed distributed training, a pipeline would be a natural fit. Your pipeline steps might look something like this:

    I.      Upload new data.

    II.     Run preprocessing.

    III.    Train the model.

    IV.     Tune the model.

    V.      Trigger the deployment pipeline.

- **Environment promotion pipeline**: Some customers, particularly in security-sensitive settings such as highly regulated industries, require that applications are upgraded through increasingly more secure environments. Here, the word *environment* means an isolated compute boundary, usually either a full new AWS account or, more simply, a different region. The steps for this pipeline might look something like this:

    I.      Trigger the pipeline from data scientists in the development account.

    II.     Promote the resources to a test account.

    III.    Test the endpoint.

IV.    If the endpoint passes, promote it to a production account. If the endpoint fails, notify the data scientists.

V.    In the production account, create the endpoint.

VI.    Set production traffic to the endpoint.

As you have no doubt noticed, each of these pipelines can interact with each other. They can trigger each other as unique steps, interact with other components, and continuously add value. Their basic components are also interchangeable – you can easily substitute some steps with others, defining whatever overall system you need.

A concept underlying much of this is **microservices**. You can think of each of these pipelines as a microservice, starting with some input and delivering an output. To maximize value across teams, you might build and maintain a base set of templates for each step, or for entire pipelines, to make it easier for future teams to use them.

As we learned earlier in *Chapter 12, How to Deploy Your Model*, there are quite a few techniques you can use to improve your model for deployment. This includes quantization and compression, bias detection, and adversarial hardening *(1)*. Personally, I tend to see many of the methods executed rarely on a model, such as when it first moves from the R&D team to the deployment team. For regular retraining, I'd avoid extensive compute resources, assuming that much of the basic updates incorporated into the model work in more recent versions.

# Continuous integration and continuous deployment

In machine learning, we tend to look at two somewhat different stacks. On the one hand, you have the model creation and deployment process. This includes your model artifacts, datasets, metrics, and target deployment options. As we discussed previously, you might create a pipeline to automate this. On the other hand, you have the actual software application where you want to expose your model. This might be a visual search mobile app, a question/answering chat, an image generation service, a price forecasting dashboard, or really any other process to improve using data and automated decisions.

Many software stacks use their own **continuous integration and continuous deployment (CI/CD)** pipelines to seamlessly connect all the parts of an application. This can include integration tests, unit tests, security scans, and machine learning tests. **Integration** refers to putting the application together, while **deployment** refers to taking steps to move the application into production.

Many of the pipelines we looked at previously could be considered CD pipelines, especially when they refer to updating the service in production. A continuous integration pipeline might include steps that point to the application, testing a variety of responses, and ensuring that the model responds appropriately. Let's take a closer look.

- Test compatibility of training scripts
- Combine data preprocessing methods
- Combine model validation methods
- Run any hyperparameter tuning
- Run bias detection and mitigation

**Continuous integration**

- Optimize model for resources
- Ensure model deploys onto target resources
- Ensure model passes all final validation checks
- Test model endpoint interaction with live application
- Ensure live application users respond well

**Continuous deployment**

Figure 14.2 – CI/CD options for machine learning

What I'm trying to convey here is that *you have many options for how to set up your pipelines*. For a large-scale foundation model, such as your own pretrained LLM or text-to-vision model, you might possibly have handfuls of extremely robust repositories that each team develops for different pieces of the puzzle. Integrating these, using slices of them to support each other, and automating as much as you can with robust unit testing to ensure the highest performance across the board is in your best interest. Separately from the model development, you'll likely have a deployment pipeline that checks all the boxes to prepare your model for real-time traffic and successful communication with your client application.

Now that we've covered a few foundational topics in general operations, let's take a closer look at two key aspects that relate especially to machine learning – model monitoring and human-in-the-loop.

# Model monitoring and human-in-the-loop

In *Chapter 11*, we explored topics around bias detection, mitigation, and monitoring for large vision and language models. This was mostly in the context of evaluating your model. Now that we've made it to the section on deploying your models, with an extra focus on operations, let's take a closer look at model monitoring.

Once you have a model deployed into any application, it's extremely useful to be able to view the performance of that model over time. This is the case for any of the use cases we discussed earlier – chat, general search, forecasting, image generation, recommendations, classification, question answering, and so on. All of these applications benefit from being able to see how your model is trending over time and provide relevant alerts.

Imagine, for example, that you have a price forecasting model that suggests a price for a given product based on economic conditions. You train your model on certain economic conditions, maybe those in January, and deploy the model in February. While deployed, the model continues to look at those same conditions and help price your project. However, you may not realize that in March, the entire market conditions changed. Things in our world change so rapidly that entire sectors may have inverted. Your model came into the world thinking that everything looks exactly the same as when it was trained. Unless you recalibrate your model, it won't realize that things are different.

But how are you supposed to know when to recalibrate your model? Through Model Monitor! Using Amazon SageMaker, including our fully managed Model Monitor capabilities, you can easily run tests that learn summary statistics of your training data. You can then schedule jobs to compare these summaries with the data hitting your endpoint. This means that as the new data interacts with your model, you can store all of these requests in S3. After the requests are stored, you can use the model monitor service to schedule jobs that compare these inference requests with your training data. This is useful because you can use it to send yourself alerts about how your model is trending on inference, especially if you need to trigger a retraining job. The same basic concepts of Model Monitor should also apply to vision and language; the only question is how we generate summary statistics.

Now, how does Model Monitor relate to human-in-the-loop? It's because you can also use triggers from your hosted model to *trigger a manual review*. As shown in the following figure, you can bring in some software checks to confirm that your model outputs content that is mostly in line with your expectations. If not, you can trigger a manual review. This uses another option on SageMaker, **Augmented Artificial Intelligence** (**A2I**), which in turn relies on SageMaker Ground Truth. Put another way, if the model doesn't act as you expect, you can send the prediction request and response to a team for manual review. This helps your teams build more trust in the overall solution, not to mention improving your dataset for the next iteration of the model! Let's take a look at this visually.

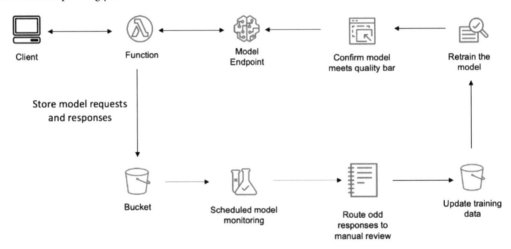

Figure 14.3 – Model monitoring with human-in-the-loop

In the preceding figure, you can see a variety of components, or microservices, that you can combine to provide a complete pipeline with model monitoring and humans kept in the loop. First, your client application can interact with a Lambda function that, in turn, invokes a SageMaker model. You might store the model requests and responses in an S3 bucket by writing it in Lambda yourself, or you could set the SageMaker endpoint to do this for you. Once you have records stored in S3, you can run **model monitoring** jobs. This can use a feature of SageMaker, model monitor, to learn the statistical differences between your training and inferencing data, sending you alerts if these fall out of a large range. Alternatively, you could write your own comparison script and run these jobs yourself on SageMaker training or processing jobs.

Once you have some visibility into how your model is responding on aggregate, your best move is to incorporate human feedback as much as you can. This is increasingly true in the generative space, where accuracy, style, and tone of the content are top criteria for most organizations. A great option for this is **SageMaker Ground Truth**! As we learned in *Chapter 2* on preparing data, this is a fully managed service you can use to both increase your labeled datasets and augment your model responses in real time.

A similar approach here is to use multiple models to confirm the prediction result. Imagine that you process a document quickly and want to extract content from it accurately. Your customer uploads a PDF to your website, you parse it using ML models, and you want to confirm or deny the contents of a given field. One way to increase your stakeholder's confidence in the accuracy of your system is to just use more than one model. Maybe you use your own, a custom deep learning model hosted in SageMaker, while at the same time, you point to a fully managed AWS service such as Textract that can extract digital natural language from visual forms. Then, you might have a Lambda function to see whether both models agree on the response. If they do, then you could respond to the customer directly! If they don't, then you could route the request for manual review.

There are countless other ways to monitor your models, including ways to integrate these with people! For now, however, let's move on to components of MLOps that are specifically scoped to vision and language.

# MLOps for foundation models

Now that you have a good idea of MLOps, including some ideas about how to use human-in-the-loop and model monitoring, let's examine specifically what aspects of vision and language models merit our attention from an MLOps perspective.

The answer to this question isn't immediately obvious because, from a certain angle, vision and language are just slightly different aspects of machine learning and artificial intelligence. Once you have the right packages, images, datasets, access, governance, and security configured, the rest should just flow naturally. Getting to that point, however, is quite an uphill battle!

Building a pipeline for large language models is no small task. As I mentioned previously, I see at least two very different aspects of this. On one side of the equation, you're looking at the entire model development life cycle. As we've learned throughout this book, that's a massive scope of development. From dataset, model, and script preparation to the training and evaluation loops, and performance and hyperparameter optimizations, there are countless techniques to track in order to produce your foundation model.

Once you have the foundation model, preparing it for development is a different beast. As we discussed previously, *adversarial hardening* includes a variety of techniques you can use to improve the performance of your model for the target domain. Everything we learned about in fine-tuning and evaluation from *Chapter 10*, bias detection and mitigation in *Chapter 11*, and deployment techniques in *Chapter 12* come right to the forefront. To me, it seems natural to locate these in a different pipeline that is focused squarely on deployment. Let's take a look at these in the following visual.

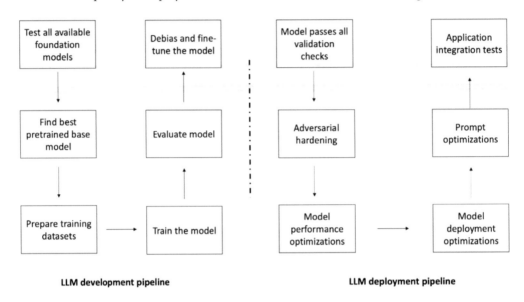

Figure 14.4 – LLM development and deployment pipelines

What makes this much more complicated is that *many of these disparate steps use similar packages and functions.* This means that to implement each of these steps, you're looking at pointing to at least one, and possibly a few `git` repositories and packages. When you decouple these, using different containers, resources, and steps to manage each piece, it helps each team work on them independently. We all know that the pace of foundation model development is only going to increase over the next few years, so assume that each step here will mean you need to pause periodically, capture the latest open source scripts or research techniques, develop and test them, and integrate them back into the larger pipeline.

Now, let's learn about MLOps for vision.

## MLOps for vision

How do vision foundation models compare with what we suggested previously for language models? To some degree, not much. You're still working with images, scripts, packages, datasets, and model quality. You still want to keep your models up to date, and you still want to incorporate as much human feedback in the best way you can. As we've seen in the book so far, models and evaluation metrics will vary, datasets will be quite different, and tasks are not entirely the same. A lot of the basic logic, however, carries over. One quick word of caution though – fine-tuning in language is not at all the same as fine-tuning in vision.

### A word of caution on overfitting in vision and a call for common sense

Please keep in mind that vision *is much more sensitive to overfitting than language*. To understand this, let's consider the fundamental differences between the two modalities. Language is inherently discrete; we represent the entire world with only letters and words, items that are noncontinuous by default. You could say that the entire modality of language is equal to the sum of all dictionaries in all languages around the world, to the extent that dictionaries themselves are only approximations of words spoken, used, and developed by humans constantly. The arrangement of these words, and the interpretation and meaning of them across the wide breadth of lived human experiences, is infinite.

Vision is completely different. The modality itself is continuous; while pixels themselves of course start and stop, the delineation between objects in a picture is almost a matter of opinion. We use metrics to quantify the quality of and discrepancy between labeled objects, such as *intersection over union*. Objects rotate; they seem to change completely in different lighting and backgrounds. Their patterns might seem to be the same even across totally different types, such as animals and cups, street signs and clothing, furniture, and natural landscapes. While both vision and language decompose into embeddings on their way into a model, the ability of neural nets to capture the meaning of the content provided and extrapolate this into other settings seems to be very different in language than in vision. Language fine-tuning works well in many cases, while vision fine-tuning very commonly results in poor performance at first blush.

Personally, I find another machine learning technique very interesting, which appears to operate, in essence, at the core of these combined modalities – common sense reasoning. Machine common sense refers to ensuring logical consistency between concepts, objects, and the defining characteristics of those objects. Most humans excel at this, such as knowing that water is wet, that heavy objects fall when dropped into open space, that fire produces heat, and so on.

Computers, however, are terrible at this. It's almost as if the physical dimension doesn't exist; certainly, the biological plain is a complete anomaly to them. Image generators don't understand that food has to go into a mouth to constitute eating. Image classifiers routinely miscategorize zebras with furniture. Language models don't appreciate the pace of human communication, occasionally overwhelming their operators. Movie generators regularly cause more disgust than delight because they fail to recognize the first basic discrimination mastered by infants – humans and their movement. To humans, it's immediately obvious that a cup and an animal are both objects, and might even occasionally share some stylistic traits, but in the physical world, they come from completely different domains. To computers, it's as if this physical dimension doesn't exist. They are quite literally only learning what exists inside the two-dimensional frames you provide. This is why we use labels in the first place – to give your model some meaning by translating the physical world into pixels.

I had the distinct pleasure of meeting and briefly chatting with Yejin Choi *(2)* last year. She delivered a keynote to the general assembly of the Association of Computational Linguists, one of the best NLP conferences in the world, on a fascinating hypothetical forecast of the next 60 years of natural language research. I was completely blown away by her passion for the humanities, philosophy, and deep scientific discoveries. She started exploring machine common sense in an era when it was extremely unpopular to do so, and in fact, she jokes today that she was actively discouraged from doing so, since everyone thought it would be impossible to get published on this topic. Since then, she's turned into probably the world's leading expert in this area, largely operating with language and vision as her modalities. Since then, I've been curious about common sense and wanted to explore it in more detail.

I wonder if human knowledge itself is inherently relational and possibly multimodal. We build concepts in our minds based on experiences – lived, perceived, imagined, and understood. These mental concepts guide our words and actions, expressing themselves in some cases verbally, and other times purely physically. Perhaps we need deeper representations to guide the intermingling of modalities. Perhaps language might help our vision models adapt to new domains more quickly. Perhaps this is because it provides a bit of common sense.

Practically, I'm bringing this up because, if you're about to embark on a vision fine-tuning exercise, I want you to go in knowing that it won't be easy, and what worked for you in language probably won't translate as well as you thought. I'm also bringing this up because I want you future researchers out there to take courage, trust your intuition, and challenge your assumptions. Now that we've learned a bit about MLOps for foundation models, let's take a look at some AWS offerings to help simplify and speed you up to nail this subject!

## AWS offerings for MLOps

Happily, AWS provides a variety of tools to help simplify this! One nice feature is called **lineage tracking**. SageMaker can automatically create the lineage *(3)* for key artifacts, including across accounts. This includes dataset artifacts, images, algorithm specifications, data configs, training job components, endpoints, and checkpoints. This is integrated with the **Experiments SDK**, letting you compare experiments and results programmatically and at scale. Let's explore this visually. We'll even generate a visualization for you to see how all of these are connected! Check it out in the following figure.

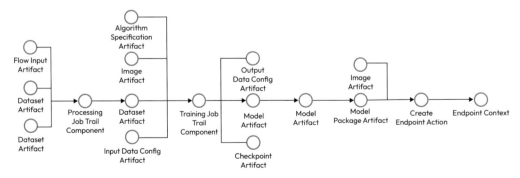

Figure 14.5 – SageMaker automatically creates lineage tracking

As you can see, the first step in tracking your lineage is running on key SageMaker resources such as training jobs, images, and processing jobs. You can use the entities that are automatically tracked, or you can define your own entities. To generate the lineage view as shown in the previous figure, you can interact with the **lineage query language**. If you want to jump straight into the notebook, which ships with a visualization solution, that's available as point *(4)* in the *References* section. The lineage tracking is explained in more detail here – *(5)*, and the querying is defined here – *(6)*. Using SageMaker Lineage, you can easily trace how a model was trained and where it was deployed.

How does it work? You can use the *LineageFilter API* to look for different objects, such as endpoints, that are associated with a model artifact. You can also search for trial components associated with endpoints, find datasets associated with models, and traverse forward and backward through the graph of associated items. Having these relationships available programmatically makes it much easier to take all of the necessary resources and put them into pipelines and other governance structures.

Once you have the resources identified, how do you wrap them into a pipeline? As we mentioned earlier in the chapter, many of the basic AWS and SageMaker resources are available as discrete building blocks. This includes the model, relevant model artifacts, deployment configurations, associated training and processing jobs, hyperparameter tuning, and containers. This means you can use the AWS SDK for Python, **boto3**, and the **SageMaker Python SDK** to point to and execute all of your resources and tasks programmatically. Wrapping these in a pipeline then means using whatever tooling stack you prefer to use to operationalize these automatically. One option for doing so is **SageMaker Pipelines**!

## A quick introduction to SageMaker Pipelines

If you're working with SageMaker-native resources, such as jobs, endpoints, model artifacts, and Docker images, then connecting them through the Pipelines SDK construct *(7)* should not be too much of an additional lift. SageMaker Pipelines is a managed feature you can use to create, run, and manage complete workflows for machine learning on AWS. Once you've defined your base Python SDK objects for SageMaker, such as a training job, evaluation metrics, hyperparameter tuning, and an endpoint, you can pass each of these objects to the Pipelines API and create it as a graph! Let's explore this in more detail in the following figure.

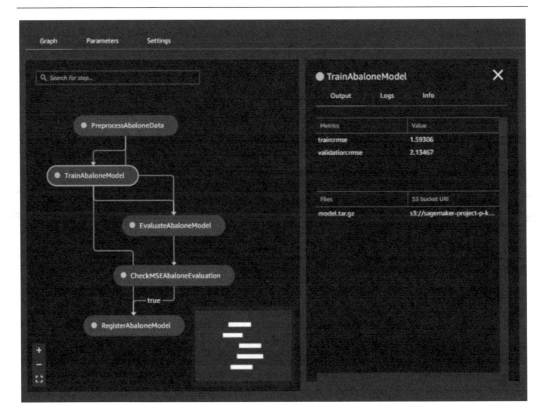

Figure 14.6 – SageMaker Pipelines

For a notebook walk-through of creating a graph very similar to the one in the preceding figure, there is a resource on GitHub *(8)*. The core idea is that you build each part of the pipeline separately, such as the data processing, training, and evaluation steps, and then pass each of these to the SageMaker Pipelines API to create the connected graph.

As you can see in the preceding figure, this is presented visually in SageMaker Studio! This makes it much easier for data scientists to develop, review, manage, and execute these pipelines. Studio also has a handful of other relevant features for MLOps, such as a feature store, model registry, endpoint management, model monitoring, and inference recommender. For a deeper dive into these topics, there's a full white paper from the AWS Well-Architected Framework on machine learning *(9)*.

Now that we've learned about the AWS offerings for MLOps, let's close out the chapter with a full recap.

## Summary

In this chapter, we introduced the core concept of MLOps, especially in the context of vision and language. We discussed machine learning operations, including some of the technologies, people, and processes that make it work. We especially focused on the pipeline aspect, learning about technologies useful to build them, such as SageMaker Pipelines, Apache Airflow, and Step Functions. We looked at a handful of different types of pipelines relevant to machine learning, such as model deployment, model retraining, and environment promotion. We discussed core operations concepts, such as CI and CD. We learned about model monitoring and human-in-the-loop design patterns. We learned about some specific techniques for vision and language within MLOps, such as common development and deployment pipelines for large language models. We also looked at how the core methods that might work in language can be inherently less reliable in vision, due to the core differences in the modalities and how current learning systems operate. We took a quick tour down the philosophical route by discussing common sense reasoning, and then we closed out the chapter with key AWS offerings for MLOps, such as SageMaker Lineage, Experiments, and Pipelines.

Now, let's conclude the book with one final chapter on future trends.

# References

Please go through the following content for more information on a few topics covered in the chapter:

1.  *Hardening Deep Neural Networks via Adversarial Model Cascades*: `https://arxiv.org/pdf/1802.01448.pdf`

2.  *Yejin Choi*: `https://homes.cs.washington.edu/~yejin/`

3.  *Amazon SageMaker ML Lineage Tracking*: `https://docs.aws.amazon.com/sagemaker/latest/dg/lineage-tracking.html`

4.  *aws/amazon-sagemaker-examples*: `https://github.com/aws/amazon-sagemaker-examples/blob/main/sagemaker-lineage/sagemaker-lineage.ipynb`

5.  *Lineage Tracking Entities*: `https://docs.aws.amazon.com/sagemaker/latest/dg/lineage-tracking-entities.html`

6.  *Querying Lineage Entities*: `https://docs.aws.amazon.com/sagemaker/latest/dg/querying-lineage-entities.html`

7.  *SageMaker Pipelines*: `https://sagemaker.readthedocs.io/en/stable/workflows/pipelines/index.html`

8.  *aws/amazon-sagemaker-examples*: `https://github.com/aws/amazon-sagemaker-examples/blob/main/sagemaker-pipelines/tabular/train-register-deploy-pipeline-model/train%20register%20and%20deploy%20a%20pipeline%20model.ipynb`

9.  *Machine Learning Lens AWS Well-Architected Framework*: `https://docs.aws.amazon.com/pdfs/wellarchitected/latest/machine-learning-lens/wellarchitected-machine-learning-lens.pdf`

# 15

# Future Trends in Pretraining Foundation Models

In this chapter, we'll close out the book by pointing to where trends are headed for all relevant topics presented in this book. We'll explore trends in foundation model application development, like using LangChain to build interactive dialogue applications, along with techniques like retrieval augmented generation to reduce LLM hallucination. We'll explore ways to use generative models to solve classification tasks, human-centered design, and other generative modalities like code, music, product documentation, powerpoints, and more! We'll talk through AWS offerings like SageMaker JumpStart Foundation Models, Amazon Bedrock, Amazon Titan, and Amazon Code Whisperer, and top trends in the future of foundation models and pretraining itself.

In particular, we'll dive into the following topics:

- Techniques for building applications for LLMs
- Generative modalities outside of vision and language
- AWS offerings in foundation models
- The future of foundation models
- The future of pretraining

## Techniques for building applications for LLMs

Now that you've learned about foundation models, and especially large language models, let's talk through a few key ways you can use them to build applications. One of the most significant takeaways of the ChatGPT moment in December 2022 is that customers clearly love for their chat to be knowledgeable about every moment in the conversation, remember topics mentioned earlier and encompassing all the twists and turns of dialogue. Said another way, beyond generic question answering, there's a clear consumer preference for chat to be *chained*. Let's take a look at an example in the following screenshot:

| Human: Who was the first president of the United States? | Human: Who was the first president of the United States? |
| Agent: George Washington. | Agent: George Washington. |
| Human: Where did he go to school? | Human: Where did he go to school? |
| Agent: I'm sorry, I don't know who "he" refers to. | Agent: George Washington was largely self-educated, after inheriting ownership of his family's farm at a young age. |
| Traditional question answering | Question answering with chains |

Figure 15.1 – Chaining questions for chat applications

The key difference between the left- and the right-hand side of *Figure 15.1* is that on the left-hand side, the answers are **discontinuous**. That means the model simply sees each question as a single entity before providing its response. On the right-hand side, however, the answers are **continuous**. That means the entire dialogue is provided to the model, with the newest question at the bottom. This helps to ensure the continuity of responses, with the model more capable of maintaining the context.

How can you set this up yourself? Well, on the one hand, what I've just described isn't terribly difficult. Imagine just reading from your HTML page, packing in all of that call and response data into the prompt, and siphoning out the response to return it to your end user. If you don't want to build it yourself, however, you can just use a few great open source options!

## Building interactive dialogue apps with open-source stacks

If you haven't seen it before, let me quickly introduce you to LangChain. Available for free on GitHub here: `https://github.com/hwchase17/langchain`, LangChain is an open source toolkit built by Harrison Chase and more than 600 other contributors. It provides functionality similar to the famous ChatGPT by pointing to OpenAI's API, or any other foundation model, but letting you as the developer and data scientist create your own frontend and customer experience.

Decoupling the application from the model is a smart move; in the last few months alone the world has seen nothing short of hundreds of new large language models come online, with teams around the world actively developing more. When your application interacts with the model via a single API call, then you can more easily move from one model to the next as the licensing, pricing, and capabilities upgrade over time. This is a big plus for you!

Another interesting open-source technology here is Haystack (*26*). Developed by the German start-up, Deepset, Haystack is a useful tool for, well, finding a needle in a haystack. Specifically they operate like a interface for you to bring your own LLMs into expansive question/answering scenarios. This was their original area of expertise, and since then have expanded quite a bit!

At AWS, we have an open source template for building applications with LangChain on AWS. It's available on GitHub here: `https://github.com/3coins/langchain-aws-template`. In the following diagram, you can see a quick representation of the architecture:

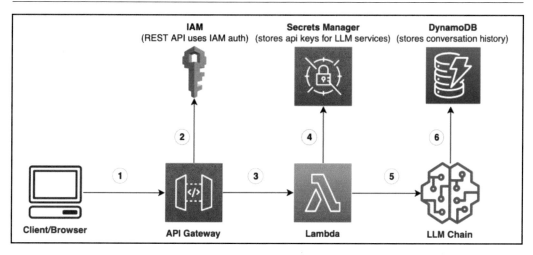

Figure 15.2 – Hosting LangChain on AWS

While this can point to any frontend, we provide an example template you can use to get off the ground for your app. You can also easily point to *any* custom model, whether it's on a SageMaker endpoint or in the new AWS service, Bedrock! More on that a bit later in this chapter. As you can see in the previous image, in this template you can easily run a UI anywhere that interacts with the cloud. Let's take a look at all of the steps.:

1. First, the UI hits the API gateway.

2. Second, credentials are retrieved via IAM.

3. Third, the service is invoked via Lambda.

4. Fourth, the model credentials are retrieved via Secrets Manager.

5. Fifth, your model is invoked through either an API call to a serverless model SDK, or a custom model you've trained that is hosted on a SageMaker endpoint is invoked.

6. Sixth, look up the relevant conversation history in DynamoDB to ensure your answer is accurate.

How does this chat interface ensure it's not hallucinating answers? How does it point to a set of data stored in a database? Through **retrieval augmented generation** (**RAG**), which we will cover next.

## Using RAG to ensure high accuracy in LLM applications

As explained in the original 2020 *(1)* paper, RAG is a way to retrieve documents relevant to a given query. Imagine your chat application takes in a question about a specific item in your database, such as one of your products. Rather than having the model make up the answer, you'd be better off retrieving the right document from your database and simply using the LLM to *stylize* the response. That's where RAG is so powerful; you can use it to ensure the accuracy of your generated answers stays high, while keeping the customer experience consistent in both style and tone. Let's take a closer look:

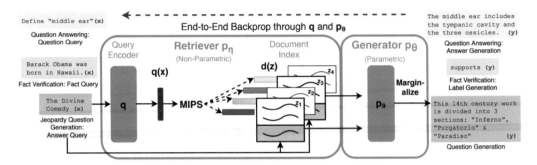

Figure 15.3 – RAG

First, a question comes in from the left-hand side. In the top left, you can see a simple question, **Define "middle ear"**. This is processed by a query encoder, which is simply a language model producing an embedding of the query. This embedding is then applied to the index of a database, with many candidate algorithms in use here: **K Nearest Neighbors**, **Maximum Inner Product Search** (**MIPS**), and others. Once you've retrieved a set of similar documents, you can feed the best ones into the generator, the final model on the right-hand side. This takes the input documents and returns a simple answer to the question. Here, the answer is **The middle ear includes the tympanic cavity and the three ossicles.**

Interestingly, however, the LLM here doesn't really define what the middle ear is. It's actually answering the question, "what objects are contained within the middle ear?" Arguably, any definition of the middle ear would include its purpose, notably serving as a buffer between your ear canal and your inner ear, which helps you keep your balance and lets you hear. So, this would be a good candidate for expert **reinforcement learning with human feedback**, or **RLHF**, optimization.

As shown in *Figure 15.3*, this entire RAG system is tunable. That means you can and should fine-tune the encoder and decoder aspects of the architecture to dial in model performance based on your datasets and query types. Another way to classify documents, as we'll see, is generation!

## Is generation the new classification?

As we learned in *Chapter 13*, *Prompt Engineering*, there are many ways you can push your language model to output the type of response you are looking for. One of these ways is actually to have it classify what it sees in the text! Here is a simple diagram to illustrate this concept:

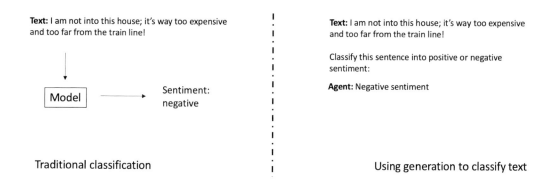

Figure 15.4 – Using generation in place of classification

As you can see in the diagram, with traditional classification you train the model ahead of time to perform one task: **classification**. This model may do well on classification, but it won't be able to handle new tasks at all. This key drawback is one of the main reasons why foundation models, and especially large language models, are now so popular: they are extremely flexible and can handle many different tasks without needing to be retrained.

On the right-hand side of *Figure 15.4*, you can see we're using the same text as the starting point, but instead of passing it to an encoder-based text model, we're passing it to a decoder-based model and simply adding the instruction **classify this sentence into positive or negative sentiment**. You could just as easily say, "tell me more about how this customer really feels," or "how optimistic is this home buyer?" or "help this homebuyer find a different house that meets their needs." Arguably each of those three instructions is slightly different, veering away from pure classification and into more general application development or customer experience. Expect to see more of this over time! Let's look at one more key technique for building applications with LLMs: keeping humans in the loop.

## Human-centered design for building applications with LLMs

We touched on this topic previously, in *Chapter 2, Dataset Preparation: Part One, Chapter 10, Fine-Tuning and Evaluating, Chapter 11, Detecting, Mitigating, and Monitoring Bias*, and *Chapter 14, MLOps for Vision and Language*. Let me say this yet again; I believe that human labeling will become even more of a competitive advantage that companies can provide. Why? Building LLMs is now incredibly competitive; you have both the open source and proprietary sides actively competing for your business. Open source options are from the likes of Hugging Face and Stability, while proprietary offerings are from AI21, Anthropic, and OpenAI. The differences between these options are questionable; you can look up the latest models at the top of the leaderboard from *Stanford's HELM (2)*, which incidentally falls under their human-centered AI initiative. With enough fine-tuning and customization, you should generally be able to meet performance.

What then determines the best LLM applications, if it's not the foundation model? Obviously, the end-to-end customer experience is critical, and will always remain so. Consumer preferences wax and wane over time, but a few tenets remain for general technology: speed, simplicity, flexibility, and low cost. With foundation models we can clearly see that customers prefer explainability and models they can trust. This means that application designers and developers should grapple with these long-term consumer preferences, picking solutions and systems that maximize them. As you may have guessed, that alone is no small task.

Beyond the core skill of designing and building successful applications, what else can we do to stay competitive in this brave new world of LLMs? I would argue that amounts to customizing your data. Focus on making your data and your datasets unique: singular in purpose, breadth, depth, and completeness. Lean into labeling your data with the best resources you can, and keep that a core part of your entire application workflow. This brings you to **continuous learning**, or the ability of the model to constantly get better and better based on signals from your end users.

Next, let's take a look at upcoming generative modalities.

## Other generative modalities

Since the 2022 ChatGPT moment, most of the technical world has been fascinated by the proposition of *generating novel content*. While this was always somewhat interesting, the meeting of high-performance foundation models with an abundance of media euphoria over the capabilities, combined with a post-pandemic community with an extremely intense fear of missing out, has led us to the perfect storm of a global fixation on generative AI.

s this a good thing? Honestly, I'm happy to finally see the shift; I've been working on generating content with AI/ML models in some fashion since at least 2019, and as a writer and creative person myself, I've always thought this was the most interesting part of machine learning. I was very impressed by David Foster's book *(3)* on the topic. He's just published an updated version of this to include the latest foundation models and methods! Let's quickly recap some other types of modalities that are common in generative AI applications today.

> **Key modalities for generation outside of vision and language**
>
> Here is my shortlist for the most interesting type of content generation outside of what we've seen throughout the book:
>
> - Generating code
> - Generating music
> - Generating PowerPoint slides, ads, and visuals
> - Generating product documentation
> - Generating architectural designs, and then building the application
> - Generating movies, TV shows, and entertainment
> - Generating websites, games, and mobile apps

Generating code should be no surprise to most of you; its core similarities to language generation make it a perfect candidate! Fine-tuning an LLM to spit out code in your language of choice is pretty easy; here's my 2019 project *(4)* doing exactly that with the SageMaker example notebooks! Is the code great? Absolutely not, but fortunately, LLMs have come a long way since then. Many modern code-generating models are excellent, and thanks to a collaboration between Hugging Face and ServiceNow we have an open source model to use! This is called *StarCoder* and is available for free on Hugging Face right here: `https://huggingface.co/bigcode/starcoder`.

What I love about using an open source LLM for code generation is that you can *customize it*! This means you can point to your own private code repositories, tokenize the data, update the model, and immediately train this LLM to generate code in the style of your organization! At the organizational level you might even do some continued pretraining on a open-source LLM for code generation on your own repositories to speed up all of your developers. We'll take a look at more ways you can use LLMs to write your own code faster in the next section when we focus on AWS offerings, especially **Amazon Code Whisperer**. *(27)*

The rest of the preceding content can all be great candidates for your own generative AI projects. Truly, just as we saw general machine learning moving from the science lab into the foundation of most businesses and projects, it's likely that generative capabilities in some fashion will do the same.

Does that mean engineering roles will be eliminated? Honestly, I doubt it. Just as the rise of great search engines didn't eliminate software engineering roles but made them more fun and doable for a lot of people, I'm expecting generative capabilities to do the same. They are great at searching many possibilities and quickly finding great options, but it's still up to you to know the ins and outs of your consumers, your product, and your design. Models aren't great at critical thinking, but they are good at coming up with ideas and finding shortcomings, at least in words.

Now that we've looked at other generative modalities at a very high level, let's learn about AWS offerings for foundation models!

## AWS offerings in foundation models

On AWS, as you've seen throughout the book, you have literally hundreds of ways to optimize your foundation model development and operationalization. Let's now look at a few ways AWS is explicitly investing to improve the customer experience in this domain:

- **SageMaker JumpStart Foundation Model Hub**: Announced in preview at re:Invent 2022, this is an option for pointing to foundation models nicely packaged in the SageMaker environment. This includes both open source models such as BLOOM and Flan-T5 from Hugging Face, and proprietary models such as AI21 Jurassic. A list of all the foundation models is available here *(5)*. To date, we have nearly 20 foundation models, all available for hosting in your own secure environments. Any data you use to interact with or fine-tune models on the Foundation Model Hub is not shared with providers. You can also optimize costs by selecting the instances yourself. We have tens of example notebooks pointing to these models for training and hosting across a wide variety of use cases available here *(6)* and elsewhere. For more information about the data the models were trained on, you can read about that in the playground directly.

- **Amazon Bedrock**: If you have been watching AWS news closely in early 2023, you may have noticed a new service we announced for foundation models: Amazon Bedrock! As discussed in this blog post *(7)* by Swami Sivasubramanian, Bedrock is a service that lets you interact with a variety of foundation models through a serverless interface that stays secure. Said another way, Bedrock provides a point of entry for multiple foundation models, letting you get the best of all possible providers. This includes AI start-ups such as AI21, Anthropic, and Stability. Interacting with Bedrock means invoking a serverless experience, saving you from dealing with the lower-level infrastructure. You can also fine-tune your models with Bedrock!

- **Amazon Titan**: Another model that will be available through Bedrock is *Titan*, a new large language model that's fully trained and managed by Amazon! This means we handle the training data, optimizations, tuning, debiasing, and all enhancements for getting you results with large language models. Titan will also be available for fine-tuning.

Amazon Code Whisperer: As you may have seen, Code Whisperer is an AWS service announced in 2022 and made generally available in 2023. Interestingly it seems to tightly couple with a given development environment, taking the entire context of the script you are writing and generating recommendations based on this. You can write pseudo-code, markdown, or other function starts, and using keyboard shortcuts invoke the model. This will send you a variety of options based on the context of your script, letting you ultimately select the script that makes the most sense for you! Happily, this is now supported for both Jupyter notebooks and SageMaker Studio; you can read more about these initiatives from AWS Sr Principal Technologist Brain Granger, co-founder of Project Jupyter. Here's Brian's blog post on the topic: `https://aws.amazon.com/blogs/machine-learning/announcing-new-jupyter-contributions-by-aws-to-democratize-generative-ai-and-scale-ml-workloads/` Pro tip: Code Whisperer is free to individuals! Close readers of Swami's blog post above will also notice updates to our latest ML infrastructure, like the second edition of the *inferentia chip*, *inf2*, and a trainium instance with more bandwidth, *trn1n*.

Close readers of Swami's blog post will also notice updates to our latest ML infrastructure, such as the second edition of the *inferentia chip*, *inf2*, and a Trainium instance with more bandwidth, *trn1n*. We also released our code generation service, *CodeWhisperer*, at no cost to you!

Now that we've learned about some of the AWS offerings in this space, let's hypothesize about the future of foundation models.

# The future of foundation models

To me, a few key points seem incredibly obvious for where foundation models are trending:

- *Intense competition will continue between open source and proprietary model providers.* As mentioned previously, right now we are in a perfect storm of hyper-focus on foundation models from most of the technology industry worldwide. A key axis here is proprietary versus open source. As suggested by this leaked Google document on May 4 *(8)*, the capabilities of the open source world are advancing and in many cases, open source options are better than proprietary ones. They actually describe open source models as "pound-for-pound more capable." This means that for the size of the model itself, the smaller ones produced by the open source world are better in a per-byte-size comparison.

- *Model consumers will get more options at a lower cost if they are flexible about model providers.* To me, the result of this intense competition is clear; you'll get more and more options at a lower price point as time goes by! This means the clear right choice here, as a model consumer, is not getting locked into a single model. As the brave new world of foundation models swims on, put you and your teams in the best possible scenario and stay flexible to new models as they emerge.

- *Models are getting smaller and stronger.* In no small part thanks to the drive enthusiasm in the open-source community coming from Stable Diffusion, foundation models are now decreasing in size but increasing in accuracy. This means today you can accomplish with a 13B-parameter model, like *StableVicuna (28)* what a few years ago took a 175B-parameter model to do. Keep this in mind as you're designing apps!

- *Make proprietary data and human feedback your strength.* To best take advantage of all this competition, I'd suggest leaning into your data. As long as you're open to the latest and greatest model backbone, using your own proprietary data and human feedback as a key investment area lets you differentiate from the rest of the market. Make sure you and your teams are labeling data early and often, using as much of your unique perspectives and expertise as possible.

- *Security is critical for interacting with foundation models.* This signal shows up so clearly across the market, consumers very strongly prefer environments that secure their data and do not allow sharing with model providers, including both model queries and fine-tuning assets. This is in some sense a derivative of making proprietary data and human feedback your strength; in tomorrow's world, your data becomes your selling point. Protecting this in the form of your own foundation model, in terms of keeping your model unbiased, safe from jailbreak attacks, and not able to generate hate speech will continue to be important. It seems like an entirely new portfolio of security measures is necessary to ensure foundation model applications.

- *Foundation models are becoming the new database, and natural language is the new programming language.* I am expecting most applications in the next twelve months to include foundation models as a new type of database. Rather than just storing your records on disk, now you can crunch through them with neural networks, learn mappings and relationships at scales that single humans can't compete with, and interact with humans in natural language. Optimizing, scaling, debiasing, ensuring accuracy, and taking costs out of this equation will be the work of the next few years.

I'm also expecting many more foundation models, across modalities, user bases, languages, technologies, goals, and domains. As the cost of training and producing them goes down, thanks to intense competition, we might see more and more entry-level developers entering this market. With that in mind, let's close out the book with parting thoughts on the future of pretraining.

# The future of pretraining

In a full roundabout, let's take a look at some skeptical trends that provide a sense of caution and critical evaluation of the recent goldrush in foundation models. One of the most prominent examples is Geoffrey Hinton quitting Google (29) to warn about the dangers of AI development, calling for a 6-month moratorium (30) on all foundation model research.

Personally, I think this pause fails to recognize what drove the hype in the first place: the invisible hand of AI economics. Landing high-paying tech jobs is not easy; getting and maintaining visas for the US and similar countries is non-trivial. Growing your career in an industry with some of the most intelligent and driven people, with ground-shattering fast-paced changes is anything but simple. Foundation models and all improvements in technology evolve because humans need to prove themselves, grow their careers, and provide for their families. Asking to pause experiments on large-scale training is almost the same as asking massive swaths of young people to stop putting all of their passion, skills, and time into some of the best possible options for their own career development. Obviously, that's the opposite of what's in their best interest to do!

However, even within the camp of those who do support continued research on foundation models, not everyone is overly optimistic about the continued value of pretraining Transformers. Yann LeCun, the same scientist we mentioned in *Chapter 1* who developed MNIST, considers self-supervised learning to be "*the dark matter of intelligence. (9)*" Since the viral ChatGPT global moment LeCun has been very critical about the bounded performance of large language and auto-regressive models, given their core strength is simply predicting the next most likely token in a sequence and not actually understanding the world in any reliable way. Instead, he suggests we build AI models that learn how to reason, including developing hierarchical representations of action plans.

He's not alone in this cautionary note. MacArthur Fellow at the University of Washington and the Allen Institute for Artificial Intelligence Yejin Choi (10) recently shared her thoughts in a TED talk about why "AI is incredibly smart – and shockingly stupid." (11) Choi's multiple decades of work on common sense reasoning shows that while NLP models may solve some limited tasks well, they still struggle with extremely basic human tasks, such as understanding the difference between reality and fiction or hypothesizing and planning, the value of simplicity, and basic logical mapping of the world around them.

To me, the divide here is clear. On the one hand, we have a decades-long push for the best and most impressive artificial representations of intelligence. On the other hand, we have massive industries of business, technology, and academia with millions of human beings actively trying to build applications and provide value that serve as the foundation for their careers and their team's longevity. Will this economy of technological development create the most intelligent machines? Possibly. Will it build applications and businesses that provide value to consumers? Certainly. Will these two related and yet distinct vectors continue to overlap for decades to come? Without a doubt.

Before we close things out, let me mention a few interesting technical trends of note to pretraining in particular:

- **Continuous pretraining**: If your foundation model benefits from the latest data, and this is available in a constant stream of updates, why not build a continuous loop of ingestion and training to keep your application performant? That's the core proposal in this 2022 paper *(12)*. I'd imagine that some applications benefit from this constant stream of training, especially when parameter-efficient fine-tuning *(31)* makes the cost of this more appealing.

- **Retrieval pretraining**: The demand for accurate generated text will continue increasing as generative AI applications expand. This approach, suggested by DeepMind, applies the retrieval process *(14)* to pretraining and gets similar performance to GPT-3 while using 25x fewer parameters, making it much more efficient and appealing for both training and hosting. I'm expecting this basic concept of retrieving tokens during pretraining to evolve with RAG *(15)* to create LLMs that provide much higher accuracy guarantees.

- **More universal pretraining regimes**: As you are probably aware, much of the media and open source attention seems to focus only on the models and new state-of-the-art performance in low-level tasks. I think this is a problem because it misses the foundation of where these models come from and how they are built: pretraining itself. This indicates that if pretraining can become more accessible and more universal, we can move from a fixation on the model to broad support for pretraining more generally. A few steps exist already in this direction, such as Data2Vec *(16)*, which proposes a general framework for self-supervised learning across vision, speech, and language. Another attempt is **UL2**, **Unifying Language Learning Paradigms**. This Google Brain team suggests combining diverse pretraining paradigms and then switching to different paradigms during fine-tuning.

- **More languages, please**! One of the first conferences I attended in person after the pandemic was the Association of Computational Linguists in 2022 *(18)*. I was happily surprised by their focus on being multi-lingual, strongly and admirably pushing for capabilities that bridge languages and extend NLP capabilities across endangered languages and communities worldwide. Admirably the UN declared 2022-2023 the International Decade of Indigenous Languages, estimating that at least 50% of spoken languages today will be extinct or seriously endangered by 2100. *(32)*. This will continue to be an important topic in foundation models because it serves as a bottleneck for technical adoption and innovation. One step in this direction is Tsinghua's GLM-130B *(19)*, a model explicitly pretrained with Chinese and English. Another notable bilingual model is Hugging Face's BLOOM *(20), which was trained on 46 natural and 13 programming languages.* Other similar projects provide capabilities in singular non-English languages, such as LightOn's French model PAGnol *(21)*, a Japanese masked-language model *(22)*, a German LLM *(23)*, and more. There are even calls for a BritGPT *(24)*, to bring generative capabilities into British styles of speaking and conversing.

On that note, let's close out the book with the final conclusion.

## Summary

What a journey! To those of you who made it to the end with me, thank you so much for the time, creativity, and energy you've put into studying my words and thoughts. I hope at least some of the insights were worth your time, and that the mistakes weren't too glaring.

In this book, we walked through the entire process of pretraining foundation models, looking at key use cases and examples from vision and language, and understanding core capabilities on AWS to build your applications and projects. I love hearing from my audience, so please, reach out to me and stay in touch! I'm active on LinkedIn; you can always ping me with questions or comments. I run a weekly Twitch show on Generative AI, so you can always find there me and hop in with feedback or comments. *(25)*

And of course, you can always talk to your teams at AWS to reach out to me directly! I love meeting customers, thinking through architectural choices, communicating your needs to our service teams, and thinking big with you about how we can build a better tomorrow. Let me know what you're itching to build!

## References

Please go through the following content for more information on the topics covered in the chapter:

1.  Retrieval-Augmented Generation for Knowledge-Intensive NLP Tasks: `https://arxiv.org/pdf/2005.11401.pdf`

2.  HELM: `https://crfm.stanford.edu/helm/latest/`

3.  Generative Deep Learning: Teaching Machines to Paint, Write, Compose, and Play 1st Edition: `https://www.amazon.com/Generative-Deep-Learning-Teaching-Machines/dp/1492041947`

4.  aws-samples/amazon-sagemaker-architecting-for-ml: `https://github.com/aws-samples/amazon-sagemaker-architectingfor-ml/tree/master/Example-Project`

5.  Getting started with Amazon SageMaker JumpStart: `https://aws.amazon.com/sagemaker/jumpstart/gettingstarted/?sagemaker-jumpstart-cards.sort-by=item.additionalFields.priority&sagemaker-jumpstart-cards.sort-order=asc&awsf.sagemakerjumpstart-filter-product-type=*all&awsf.sagemaker-jumpstartfilter-text=*all&awsf.sagemaker-jumpstart-filter-vision=*all&awsf.sagemaker-jumpstart-filter-tabular=*all&awsf.sagemaker-jumpstartfilter-audio-tasks=*all&awsf.sagemaker-jumpstart-filtermultimodal=*all&awsf.sagemaker-jumpstart-filter-RL=*all`

6.  aws/amazon-sagemaker-examples: `https://github.com/aws/amazon-sagemaker-examples/tree/main/`

7.  Announcing New Tools for Building with Generative AI on AWS: `https://aws.amazon.com/blogs/machine-learning/announcing-new-tools-for-building-with-generative-ai-on-aws/`

8.  Google "We Have No Moat, And Neither Does OpenAI": `https://www.semianalysis.com/p/google-we-have-no-moat-and-neither`

9.  Self-supervised learning: The dark matter of intelligence: `https://ai.facebook.com/blog/self-supervised-learning-the-dark-matter-of-intelligence/`

10. Yejin Choi: `https://homes.cs.washington.edu/~yejin/`

11. Why AI is incredibly smart and shockingly stupid: `https://www.ted.com/talks/yejin_choi_why_ai_is_incredibly_smart_and_shockingly_stupid/c?language=en`

12. Continual PreTraining Mitigates Forgetting in Language and Vision: `https://arxiv.org/pdf/2205.09357.pdf`

13. LoRA: Low-Rank Adaptation of Large Language Models: `https://arxiv.org/abs/2106.09685`

14. Improving language models by retrieving from trillions of tokens: `https://arxiv.org/pdf/2112.04426.pdf`

15. Retrieval-Augmented Generation for Knowledge-Intensive NLP Tasks: `https://arxiv.org/pdf/2005.11401.pdf`

16. data2vec: A General Framework for Self-supervised Learning in Speech, Vision and Language: `https://arxiv.org/pdf/2202.03555.pdf`

17. UL2: Unifying Language Learning Paradigms: `https://arxiv.org/pdf/2205.05131.pdf`

18. ACL 2022: `https://www.2022.aclweb.org/`

19. GLM-130B: AN OPEN BILINGUAL PRE-TRAINED MODEL: `https://openreview.net/pdf?id=-Aw0rrrPUF`

20. BLOOM: A 176B-Parameter Open-Access Multilingual Language Model: `https://arxiv.org/pdf/2211.05100.pdf`

21. LightOn releases PAGnol, the largest French Language Model: `https://medium.com/@LightOnIO/lighton-releases-pagnol-the-largest-french-language-model-f50b719352ab`

22. A Japanese Masked Language Model for Academic Domain: `https://aclanthology.org/2022.sdp-1.16.pdf`

23. Cedille.ai launches the largest language model in German for text generation: `https://cedille.ai/blog/cedille-ai-launches-the-largest-language-model-in-german-for-text-generation`

24. UK needs its own 'BritGPT' or will face an uncertain future, MPs hear: `https://www.theguardian.com/business/2023/feb/22/uk-needs-its-own-britgpt-or-will-face-an-uncertain-future-mps-hear`

25. AWS Schedule: `https://www.twitch.tv/aws/schedule?seriesID=340be301-27dc-42c6-890a-302cd13899af`

26. deepset-ai/haystack: `https://github.com/deepset-ai/haystack`

27. AWS- Overview: `https://aws.amazon.com/codewhisperer/`

28. Hugging Face: `https://huggingface.co/CarperAI/stable-vicuna-13b-delta`

29. Godfather of AI: `https://www.theguardian.com/technology/2023/may/02/geoffrey-hinton-godfather-of-ai-quits-google-warns-dangers-of-machine-learning`

30. Pause Giant AI Experiments: An Open Letter: `https://futureoflife.org/open-letter/pause-giant-ai-experiments/`

31. huggingface/peft: `https://github.com/huggingface/peft`

32. Department of Economic and Social AffairsIndigenous Peoples: `https://www.un.org/development/desa/indigenouspeoples/indigenous-languages.html`

# Index

# D

`Packtpub.com`

Subscribe to our online digital library for full access to over 7,000 books and videos, as well as industry leading tools to help you plan your personal development and advance your career. For more information, please visit our website.

## Why subscribe?

- Spend less time learning and more time coding with practical eBooks and Videos from over 4,000 industry professionals

- Improve your learning with Skill Plans built especially for you

- Get a free eBook or video every month

- Fully searchable for easy access to vital information

- Copy and paste, print, and bookmark content

Did you know that Packt offers eBook versions of every book published, with PDF and ePub files available? You can upgrade to the eBook version at `packtpub.com` and as a print book customer, you are entitled to a discount on the eBook copy. Get in touch with us at `customercare@packtpub.com` for more details.

At `www.packtpub.com`, you can also read a collection of free technical articles, sign up for a range of free newsletters, and receive exclusive discounts and offers on Packt books and eBooks.

# Other Books You May Enjoy

If you enjoyed this book, you may be interested in these other books by Packt:

**Hands-On Graph Neural Networks Using Python**

Maxime Labonne

ISBN: 978-1-80461-752-6

- Understand the fundamental concepts of graph neural networks
- Implement graph neural networks using Python and PyTorch Geometric
- Classify nodes, graphs, and edges using millions of samples
- Predict and generate realistic graph topologies
- Combine heterogeneous sources to improve performance
- Forecast future events using topological information
- Apply graph neural networks to solve real-world problems

**Modern Time Series Forecasting with Python**

Manu Joseph

ISBN: 978-1-80324-680-2

- Find out how to manipulate and visualize time series data like a pro
- Set strong baselines with popular models such as ARIMA
- Discover how time series forecasting can be cast as regression
- Engineer features for machine learning models for forecasting
- Explore the exciting world of ensembling and stacking models
- Get to grips with the global forecasting paradigm
- Understand and apply state-of-the-art DL models such as N-BEATS and Autoformer
- Explore multi-step forecasting and cross-validation strategies

## Packt is searching for authors like you

If you're interested in becoming an author for Packt, please visit `authors.packtpub.com` and apply today. We have worked with thousands of developers and tech professionals, just like you, to help them share their insight with the global tech community. You can make a general application, apply for a specific hot topic that we are recruiting an author for, or submit your own idea.

## Share Your Thoughts

Now you've finished *Pretrain Vision and Large Language Models in Python*, we'd love to hear your thoughts! Scan the QR code below to go straight to the Amazon review page for this book and share your feedback or leave a review on the site that you purchased it from.

`https://packt.link/r/1-804-61825-X`

Your review is important to us and the tech community and will help us make sure we're delivering excellent quality content.

# Download a free PDF copy of this book

Thanks for purchasing this book!

Do you like to read on the go but are unable to carry your print books everywhere?

Is your eBook purchase not compatible with the device of your choice?

Don't worry, now with every Packt book you get a DRM-free PDF version of that book at no cost.

Read anywhere, any place, on any device. Search, copy, and paste code from your favorite technical books directly into your application.

The perks don't stop there, you can get exclusive access to discounts, newsletters, and great free content in your inbox daily

Follow these simple steps to get the benefits:

1.  Scan the QR code or visit the link below

https://packt.link/free-ebook/9781804618257

2.  Submit your proof of purchase
3.  That's it! We'll send your free PDF and other benefits to your email directly

Made in the USA
Columbia, SC
21 December 2023

29297561R00144